Praise for *Fortune Makers*

"*Fortune Makers* provides an extremely interesting perspective on a new breed of global companies with roots in China. As the chief marketing officer of Lenovo for four years, I had the unique privilege to observe and engage in the operations of one such company. Made me a huge believer in the massive impact companies like Lenovo will continue to make on the global stage. To understand how China's great private companies are being directed and led, this is *the* book to read."

—Deepak Advani, managing director of Hellman & Friedman,
former global chief marketing officer of Lenovo,
and former general manager of IBM Commerce

"For almost a hundred years, our thinking about management and leadership was dominated by the practices of American companies. Since the 1980s, we have started to see new models emerge—the Japanese way, the German way, the Indian way. Now, for the first time, a book that exposes the Chinese way of managing, an approach that will become increasingly influential in the years ahead. This is a must-read for any company that seeks to do business in China, or to compete against Chinese companies."

—Julian Birkinshaw, professor of strategy and entrepreneurship and
academic director of the Deloitte Institute, London Business School

"*Fortune Makers* offers unparalleled insight into the distinctly Chinese approach to competition that is reshaping the global business landscape. Combining illuminating commentary from top Chinese business leaders with first-rate research and analysis, the authors deliver lessons for Western business practitioners that are both utterly timely and absolutely timeless."

—Ming-Jer Chen, professor of business administration,
University of Virginia, and author of *Inside Chinese Business*

"*Fortune Makers* chronicles how a new brand of Chinese business leaders have thrown off the shackles of the Cultural Revolution and state-owned enterprises to lead aggressive private companies into the global business arena. The authors—Useem, Singh, Liang, and Cappelli—provide a fascinating glimpse [into] what makes these CEOs and the companies they lead tick, while sounding an alarm bell for all those Western competitors that will need to up their game to be successful in the future. This is a book that should be required reading for anyone conducting international business inside or outside of China."

—Arthur D. Collins Jr., former chairman and CEO of Medtronic
and managing partner of Acorn Advisors

"China's geopolitical and business impact is a force to reckon with now and will continue to grow. For business firms, China represents an incredible opportunity as well as poses new threats. *Fortune Makers* provides truly unique and valuable insights into the philosophy and approach of doing business the China way. This is a book that must be read by anyone doing or planning to do business in China or dealing with Chinese business leaders."

—Raj L. Gupta, former CEO of Rohm and Haas,
chair of Delphi Automotive, and lead independent director of
Hewlett Packard Enterprise Co.

"It is no secret that the miraculous growth of China's economy in the last thirty-five years is due largely to the flourishing of a private sector, which operated in the most unfavorable if not hostile environment, and which now contributes a lion share of China's economy, employs more than two-thirds of China's workforce, with a strong presence on both the Fortune 500 and Forbes billionaire lists. How did these entrepreneurs manage to survive and thrive and collectively elevate China to a significant position on the global economic stage? *Fortune Makers* provides an inside look into the arduous journeys of these companies and offers seven distinguishing features of their leadership."

— Anne S. Tsui, founding president of the International Association for
Chinese Management Research, and founding editor of
Management and Organization Review and Management Insight

"How did an entrepreneurial ideology find expression in the particular milieu that is the China of the recent decades? The authors build on their prior work on Indian businesses to provide a similarly compelling picture of what they call the Fortune Makers, a Chinese way of private-sector entrepreneurship. A profoundly useful and readable account of interest to managers and entrepreneurs competing or collaborating with the Chinese."

—Tarun Khanna, professor, Harvard Business School,
and author of *Billions of Entrepreneurs: How China and India
Are Reshaping Their Futures, and Yours*

FORTUNE MAKERS

FORTUNE MAKERS

The Leaders Creating
China's Great Global Companies

MICHAEL USEEM,
HARBIR SINGH,
NENG LIANG, AND
PETER CAPPELLI

PUBLICAFFAIRS
New York

Book design by Jeff Williams

Library of Congress Cataloging-in-Publication Data
Names: Useem, Michael, author.
Title: Fortune makers : the leaders creating China's great global companies / Michael Useem, Harbir Singh, Neng Liang, and Peter Cappelli.
Description: First Edition. | New York : PublicAffairs, [2017] | Includes bibliographical references and index.
Identifiers: LCCN 2016040752 (print) | LCCN 2016053935 (ebook) | ISBN 9781610396585 (hardcover) | ISBN 9781610396592 (ebook)
Subjects: LCSH: International business enterprises—China—Case studies. | Corporations—China—Case studies. | Leadership—China—Case studies. | Businesspeople—China—Case studies.
Classification: LCC HD2910 .U84 2017 (print) | LCC HD2910 (ebook) | DDC 338.092/251—dc23
LC record available at https://lccn.loc.gov/2016040752

First Edition

10 9 8 7 6 5 4 3 2 1

CONTENTS

6. The Big Boss

"The Chinese leader is always top down."

129

7. Growth as Gospel

*"The most important thing is to grow the cake
and let everyone take a piece from it."*

149

8. Governance as Partnership

*"I disagree with maximizing shareholder value. . . .
The most important stakeholder is our customers."*

173

9. What's Distinctive, What's Sustainable

*"It's our responsibility to shift
from 'made in China' to 'designed in China.'"*

199

CHAPTER 1

Introduction

Not the American Way

It seems surely just a matter of time before a
"China Way" emerges.

The rise of China has been the most remarkable development of the modern era. In twenty-five years, a country that had long lectured the Soviet Union about being soft on capitalist and Western values, that suffered through a decade-long purge of anything associated with modernity, and that competed with countries like Chad for the world's lowest per capita GDP has used capitalism to pull 600 million people out of poverty and is on track to soon be the largest economy in the world. It is an astonishing turn of events.

Anyone who believes that this development was the inevitable result of throwing off communist economic principles should consider the experience of the former Soviet Union, which has made little economic progress post-communism despite being a resource-rich country.

Furthermore, China has not adopted many of the other practices often associated with capitalism in the West, such as a substantial role for civil society, including a free press, democratic institutions, and significant personal rights. The Communist Party remains firmly in control—even more so now, under President Xi Jinping, than before. There is no doubt that changes in government policy and practices made the transformation possible, and the restructuring of state-owned enterprises has had an enormous effect. But the economic growth of China has been and is being led by a remarkable group of entrepreneurs and executives running private companies who were born and raised in the context of a rigidly anticapitalist system.

Consider the experience of Zhang Ruimin, now one of China's most important business leaders and the CEO of the Haier Group, the world's largest appliance company. He is also an official of the Communist Party, something that might have made Chairman Mao's head spin. Zhang is the son of factory workers and, as a young man, was caught up in the Cultural Revolution. He joined the Red Guards, Mao's shock troops charged with bringing down bourgeois elements within society, especially anybody associated with capitalism.

After the army was called in to bring the Cultural Revolution to a close, Zhang ended up working in a government-run construction company. He slowly advanced through the bureaucracy there, reading management books and taking classes in his spare time, then moved to the Qingdao city government and its appliance division in 1982. From there, he moved to a government factory making refrigerators, taking it over in 1984 just at the time when the country was prodding these operations to run more like businesses. It is easy to imagine Zhang being seen at this point as a civil servant—an ambitious one, but still a bureaucrat.

As with many of the business leaders we interviewed, Zhang's eyes were opened by his first interaction with Western business, in his case a trip to Germany to visit one of his company's suppliers. The comparison between this supplier and his home operations, particularly regarding the quality of his own refrigerators, was a shock and something of an embarrassment both to his company and, he noted, to his country.

What happened when Zhang returned from Germany is one of the most famous stories in Chinese business. He pulled all the defective refrigerators out of his inventory, brought them to the front of the factory floor, and had the employees smash them with sledgehammers. The message, which went out from the factory to the customers, was as dramatic a statement of a change in company culture as business has ever seen: we will no longer tolerate bad products.

Except for that limited exposure to the German company Liebherr Group (from which the Qingdao Refrigerator Company would be renamed "Qingdao Haier" and then just "Haier," a transliteration of the last syllable of the German company's name), Zhang had no real model to follow to reform his company. He changed the pay system, rewarding employees in part based on company performance, but he also pioneered the now common practice in China of "shaming" bad performers by having them stand before fellow employees and explain their mistakes. Along the way, he created marketing by checking with customers to see what they thought of the company's products. The government gave him other appliance companies to run, which he then consolidated into the new Haier Group. Zhang himself went back to school while running the business and, despite never having been to college, secured an MBA degree in 1994, continuing to search for better answers to company problems.[1]

As the economy opened up, the Haier Group followed suit, securing capital through private markets, expanding into export markets, and then acquiring businesses in other countries and establishing factories abroad. It might be tempting to imagine Zhang as a brash paradigm-buster, but it also seems that his experience of living through the cataclysm of the Cultural Revolution made him a cautious leader. Consider his motto for running a business: "Tread on eggs always, run scared always."[2]

The rise of Haier and other private companies in China was surely not inevitable. The most elementary ownership rights that Western entrepreneurs have long taken for granted were not in place when the first companies began. China did not promulgate its first law governing private companies until 1994, and it did not offer constitutional protection of private property until 2007. Imagine being an entrepreneur with no assurance that you would own any of it, even if you could somehow build a company that countered the prevailing winds. It is fair to say that when entrepreneurs like Zhang Ruimin arose in the 1980s, private enterprise was tolerated rather than officially permitted. The ability to make the decisions that most Western entrepreneurs take for granted, such as setting prices, entering new markets, and fixing wages, was in doubt throughout most of that decade since private enterprise had not yet been countenanced. Entrepreneurs had to fight not only for market share but also for the basic right to exist.

The story ahead is about how leaders like Zhang who are running—and in many cases founded—the most important companies in China think about business and how they manage their operations. Their businesses typically started in an environment that was utterly hostile to private enterprise, and the founders—unlike entrepreneurs in the West—not only had few direct models to follow but also no investment bankers or management consultants to render advice. What did they come up with as a system for running their businesses?

In fact, Chinese business leaders have evolved a cluster of ideas and methods for taking action that constitute a distinctive mindset: a combination of both cognitive and emotional factors that shape how executives see their market, their firm's place in it, and their leadership of it. Business mindsets, though not immutable, are enduring and encompassing, and over substantial periods they shape how business is approached and companies are led. The approach of Chinese business leaders is not the American model, the European model, or the Japanese model. These fortune makers invented their own way forward.[3]

China Matters

We should be interested in China's emerging management mindset for two major reasons: first, because China matters. Compared to its gross domestic product of 1978, China's GDP in 2015 had grown twenty-six-fold—contrasting with less than a three-fold growth over the same period in the United States. In so expanding, China has lifted more than 600 million people out of poverty. China already accounts for one-fifth of the global economy (see Table 1.1), and its gross domestic product is forecast to become the world's largest in just a few short years.

As a result of China's prodigious growth, companies of all stripes are increasingly shipping their products and services outside the country. Chinese steel production, for instance, soared from 37 million metric tons in 1980 to 822 million in 2014, up from 5 percent of global production to 48 percent of the world's output. Over the same period, US steel production declined from 102 to 87 million metric tons, and European production sagged from 208 to 166 million metric tons.[4]

From 1978 to 2013, Chinese exports as a fraction of the country's GDP rose from 4 to 24 percent. In 1978, exports and imports combined constituted the equivalent of 10 percent of China's gross domestic product, but that fraction had ratcheted up by a factor of four, reaching 46 percent of

TABLE 1.1 Chinese and Global Economies, 1700–2015

	1700	1820	1900	1950	2001	2015
Population (in millions)						
China	138	381	400	547	1,275	1,387
World	603	1042	1,564	2,521	6,149	7,154
China %	23	37	26	22	21	19
GDP*						
China	83	229	218	240	4,570	11,463
World	371	696	1,973	5,326	37,148	57,947
China %	22	33	11	5	12	20
GDP/capita**						
China	600	600	545	439	3,583	8,265
World	615	668	1,262	2,110	6,041	7,154
China/World	0.98	0.90	0.43	0.21	0.59	1.16

Source: Yao, 2016. *GDP in billions of 1990 dollars; **GDP per capita in 1990 dollars.

GDP by 2013—making China an extremely international economy (see Figure A1.1 in Appendix 1).

One tangible and obvious result for US consumers has been a startling flow of China-made products onto US shelves. It is estimated that 70 percent of the items sold in Walmart's American stores by the early 2010s were manufactured in China. Many US customers had already become aware of this pedigree, and some were even coming to appreciate and ask for such branded products as Haier refrigerators, Huawei connectors, and Lenovo laptops. That familiarity is sure to increase as Chinese-made automobiles arrive in the US market, led in 2015 by Volvo, the formerly Swedish nameplate acquired from Ford Motor Company in 2009 by China's Zhejiang Geely Holding Group. Cars from other Chinese automakers such as Chery and Great Wall are coming to American showrooms, too. Even General Motors was importing its China-manufactured Buick compact sport-utility vehicle, Envision, to the US market beginning in 2016.[5]

The other obvious effect of the shift toward Chinese-made merchandise has been a decline in manufacturing goods and jobs in the United States and other Western countries. This effect is most notable in products like personal apparel, injection molded plastics, and consumer goods. The political fallout from the effects on American jobs became a central theme of the 2016 US presidential race.

Chinese businesses are even beginning to enter more sophisticated product markets where the West has long held a monopoly. In 2015, for example, the Commercial Aircraft Corporation of China—Comac—introduced a single-aisle airliner, C919, with seats for up to 174 passengers, as a direct competitor to Boeing's 737 and Airbus's 320. Though fully ramped-up production was not expected until 2018, by 2015 Comac had already received more than 500 orders from 21 airlines. As we note elsewhere, China has a huge advantage over other countries in developing viable multinational competitors in that its domestic market is so large. Comac's home demand is expected to reach 4,600 single-aisle aircraft by 2034. America's Boeing and Europe's Airbus booked more than 90 percent of all commercial aircraft sales worldwide in the mid-2010s, but that dominance will surely be threatened by China's emergent aircraft industry in the years ahead.[6]

Chinese real-estate developers have been ramping up their footprint outside China as well. Greenland Holdings Group, Dalian Wanda Group, and other property companies poured billions of dollars into buildings from New York to Chicago to Los Angeles. A Brooklyn apartment investment totaled $5 billion, a Chicago investment included a ninety-four-story condo-hotel building, and the Los Angeles stakes included $3 billion in condos, retail space, and hotel properties. Chinese acquisitions of US commercial properties in 2010 stood at $1 billion, but the value of these properties more than doubled by 2014 to $2.5 billion and then tripled a year later to $8.6 billion.[7]

Investments and acquisitions by Chinese companies abroad accelerated more generally in the mid-2010s, with the United States a primary target. Chinese private-company foreign direct investment in the United States rose from virtually zero during the 2000s to more than $13 billion by 2015 (see Figure A1.2). The Haier Group, a case in point, agreed to acquire General Electric's appliance division in 2016 for $4.5 billion. Haier already held a 5.6 percent share of the US market for major household appliances, and in acquiring GE's 12,000 employees and the right to use the GE brand on its appliances for forty years, CEO Zhang Ruimin was determined to significantly expand his American footprint.[8]

China's commercial engagements elsewhere have displayed much the same expansion. Latin American trade with China from 2000 to 2015 rose by a factor of twenty-two, leading the Organisation of Economic Co-operation and Development (OECD) to characterize China's engagement as "a game changer in the region's external environment." Similarly, Chinese companies acquired twenty-eight German companies in 2014 for a total value of $2.6 billion, and during the first five months of 2016, Chinese firms bought twenty-four companies valued at $9.1 billion. Chinese buying surges in 2016 were also evident in France, Switzerland, and Spain. The total value of mergers and acquisitions both within and outside China by Chinese companies rose from less than $10 billion in 2005 to more than $110 billion in 2015 (see Figure A1.3). During the first five months of 2016, China had overtaken the United States as the number-one acquirer of foreign companies worldwide.[9]

At the heart of China's global expansion and increasingly a driver of it has been a host of privately incorporated enterprises. If we are to appreciate what has been fueling China's extraordinary development during the past four decades, we have to understand how its fortune makers have helped map, build, and sustain it. And they have done so despite the dominating role of the state and its continuing tolerance of anti-competitive practices.[10]

National differences in management models, especially when combined with other methods such as Toyota's "lean manufacturing" or General Electric's "leadership engine," were of great interest in earlier periods to company leaders in other national settings. American focus on Japanese management practices, for instance, soared when Japanese companies were on a tear during the 1980s, epitomized by best-selling books such as William G. Ouchi's *Theory Z: How American Business Can Meet the Japanese Challenge* (1982) and Ezra Vogel's *Japan as Number One: Lessons for America* (1979). In the case of China, worldwide interest in its business practices is now already high and likely to further intensify as its economy continues to expand and its companies become increasingly important, if not dominant, players worldwide.

The second reason to care about the Chinese model is that it may have much to instruct the West. Though large American companies have had a century-long head start, China's commercial upstarts—many now already counted among the Global 500—achieved scale with remarkable speed. While it is undoubtedly easier to catch up with rivals than to surpass them, Chinese companies show no signs of slowing down. Unlike most of their Western counterparts, they grew up in the current era and thus carry none of the legacies that can weigh on those from an earlier time when markets were very different. As a result, the ways they operate may be better suited for the new global order. Just as traditional carmakers worldwide have fruitfully incorporated ground-breaking concepts from Japan's postwar auto-making methods, we believe that Western companies can learn much from how the new Chinese companies manage and run their freshly devised operations.[11]

Research on companies in the United States has found that their executives have greater impact on the enterprises if they are facing greater uncertainty in their markets. That stands to reason: when company executives are less clear about what should be expected because of uncertainty, their decisions are likely to have greater consequences for the enterprise, for better or for worse. As we describe in more detail below, Chinese companies are run much more by the person at the top than by staff or procedures—an approach that makes their individual executives much more important. The lessons of how these executives operate may therefore be more important for companies and executives worldwide as uncertainty becomes a more pervasive attribute of modern business.[12]

Company managers everywhere will also want to better understand Chinese leaders' distinct way of doing business if they are to compete against—or partner with—the companies that already dominate the Chinese market and are increasingly coming to the fore on the world stage.

•

The approach we take to tell this story is one we have used elsewhere in identifying the distinctive facets of Indian business leadership. Specifically, in *The India Way: How India's Top Business Leaders Are Revolutionizing Management* (Harvard Business Review Press, 2010), we interviewed a number of founders and executives of India's largest publicly traded companies, including those of Infosys, Reliance, and Tata. We worked to understand the mindset of the leaders of these companies through direct contact with the founders and executives themselves.

We have pursued the same path here, interviewing the top executives at China's largest private companies. With virtually unprecedented access, we have sought to see the founders and executives close in. We quizzed the leaders of the largest and most prominent private companies in China—including not only the already well-known icons such as

Alibaba and Lenovo but also companies like Geely and Vanke that are still unknown to most Americans and Europeans. And in doing so, we found a different business mentality that contrasts sharply with the executive mindsets so prevalent in the West. The executives we talked with are identified at the back of the book, and their companies include the following:

Alibaba Group. Alibaba is an Internet-driven e-commerce company founded in 1999 whose annual sales in recent years have exceeded $15 billion. It has more than 35,000 employees, and its 2014 initial public offering in the United States raised more than $21 billion, far exceeding Facebook's $16 billion initial public offering in 2012. We interviewed Alibaba chief executive Jack Ma.

Geely Automobile. Created in 1986 as a refrigerator company, Geely is a leading maker of automobiles, motorcycles, engines, and parts. It acquired Volvo Cars in 2010 and the London Taxi Company in 2012, and by 2016 it was selling its products in twenty-four countries, including the United States. Geely had revenue of $4.5 billion, more than 18,000 employees, and a market value of $37 billion in 2015. We interviewed senior executive Shen Freeman.

Lenovo Group. Now the world's largest maker of personal computers, outselling both Dell Computer and Hewlett-Packard, Lenovo is also a major producer of tablets, smartphones, and servers. Founded in 1984, Lenovo had more than 60,000 employees as of 2015 and drew an annual revenue of more than $46 billion. We interviewed Lenovo founder Liu Chuanzhi several times, along with CEO Yang Yuanqing and other company executives.

Vanke Group. Also established in 1984, Vanke has emerged as China's largest real-estate developer and property manager. With a market value of $25 billion in 2015, it had more than 40,000 employees and owned and managed real estate throughout greater China and abroad. We interviewed Vanke founder and chairman Wang Shi.

We supplemented those interviews with information on the executives and their firms from a range of public and private sources. In addition, we

excluded government-owned corporations because state-owned enterprises are largely government operations whose leaders are state officials.
Much of the production of state-owned enterprises (SOEs) is government
directed, with public objectives overlaid on commercial aims. The goals of
non-state-owned enterprises, by contrast, are more similar to the traditional self-interested objectives of privately held companies in the West,
making comparison of their leadership styles more direct. The state-owned
enterprises are still important, of course, and rank among the largest employers on earth in terms of the number of employees. Of the twenty-five
largest publicly traded companies in 2015, for example, the United States
was home to eight, topped by WalMart with 2.2 million on payroll, but
China counted six, led by PetroChina with 534,000 employees.

It is worth noting that many of the state-owned companies are following the lead of the private companies into world markets. Consider the
state-owned China National Chemical Corporation, often called Chem-
China, which acquired one of the world's largest agricultural chemical and
seed companies, Switzerland's Syngenta, for $43 billion in 2016, having
also purchased the Italian tire maker Pirelli a year earlier for $7.7 billion.[13]

The government had resolved in 1995 to end state ownership of most
companies, retaining just several hundred large state-owned enterprises,
and over the next ten years it privatized more than 90 percent of the country's SOEs. In that year, over half of China's urban employees were still on
the payroll of a state-owned enterprise, but by 2014 just 14 percent of urban employees were working for a state-owned enterprise (see Figure
A1.4). In rural China, only 1 million people had found work in private enterprises as of 1990, but by 2014 that figure had risen to 45 million. In metropolitan regions, one-fifth of employees worked for private companies in
1978, but four-fifths did so by 2013 (see Figure A1.5).[14]

Private firms accounted for just 10 percent of the country's industrial
output in 1965, on the eve of the Cultural Revolution, but their output bal-
looned to nearly half of the nation's industrial output by 2013 (see Figure
A1.6). The amount of annual output, the value of goods and services produced in a year, had also radically grown, from less than ¥3 trillion in 1993
to nearly ¥53 trillion just twenty years later (see Figure A1.7; ¥ = Chinese
yuan, also designated CNY, renminbi, or RMB).[15]

Privately owned companies are playing an increasingly dominant role
in China's economy, responsible by the mid-2010s for half of the country's

industrial output and three-quarters of its urban company employment—figures that are growing. (The world's second-largest employer, Hon Hai Precision Industry, better known by its trading name, Foxconn Technology Group—the maker of BlackBerries, iPhones, and Kindles among dozens of other electronic products—has most of its nearly 1.3 million employees work at facilities in China. We excluded this company from the study since it is headquartered in Taiwan.)

To appreciate the recency of the Chinese position in world business, turn the clock back to 1996, the first year that the editors of the *Financial Times* compiled a worldwide-500 list of publicly traded companies. The United States included 203 firms among the top 500—but China none. Twenty years later, China boasted 37, having vaulted ahead of France, Germany, Japan, and the United Kingdom. Of *Fortune* magazine's annual ranking of the 500 largest companies globally by revenue, none were based in China in 1980, but by 2015, 98 of the Fortune 500 were so incorporated.[16] The market value of the 37 publicly traded Chinese companies in the *Financial Times*'s global 500 is the equivalent of the economy of the seventh-largest country in the world, greater than that of Brazil, Italy, India, or Russia. Although down from its peak, China's annual growth rate is forecast to put its economy over that of the United States by the mid-2020s. In 1980, the Chinese GDP was a thin sliver of that of the United States, but by 2016 it had soared to more than two-thirds (see Figure 1.1).[17]

Despite the prodigious growth at home and significant inroads abroad, the founders and executives who lead China's private business firms are barely known even in the business community outside of their home turf. Most American readers of the business press know that Steve Jobs built Apple and Mark Zuckerberg created Facebook. But with the possible exception of Jack Ma, the founder and driver of Alibaba, one would be hard-pressed to find many people outside China who could name any Chinese business leaders.

Chinese growth has not been without its bumps, but the private companies that are the subject of this book are likely to remain robust in growth and increasing impact on markets around the world. For example, annual growth rates have been 20 percent at Lenovo, 34 percent at Vanke, and 45 percent at Alibaba. And as the Chinese government continues to press its remaining state-owned enterprises to further privatize, we

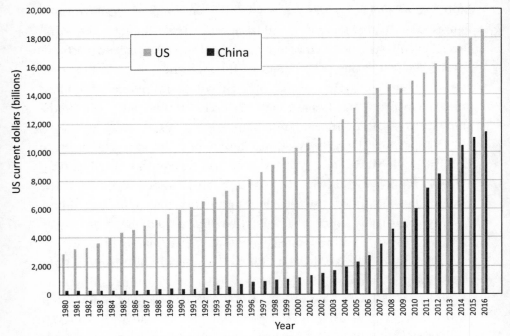

FIGURE 1.1 GDP in Current US Dollars, China and the United States, 1980–2016
Source: International Monetary Fund, 2016.

believe that the private-company model featured in this book will become increasingly important in driving China forward.

Understanding the China Way

The growth and ascendance of Chinese companies are products of the strategies and leadership of those who created, built, and now manage those enterprises. The invisible hand of the market conditioned their goals and decisions, but their actions have constituted a strong visible hand. We want to understand that visible hand, how they direct it, what they want from it, and where it is taking their enterprises.

As with business executives anywhere, the leaders of Chinese companies make hundreds of vital decisions every year, ranging from whom to hire and what to make to where to invest and what to cut. The types of decisions they make are of course not dissimilar from those made by

American managers or German managers or Indian managers. All businesses have to hire people and run production and meet payrolls and tally earnings. But how they do so is shaped by the businesses' heritage, values, and a host of other national factors.

We often talk about international business as if a giant convergence is taking place. Thomas L. Friedman's 2005 book, *The World Is Flat,* outlines many such developments, especially on the consumer side, that play out in a similar manner around the world: cellphones are ubiquitous, for example, and (more or less) work the same way everywhere. But a larger literature suggests that many national differences still matter, and indeed may be becoming more salient, as we have seen in the UK's decision to leave the European Union and the growing US reluctance to reduce trade barriers.[18]

The idea of distinctive national business leadership principles is not new. German sociologist Max Weber argued in a celebrated book, *The Protestant Ethic and the Spirit of Capitalism,* that business managers in countries in Northern Europe and North America evolved a distinctive calling whereby they demonstrated religious merit by founding a private enterprise, building the enterprise, and reinvesting in the enterprise—rather than consuming the newfound wealth. Though Weber contended that both the "ethic" and the resulting "spirit of capitalism" are rooted in the Protestant Reformation, others have suggested that they comprise an ethos also shared among business leaders in Catholic countries. Whether the ethos is rooted in Protestantism or Catholicism, it emerged as a distinctive high-octane fuel for those at the apex of enterprises in Northern Europe and North America.[19]

Later, sociologist Reinhard Bendix characterized what Weber had unearthed as just one of several "ideologies of management," systems of thought that drive the actions of executives and justify the willingness of large numbers of employees to accept direction from those executives. Such management ideologies, he argued, emerge as business leaders face and come to appreciate similar challenges across a range of companies and industries within a country.

Drawing on the period of industrialization in England, Germany, Russia, and the United States, Bendix found what he termed *entrepreneurial ideologies* to have emerged as company founders fought for acceptance by ruling aristocracies whose dominance predated the rise of private enterprise. Later, new challenges emerged as company executives faced workforces that were becoming restless and sometimes revolutionary. Even then, national differences persisted, as business entrepreneurs came to constitute a dominant and self-assured social class in the United States but remained subordinate to state authority in Russia and consequently less dominant and self-assured in its mindset.[20]

While managerial ideologies in America and England differed strikingly from those that emerged in Russia and elsewhere, subtler ideological differences also emerged between the United States and the United Kingdom. Historian Martin J. Wiener, for example, documented that the supremacy of business became far more complete in the United States than in the UK in the latter half of the nineteenth century and the first half of the twentieth century. High culture in England had not accorded business the respected status that it had achieved in America. Finance had become more of a noble calling in the UK, but young people were not encouraged by the mores of the era to enter what was deemed the more mundane world of making or marketing factory products. "This anti-industrial culture" was so strong in the United Kingdom, Wiener reported, that industrialists themselves "breathed it in ever more deeply the higher they rose in social position," in sharp contrast to the status accorded industrialists like Andrew Carnegie, Henry Ford, and John D. Rockefeller in the United States.[21]

Our colleague, sociologist Mauro Guillen, extended Weber's and Bendix's ideas with the phrase "models of management," referencing the distinct national mindsets he documented among company managers in Germany, Great Britain, Spain, and the United States. Guillen reported, for instance, that the precepts of Taylorism and scientific management found early adoption by company leaders in Germany and the United States but far less acceptance in Great Britain and Spain. Like scientific paradigms, each country model set forward the business goals most valued and the managerial precepts most expected within its territory. And each considered itself to be the one best way.[22]

Country differences in more specific leadership principles are also evident from any number of other investigations. Cross-national studies of company leadership have reported, for example, that several business principles are common to most countries. Consider the work stream of Robert House, Mansour Javidan, and their colleagues. In several major studies they appraised mid-level manager preferences for company leadership qualities in the early 2000s with survey data from 17,000 middle managers of 825 companies in 62 countries. The researchers found that managers almost everywhere favored dynamism, decisiveness, and honesty among those they follow; an ability to motivate and negotiate with others; and a focus on performance. At the same time, they reported other leadership principles that were important in some countries and not in others, including status consciousness, self-effacement, and subordinate empowerment.[23]

Our own study of Indian business leadership, which serves as a proto-type for the present book, found something similar. Since the economic reforms in 1991 that opened up the Indian economy, a new group of en-trepreneurs created and operated their companies based on a set of prac-tices that differed substantially from what characterized the previous period, when oppressive government control (the "license raj") and a cul-ture of hierarchy had stifled innovation and flexibility. These emergent practices comprise a distinctive bundle that we term "the India Way."

Cross-national investigations focused directly on businesses in China have also reported enduring differences there. Julian Birkinshaw of the London Business School, for instance, has found that Western managers emphasize creating near-term value for shareholders, while Chinese man-agers emphasize longer-term value for stakeholders; that Western manag-ers execute more through delegation and organization, while Chinese managers do so more through authority and persuasion; and that West-ern managers stress productivity and efficiency, while Chinese managers stress reflection and learning. "It seems surely just a matter of time," he concluded, "before a 'China Way' emerges."[24]

We appreciate that some business leaders freely defy their own na-tion's way. Think of Tony Hsieh, who leads US shoe seller Zappos with neither organizational charts nor job titles, or John Mackey, who leads Whole Foods Market with a focus on wholesome products and employee "happiness." Or consider Facebook and Google versus General Electric and U.S. Steel, all based in the United States but led by executives with vastly different leadership styles. That said, we are looking here for the most common threads that characterize the way that many executives of private Chinese companies have led their enterprises, recognizing that not all share all the threads.[25]

•

To understand the China Way, we have placed particular emphasis on going to company leaders themselves. Other sources of information have been invaluable, but we have especially sought to see Chinese business through the eyes of those who are creating and leading it. We appreciate of course that, like all of us, Chinese business leaders bring blinders and biases to their perceptions, so we have made every effort to take those limitations into account as we have sought to extract the guiding principles of Chinese business leadership.[26]

We refer to tangible company leadership capacities, such as thinking strategically and deciding decisively, as leadership principles. We describe a coherent and distinctive constellation of those leadership principles, widely shared among business founders and executives within a given country, as an executive mindset, a management model, or a business way. And from our interviews with the Chinese private-business leaders featured in this book, we have found several distinctive strands of an emergent management model. Taken together, these can be seen as constituting the China Way:

China's Fortune Makers

The China Way

We identify seven distinguishing features among the leaders creating China's great global companies:

- Their Own Way Forward
- The Learning Company
- Strategic Agility for the Long Game
- Talent Management
- The Big Boss
- Growth as Gospel
- Governance as Partnership

Their Own Way Forward. Business leaders in China have learned to build private enterprises in an environment where Marxist ideology and party control remained dominant through much of the reform period. Unlike Western entrepreneurs, who typically start by developing a new product or service, the early Chinese entrepreneurs often began in the trading business, serving as distributors for foreign multinationals or as brokers between suppliers and users. In the process, they taught themselves how to do business, maneuvered through political uncertainty, found their own niche, built a sustainable organization, and developed their own core competencies.

They learned pragmatically by doing and then reflecting on what they did. While the mapping of their own pathway has come of necessity, it inadvertently brought the advantage of leaving the executives unburdened by the past, giving them a free hand to lead without the limits of habit or tradition.

Their emphasis on self-improvement through education and reflection is analogous to approaches long embraced by the Communist Party. And their inclination to discover their own way forward with few precedents is akin to that of the early world explorers who traveled without the benefit of map or compass. Indeed, by finding and fashioning their own way, the founders put their own unique imprints on their enterprises.

The Learning Company. Many of these company executives were shocked by their first exposure to international competitors and realized how much they had to learn. They knew that they and their managers were woefully unprepared for operating in China, let alone against international competitors at home or abroad. Accordingly, they pursued every feasible path for organizational learning: hiring managers from abroad, engaging consultants of all stripes, and partnering with Western firms.

Chinese executives have carried their own learning experience into the firm. They have insisted that their company learn to be a learning organization with greater zeal than is common in the West, and for that they have drawn upon channels already well familiar to the West: self-directed learning, instructive experience, and personal coaching. Some have even launched their own universities.

Strategic Agility for the Long Game. The focus on finding new opportunities and going after them fast—driven by scrappy personalities and lean architectures—is similar to how start-ups have of necessity operated everywhere. Without proven models to emulate or roadmaps to follow,

Chinese executives have recurrently focused their enterprise on what they believed was a promising product or service, only to learn from experience that a different direction was more promising. They have nimbly pivoted, yet in doing so they also kept an eye on a far horizon, seeking to sustain their enterprise for the decades ahead—whatever the immediate shifts.

Underpinning this leadership principle of strategic agility is an enduring concept of market and purpose, a defining notion that shapes the firm's specific strategies but transcends them as well. Company agility, then, born of necessity, rests at the same time on a long-game platform. When Chinese CEOs decide to move into a new opening, they are thus able to take a future-term perspective, willingly accepting shareholder losses in the near term to later arrive there.

Talent Management. Business leaders in China have learned to grow big fast by drawing on a paternalistic leadership style and building a clan-like corporate culture. They have learned to oversee large workforces comprising tens of thousands of people, though managing them and their human resource systems are among the least sophisticated and developed part of the Chinese businesses we studied. Most Western corporations have well-established architectures for organizing work, appraising performance, and rewarding success, but there is far less such scaffolding among the Chinese companies.

No one would claim that these companies are sophisticated in their hiring, motivating, and employee-management practices. It is thus no surprise that problems of retention, of securing the right skills, and of moving employees to take the initiative loom larger in China than in the West. Not many Chinese companies have refined internal control systems to monitor performance and check against malfeasance.

The Big Boss. Privately owned firms are exceptionally focused on the individual at the top. While the big-boss model has faded in the West, not so in China. The special place of top executives is partly a product of their having founded the firm, but also a consequence of having no preexisting models to suggest otherwise. In a country with a relatively low level of individualism and no democratic tradition, it may not be surprising that worker willingness to defer to company leaders and identify with their interests runs high. Chinese business executives thus play an outsized role in their firm compared to executives in other countries—one that might well be described as a "big-boss presence." In the West, CEOs are powerful because they control the bureaucracy of the firm; in China, CEOs are powerful because they are at the top of it.

The focus on the big boss, however, creates a potential conflict since business culture still carries the national norm of personal modesty, stressing personal sacrifice for the common good. Consequently, Chinese business leaders have embraced a simultaneous posture of brashness and humility, emphasizing a readiness to take bold actions even when these are individually costly. The big-boss model has thus led to an ironic combination of hierarchic and ostensibly humble management.

Growth as Gospel. The leaders of private companies have defined the goals of their own Chinese ethic and spirit of capitalism very differently from what we are familiar with in the West, both historically and contemporarily. They place a greater premium on growth, believing that profitability is an end product of growing the business rather than the primary goal. It is not surprising that Chinese business leaders focus as much on business strategy as do business leaders elsewhere, but what is a surprise is how much of their attention is also concentrated on expanding their current markets and finding new ones.

Company growth rather than shareholder value has thus become the defining agenda. And that growth is anchored in and rationalized in terms of providing more of whatever the firm produces to companies and consumers who need it. This management ideology of growth may be transitory, more a historic stage than an enduring mindset, but in the meantime, company expansion has become the gospel.

Governance as Partnership. When we put the above components together—lean, low-cost operating structures, highly centralized decision making with continuous learning, and a workforce that follows the boss—we get the essence of the competitiveness of Chinese businesses. Their executives can and do move fast, with no patience for reports to be written or committees to meet.

And while American executives are pressed by their boards to maximize profits, Chinese directors place scant stress on the driving mantra of shareholder value. Corporate governance as a result is not what we have seen in the United States. For plotting their path, Chinese business leaders turn to their board for ideas and guidance far more than review and approval. Directors are pressed to help lead—and less to monitor—their company. The China Way is characterized by company boards that help build growth even if their directors are doing little to discipline management to optimize shareholder return.

What's Distinctive, What's Sustainable?

The Chinese companies we studied are distinct from Western companies in the ways described above. Though a powerful force in China's growth, this China Way also comes with a set of yet-unanswered questions about its viability. For example, will these companies be able to continue without sophisticated human resource systems and without internal control functions now that individualism is on the rise in China, and the new generations entering the workplace lack some of the compliance with authority associated with their parents' generation?

The current arrangements in China give CEOs extraordinary power. In the companies we studied—by definition, the most successful ones in the country—that power has typically been used wisely, admirably so in most cases. Will this continue into the next generation, when business leaders are no longer as concerned about the legacy of the companies and may be more focused on their own fortune than on fortune making?

At the moment, the corporate governance of these companies does not seem to be up to the job of removing failing or troublesome CEOs. Nor has succession been well planned in most firms. As Warren Buffett is fond of saying, it's only when the tide goes out that you can see who has been swimming naked, and if China's economy slows considerably, it will be much more obvious which companies are performing with poor leadership. Will anything be done to resolve those problems?

More generally, will these companies continue to be run so directly by their CEOs as they become even larger and more complex? Can they expand into international waters without giving local leaders in those countries greater autonomy? How will they develop future leaders under their current model, which gives decision making and real autonomy to very few managers? Will the competitive advantage begun in the booming domestic market of China translate into head-to-head competition abroad, where markets are growing more slowly, local competitors have deep knowledge, and business operations are more complex?

All of these questions await the next edition of *Fortune Makers*.

The spirit of capitalism . . . had to fight its way
to supremacy against a whole world of hostile forces.

MAX WEBER, *The Protestant Ethic and the Spirit of Capitalism*

CHAPTER 2

Their Own Way Forward

It's very difficult to apply the US business model
to China directly. . . . We have to develop our own.

When China first initiated its economic reforms in 1978, there were virtually no private enterprises in China and few indigenous traditions for China's would-be entrepreneurs to build upon or emulate. How should company founders go about developing their markets and building their organizations? Should they follow models already proven successful in other countries or develop their own?

Two distinct management paradigms had become dominant abroad in the 1980s. One, a Japanese model, was well summarized by academic researcher William Ouchi. After years of research on Japanese managers, Ouchi argued his case in *Theory Z: How American Business Can Meet the Japanese Challenge,* which became a *New York Times* best-seller. The secret to Japanese success, he contended, was not technology but a better way of managing people: "This is a managing style that focuses on a strong company philosophy," he wrote, "a distinct corporate culture, long-range staff development, and consensus decision-making." Ouchi marshaled evidence that his "Theory Z" model resulted in lower turnover, increased commitment, and higher productivity.[1]

Another best-seller, *In Search of Excellence: The Lessons from America's Best-Run Companies,* popularized an American model. McKinsey consultants Thomas J. Peters and Robert H. Waterman studied forty-three large American companies and identified a set of management practices accounting for their performance, including (1) a bias for action, (2) being close to the customer, (3) fostering innovation, (4) treating employees as a source of quality, (5) hands-on, value-driven management, (6) sticking to the knitting, and (7) adopting simple and lean structures. These management practices focused on building shareholder value by exploiting market opportunities, acquiring other companies, and incentivizing top management.[2]

Both the Japanese and American management models were premised on the dominance of private-company ownership and a relatively unfettered market economy. Our would-be Chinese entrepreneurs, however, enjoyed neither precondition. At the time they founded and built many of today's top Chinese private firms, the business environment was drastically different from that which had prevailed in Japan and the United States.

The Chinese Business Environment in the 1980s and 1990s

From China's revolution in 1949 until its economic reforms commencing in 1978, Beijing had insisted on a centrally planned economy. National officials set production goals, controlled wages, fixed prices, allocated resources, and directed a large share of the country's economic activity and output. From 1956 to 1978, the state allowed no private ownership or foreign business presence. Three-fourths of China's industrial output in 1978 was produced by centrally controlled state enterprises and the remainder by locally controlled collective enterprises.

The Chinese government began to test private ownership in the early 1980s. Its reform-minded leaders gradually liberalized the market, deregulating price controls and opening international trade, though they postponed privatization of the state-owned sector until the mid-1990s. One consequence of the gradualist approach was to create disparate product opportunities for those outside the state-controlled economy, allowing the entrepreneurial-minded to seek private profit independent of the state's allocation of raw materials and manufacturing equipment.

In searching for opportunities around which to launch a private enterprise, swarms of entrepreneurs experimented with management innovations that enabled them to bypass central planning and to secure their own upstream materials and downstream channels. Neither the absence of a legal or regulatory framework for private enterprises nor the challenges in accessing scarce government-controlled resources thwarted the would-be capitalists. By the time private enterprise finally received constitutional protection in 2004, guaranteeing equal status with government-owned firms, and legal protection in 2007 with China's first property-rights law, some 5.5 million private companies were already up and running with 120 million workers.

In an emergent process that academic researchers Victor Nee and Sonja Opper aptly characterized as "capitalism from below," private manufacturing arose in three phases. In the first phase, a gradual replacement of central planning by market mechanisms resulted in a power shift from state bureaucrats and government agencies to private producers. Entrepreneurs faced a widened set of choices, allowing them to experiment with new forms of production. They also informally developed new arrangements for commerce outside the reach of state planning.[3]

In the second phase, an expanding free market generated incentives for business innovations as rewards came increasingly from market performance rather than government connections. Now, private capital markets, free labor movements, industrial clusters, and distribution networks of their own making enabled private entrepreneurs to more readily surmount the daunting barriers to market entry. Despite lingering discriminatory treatment by the state and low social status, private firms grew faster than state-owned enterprises, and in time the bulk of China's urban workers came to be employed by non-state-owned companies. Finally, in the third phase, large numbers of entrepreneurs piled in, creating a tipping point as a self-reinforcing private-sector constituency emerged. Officials relaxed their rules to accommodate but also to regulate the embryonic private-sector realities.

This bottom-up process was by no means easy for those pushing it from below. In fact, starting a private business in China has been far riskier than doing so in the United States. The hazards of business failure are higher in China than in the United States, according to two analysts who drew data from China's State Statistical Bureau Annual Survey of Industrial Firms. This survey targets all state-owned enterprises and private companies with an annual sales revenue of at least ¥5 million. The entry and exit rates for the surveyed companies from 1999 to 2006 are displayed in Table 2.1, where we see an average annual entry rate of 25.8 percent and an average annual exit rate of 18.6 percent (where *exit* is defined as a registered business ceasing to exist). By comparison, the comparable entry and exit rates for US companies are only half as high as in China. For the

TABLE 2.1 Annual Percentages of Firm Entries
and Exits in China, 1999–2006

	1999	2000	2001	2002	2003	2004	2005	2006	Avg.
Entry	23.1	21.0	31.8	21.0	23.7	45.1	18.9	21.8	25.8
Exit	22.6	24.9	16.4	16.6	25.4	18.7	12.3	11.8	18.6

Source: He and Yang, 2015.

period from 1999 to 2011, for instance, one study found that the annual entry and exit rates in the United States were consistently less than 12 percent and 10 percent, respectively.[4]

Many factors in this early reform era account for the high rate of business failure rate in China, and as we detail below, four of these proved particularly problematic: institutional void, anti-business ideology and regulation, political uncertainty, and rent seeking and windfall profits. These factors point to the barriers and obstacles that the leaders of China's private companies have had to endure and surmount as they worked to create their own management model.

Institutional Void. The first nettlesome factor was what sociologists often term an "institutional void"—the absence of policies, rules, and practices that make for commercial exchange, such as market intermediaries, professional auditors, accounting rules, and government regulations. Even some of the most basic legal scaffolding was absent. China had no contract law until 1981, no commodity exchange until 1990, no stock exchange until 1992, and no corporate law until 1994. As academic researchers Tarun Khanna and Krishna Palepu have argued, such voids seriously hamper economic exchange in capital, labor, and product markets. When Michael Dell started his personal-computer business in his college dorm in 1984, he could simply call Texas Instruments to order components, but when Liu Chuanzhi founded Lenovo in China in the same year, he had to first ask the government for permission to even buy his components.[5]

Every American entrepreneur understands that if successful, he or she will own the company or at least a major share of it after an initial public offering. Yet in China, it took Lenovo founder Liu twenty years to secure just 1.4 percent of his company's equity since the very concept of private ownership could not be found in Chinese law at that time and he had to convince government agencies that his ten co-founders and key employees of Lenovo were also entitled to part of the equity they created. Virtually all firms formed during the 1980s and most in the 1990s were first owned by the state in urban areas or by collectives in the rural areas. Many of today's premier firms including Haier, Lenovo, and Vanke began as partial spin-offs from state-owned firms or rural collectives. There was simply no ready-to-use operator's manual on how to set up a private enterprise.

Anti-Business Ideology and Regulation. The absence of infrastructure for private business did not mean that the private business environment was neutral or even-handed. Rather, a second source of resistance was a deeply rooted anti-business ideology. In the Marxist doctrine of the era, private ownership was deemed a root cause of most social ills. China's central planning system was thus intended to replace private firms and their markets with an overarching scheme devised by government planners and state-owned company executives. Though the Chinese government commenced its economic reforms in 1978, most Marxist precepts persisted for years. Regulatory policies proved hostile to private business at almost every turn.

When the Chinese government first granted permission for private firms to form in 1979, it limited the number of employees at first to just five. Along with an owning married couple, the total workforce would have to be less than eight, a threshold above which exploitation of the working class would become significant, according to Marxist doctrine. Another decade passed until the Chinese government finally dropped this extreme workforce restriction in 1988. Even then, the ownership of private property was not accorded constitutional protection until 2004.

Because of the lingering anti-private-business legacy, regulators and regulations often discriminated against private firms. For example, state-owned enterprises (SOEs) could obtain their raw materials through the planning system at fixed prices. But since the inputs required by private firms were not included in China's central plan, they had to scramble for their raw materials on the open market, paying higher prices. SOEs borrowed their working capital from state-owned banks at official interest rates; private firms turned to outside providers with far higher rates.

Standard business practice in the West, such as private brokerage—making money by serving as intermediaries between buyers and sellers—was considered a crime in China since it could siphon funds away from the government's central plan, as a private-factory salesman learned in 1979. Ma Hanwen had signed a contract to sell glass-fiber fabric with a commission rate of ¥0.04 to 0.08 per meter. In one deal for 200,800 meters, Ma received a commission of ¥5,332, a vast amount compared to his monthly salary of ¥40 at the time. But because he had "served as a middle person with the purpose to make a huge profit," he was sentenced to five years in prison by a local court since China's criminal law at that time prohibited such activities as "speculation."[6]

Political Uncertainty. A third constraining factor for would-be private-business leaders was political uncertainty. Unlike Russia and other East European countries after 1989, when their economic reform came as "shock therapy," Chinese leaders adopted an incremental approach. Advocates of wholesale change contended that privatization of state-owned enterprise must go hand-in-hand with marketization and deregulation, but gradualists won the day on the premise that there was no proven blueprint for doing so and comprehensive reform must follow a learning approach. Chinese reformers would have to test their policies through trial and error.

Some have attributed China's success in its gradual economic reforms to a practice of learning from below, building local experiments into national policy. As noted in the summary of scholar Sebastian Heilmann, "central policy makers encourage local officials to try out new ways of problem-solving and then feed the local experiences back into national policy formulation." This experimental process shaped the making of policies in domains as diverse as rural de-collectivization, state-sector restructuring, and stock market regulation. But one by-product has been continuing uncertainty as contending policy makers gain the upper hand only to lose it to others several years later. A new business policy could be celebrated as a great reform today, only to be declared anti-socialist next year.[7]

The experience of the "Eight Kings of Wenzhou" offers a case in point. The Chinese government in 1980 began to experiment with private ownership, and China's State Council issued a directive in 1981 that endorsed "competition among firms of different ownership types." Eight entrepreneurs in Wenzhou, a county in Zhejiang province, jumped at this new opportunity, setting up private workshops to make and market a variety of products in short supply at that time. Their business grew rapidly, partly because the products they had chosen to produce were in high demand, and partly because they were able to adopt more flexible human resources practices—such as sales commissions and replacing nonperforming employees—than what was allowed in state-owned enterprises.

The eight entrepreneurs quickly became millionaires, but the policy allowing that prosperity was soon reversed. Because their business model and management methods were by their very nature in violation of central planning, it was not difficult for state officials to find fault with them. By 1982, seven of the eight entrepreneurs had been imprisoned for the crime of "disrupting the economic order of socialism."[8]

There were serious political risks even for government officials who dared to press for reform. Hu Yaobang, general secretary of the Chinese Communist Party, was forced to resign in 1987 for not sufficiently adhering to Marxist ideology and party oversight. What had been a political experiment in 1988 to liberalize price controls on consumer goods and insulate company management from party control had become a political crime a year later. Subsequently, the state stripped another general secretary and advocate of reform, Zhao Ziyang, of all positions and placed him under house arrest for the remainder of his life. Today's advocacy of reform could be swept into tomorrow's "anti-revolutionary conspiracy."

Rent Seeking and Windfall Profits. One key aspect of China's gradual reform program was a so-called dual-track liberalization under which contract prices among enterprises were frozen at a level specified in the central plan but were then freed for outputs above the centrally planned level. The first use of dual pricing was for crude oil in 1981, when the government allowed the export of above-quota crude oil at a higher price. In 1984, the government permitted industrial goods to be sold at market prices so long as the selling price was within 20 percent of the planned prices, though the latter restriction was finally lifted in 1985.[9]

However, dual pricing also brought with it an untoward side effect in its opening of rent seeking in the late 1980s. *Rent* does not refer here to payment on a lease but is a term stemming from Adam Smith's division of income into profit, wage, and rent. Rent seeking, then, is an attempt to obtain economic gains by manipulating the social or political environment rather than by contributing new wealth to it, extracting rather than adding value. Profit seeking depends on creating wealth, while rent seeking depends on influencing institutions such as the government to redistribute wealth among different groups without creating new wealth.[10]

According to one study, the centrally planned price of steel in 1987 was ¥905 per ton whereas the open market price had risen to ¥1,540 per ton. With a total steel production in 1987 of 43 million tons and nonplanned steel accounting for 53 percent of that production, the total differential came to ¥15.4 billion. That presented a huge rent-seeking opportunity both for government officials in charge of steel output and for company managers in charge of steel production. One study concluded that a rising wave of government corruption was partly attributable to the rent seeking from the dual-track price system. But rent seeking also proved risky to its private practitioners, as their relationship with government officials was inherently unstable.[11]

To summarize, the business environment in China in the early reform era when many of today's leading private enterprises were founded was characterized by an institutional void, an anti-private business ideology, high political uncertainty, and lucrative short-term but risky long-run temptations to engage in rent seeking. It was against this background that Liu Chuanzhi of Lenovo and Wang Shi of Vanke started their ventures in Beijing and Shenzhen, respectively. They not only had to find their own way forward in building a business but had to do so at a time when the political system was fundamentally hostile to their undertaking. As Lenovo founder Liu Chuanzhi told us in our interview, "It is very difficult to apply the US business model to China directly. . . . We have to develop our own."

Through Trial and Error

With virtually no private enterprise before 1980, few indigenous traditions to build upon or emulate, and an unfriendly environment, business leaders in China have learned to lead through trial and error. They have also learned to develop their own homegrown talent for doing so since so little was coming over the transom with the kind of management credentials that Western companies have long taken for granted.

In effect, Chinese business leaders in the 1980s and 1990s had to invent their own management methods. Almost nobody had built or run a private enterprise in China for more than a quarter century. In the absence of business models, business majors, even business magazines, the fundamentals were largely unfamiliar. They would have to be devised from scratch.

In the United States, that had happened a century earlier, with the emergence of AT&T, Montgomery Ward, and Standard Oil, soon to be followed by Carnegie Steel, General Electric, and Sears & Roebuck. As chronicled by business historian Alfred Chandler in *Strategy and Structure,* these companies had invented the American Way. They learned how to build and run large-scale enterprise, mastering the art of multidivisional management from their own experience. Later, as chronicled by corporate observers Adolf Berle and Gardiner Means, they learned how to run themselves with professional non-owning managers in place of their founding families.[12]

A century later, American Way capitalism had become part of the American way of life. Business takeovers were worthy of headline news, business majors outnumbered all others at US colleges, and new managers had the benefit of a vast canon, informed by the wisdom of Jim Collins, Peter Drucker, and Sheryl Sandberg, and the accumulated practices of generations past.

If American executives today come prewired for their leadership at the top, Chinese executives arrived at the top by creating the top. American managers could draw on more than a hundred years of codified experience served up by classrooms, textbooks, and consultants, while Chinese managers not only lacked college curricula, how-to books, and indigenous consultants but faced an environment that was systematically hostile to what they were doing. Like Meriwether Lewis and William Clark, they had knowingly ventured into terra incognita.

By way of one symptomatic example, consider the chairman of a large industrial firm who reported that he'd had to learn the art of industrial production on his own. "In the developed countries," he explained, "there are lots of management experiences, models or theories," but in China he found "few mature management theories or business models." In building his company over more than three decades, he had placed special emphasis on internal control systems in research, purchasing, production, sales, and finance, and he'd had to learn how to construct each largely from naught. Said the chairman of a developer of system programs for construction and property management that he had founded some twenty-five years earlier: "Whenever we run into issues, we learn as we go."

Another chairman had founded his company in the early 1990s, and by time of our interview, it had become one of China's largest high-technology enterprises, supporting R&D, manufacturing, and information technologies in industries ranging from aerospace and banking to telecom and transportation. He and his founding generation, he observed, had to feel their way forward, in sharp contrast to what he has seen among those presiding over the multinational companies coming into China:

> Most of the famous foreign companies hire professional managers as their chairmen. They are not founders of the company. There-fore, they do not have the opportunity to experience all the difficul-ties that we have to deal with. Chinese chairmen, who are the founders, have to cope with all kinds of unexpected and compli-cated situations to develop the business and company in an envi-ronment that does not have established rules and regulations as well as policies.

The founder and chairman of a bio-technology company that, after twenty years since its onset, was now producing more than a thousand products for diverse markets ranging from cosmetics and furniture to health care and household products, testified that when he started the en-terprise, he had virtually no comprehension of the difference that mana-gerial talent can make to a company's development. Yet from his two decades of company-building experience, he had inductively come to place great value on that talent among the 10,000 people whom he now employed in operations both in China and abroad.

The chairman of a property investment company likewise dating back two decades, who had also helped establish one of the country's premier non-state-owned financial institutions, more generally characterized a mindset that we found to be prevalent among most of the executives we studied:

> A striking common strength shared by Chinese commercial leaders is their strong learning capability and passion for self-development. They are eager to study new things at home and abroad, evidenced by the quick development of business schools in China. . . . By

learning the latest knowledge and practices, Chinese commercial leaders are able to develop business visions to quickly adapt themselves in today's volatile global market. The quest for continuous self-growth among leaders is a great competitive advantage for Chinese companies.

The chairman of a major consumer-products company with a significant market share in China and a top-selling brand in the United States learned in much the same way. The company's strategy has been to bolster its brand, and to discover how to follow this strategy he relied on his own office know-how. "A company leader can never find out the insights for competitive advantages and make the right strategy without the unique understanding of his industry," he said. "This kind of special . . . understanding is gradually developed over years of real working experience."

The consumer-products company chair had foregone other expansion strategies such as recurrent mergers and acquisitions, which have been used by several of his global rivals. In learning how to build organically, he utilized self-directed study—an endeavor to which he also devoted most of his time. "It's very important for me to learn new things through study, communication, conversation, and seminars," he noted. "As the chairman, you have to have the vision and not be confined to daily chores." And in his company's efforts to become a multinational purveyor—it ranked among the top ten in global sales in the mid-2010s—direct experience remained a wellspring.

To better describe these executives' invention of a business way and its legacy for the present era, we delve more deeply into the lives of two of China's most prominent business leaders, Liu Chuanzhi and Wang Shi. Liu created and led the largest technology enterprise in China, now the largest personal-computer maker in the world; Wang founded and built the largest residential property-development company in China, now the largest such company worldwide. The accounts ahead, which draw on our personal interviews with these and other company executives as well as on public sources, repeatedly witness instances in which the executives map their own way forward and work to control their own destinies in an uncharted world. By looking closely at the building of their enterprises, we see just how freehand that way forward has been.

Liu Chuanzhi Builds Lenovo

The founder, builder, and leader of Lenovo—Liu Chuanzhi—charted much of his own path. Born during the chaos of China's civil war and completing high school on the eve of its Cultural Revolution, which had raged from 1966 to 1976, Liu had hoped to become a military aviator. His early aspirations were dashed, however, when the Red Guard denounced a relative as a "rightist," a capitalist-roader, and Liu sought personal refuge, joining a communications institute. But even that failed to insulate him against the vagaries of the Cultural Revolution. The institute was controlled by the People's Liberation Army, and when his privately disclosed criticisms of the "revolution" reached institute officials, they dispatched him to a rice farm for "thought reform" and then to a hard-labor farm for political criminals.

Following his release from the labor camp, Liu secured a job as a computer engineer with yet another state-owned research agency, the Chinese Academy of Sciences. Though a welcome respite from political persecution, it proved intellectually exasperating. The Academy's engineers were certainly inventive—building China's first computer—but Liu found their scientific bent to be a frustrating misfit with his own instincts. Satisfied with producing just one computer, a proof of concept, his fellow engineers were eager to move on to the next new thing. Commercializing inventions was the last thing on their mind, but not on Liu's. Fortunately for Liu, Deng Xiaoping and his market reforms were emerging as a new force, opening a crack in the state's great anti-capitalist wall, and Liu chose to squeeze through it.

Owing to the social and economic calamities incurred by the Cultural Revolution, China was on the verge of bankruptcy when it finally abated in 1976. Looking for ways to make ends meet, the state significantly cut research subsidies for the National Academy of Sciences, where Liu worked. Because the academy could no longer depend on the state for full funding, it encouraged its research staff to turn to commercial enterprise as an independent source of revenue.

In 1984, Liu Chuanzhi and ten colleagues from the Academy's computer institute used this opportunity to launch what would become Lenovo. In doing so, Liu immediately appreciated that there were no known byways for capitalizing on the opening and navigating beyond it. He was entirely on his own, and he encountered plenty of barricades ahead. Those building a start-up in the West could expect Max Weber's "Protestant ethic" and the "spirit of capitalism" to at least sanction what they were doing. But Weber found that even in the West the spirit "had to fight its way to supremacy against a whole world of hostile forces," and in the East those forces were even more daunting. Liu discovered that his country's anti-capitalism still militated against pretty much everything he wanted to achieve. "It wasn't easy," he recalled. "The lowest thing you could do in the early '80s, as a scientist, was to go into business." In the face of China's planned economy at the time, "there was barely room for a freewheeling company like ours."[13]

Unsurprisingly for a new start-up in the United States, and even more so for one of the first start-ups in China, Liu and his team lurched into several dead ends, including the importing of Western televisions, certifying of computer quality for new buyers, and marketing of a digital watch. If their strategy was ill-conceived, their execution was equally so. Even the basic model was unclear. "Our management team often differed on which commercial road to travel," Liu recalled. "This led to big discussions, especially between the engineering chief and myself. He felt that if the quality of the product was good, then it would sell itself."[14]

The underlying problem, Liu found, was that he and his associates did not yet appreciate even the rudiments of what they would have to do to create a viable enterprise and sell its products. "We were mainly scientists and didn't understand the market," he confessed. "We just learned by trial and error, which was very interesting—but also very dangerous."[15]

Rather than beginning with its own core proprietary technology and gradually developing downstream capabilities in manufacturing, marketing, sales, and distribution, as many technology entrepreneurs would do in the West, Liu and his team invented a reverse development process, starting from downstream—sales and distribution—and gradually moving upstream, initially to manufacturing and then to innovation.

When Lenovo started in the 1980s, the personal-computer market in China was dominated by second-tier foreign producers, and the leading brand was California-based AST Research. Lenovo became the first distributor for AST in China and subsequently became the distributor for other international brands, including Hewlett-Packard and IBM. That served as a primary source of Lenovo's initial revenue, but even more importantly, it provided a practical and profitable avenue for mastering the market. Liu and his team intuitively came to appreciate consumer behavior, sales and marketing, accounting and receivables, and inventory and logistics—in short, doing business in China.

By 1990, Lenovo had built up its own understanding of the Chinese market and consumer behavior along with the know-how for PC making and selling. Moving up from being a sales agent of imported PCs to becoming a producer of its own, Lenovo launched its branded personal computer into the Chinese market in 1990. Ramping up rapidly, Lenovo overtook both IBM and Compaq by 1994, becoming the leading PC supplier in China—a position it has held ever since.

Lenovo's bottom-up study of consumer behavior and business barriers during the 1990s created an informed platform for growth. The Internet was still in its infancy in China, and through trial and error Liu and his staff learned to surmount its many limitations. PC owners found it cumbersome at the time even to link with the Internet, and Lenovo worked with telephone companies to streamline connecting. Lenovo even added a dedicated key to its keyboards: touch the button and the operator was taken instantly onto the web. When Liu learned that teenagers and older users were seeking specialized functionalities, he customized his PCs for those submarkets. The milestones in Lenovo's absorption of China's personal computer market are summarized in Table 2.2.

To reduce the risks of making costly mistakes, Liu early introduced a learning device that has served him ever since. Whenever he was asked to give a speech or to submit a major report, he told us, he would gather his inner circle in a closed-door session to candidly look back on the firm's progress in key areas to identify the sources of its successes and failures. He then drafted the speech or report himself, rather than delegating it to staff assistants or professional writers. In addition, he noted, he met with his inner circle on Friday afternoons to candidly discuss the week's achievements and shortfalls, seeking to understand what he and his lieutenants should do differently the following week. Many mistakes were made, he explained, but the debrief helped "to ensure that we don't make [the same] mistake in the future." Without a century of business precedent, he had to build his enterprise by learning from his *own* experience on the other side of the wall.

Even with these regular after-action reviews, a concept that is only now becoming common in the West, trying times lay ahead, resulting in recurrent cycles of deciding, revising, and improving. When Liu moved his

TABLE 2.2 Milestones in Lenovo's Development, 1984–2014

1984	Established in 1984 as ICT Co., a government-funded R&D institute under the Chinese Academy of Sciences.
1987	Became a distributor for AST and, later, for HP and other foreign branded PCs.
1988	Established Hong Kong Computer Group, a joint venture with a Hong Kong partner to produce PC motherboards and add-on cards, and operated a trading business.
1989	Renamed as Legend Group Co.
1990	Changed its role from agent for imported computer products to producer and seller of its own branded computer products.
1993	Became the largest domestic PC manufacturer in China, but still behind AST and Compaq.
1994	Listed on the Hong Kong Stock Exchange.
1996	Merged as the market leader in China with more than 30 percent market share.
1998	Established the first Legend Retail Shop.
1999	Became the first Chinese PC manufacturer to achieve the status of top seller (by units) in the Asia-Pacific region (excluding Japan).
2001	Spun off Digital China Co. Ltd. as a separate listing on the Hong Kong Stock Exchange.
2002	Changed its English name from Legend Holdings Limited to Legend Group Limited.
2004	Changed its English name from Legend to Lenovo; targeted the rural market in China.
2005	Completed acquisition of IBM's Personal Computer Division to become the world's third-largest personal computer company after Dell Computer and Hewlett-Packard.
2006	Introduced its branded products outside of greater China.
2007	Partnered with the 2008 Olympic Games in Beijing.
2008	Added "Idea" brand (e.g., IdeaPad notebooks) alongside "Think" brand (e.g., ThinkPad desktops).
2009	Led the personal computer industry in using recycled material.
2011	Named by *Forbes* as one of the world's "100 Most Reputable Companies."
2014	Became the world's largest PC maker; acquired IBM's server business and Google's Motorola Mobility division.

Sources: Compiled by the authors from the Lenovo website,
and from Xie and White, 2004, and Sun et al., 2013.

nascent enterprise, Legend, to Hong Kong in 1988, he was struggling to stay above the water line, and he and his team learned—by necessity—to be cost obsessed and threadbare, even using cheap public transport to commute to work. When the company was later scandalized by an executive who stole millions from it, Liu's memo to himself referenced the importance of ensuring impeccable character among all those he would thereafter bring into responsible positions. When he listed the company as Legend on the Hong Kong exchange in 1994, Liu learned to suppress his pique when investors and analysts questioned his strategy or results. Before going public, his primary owner, the Chinese Academy of Sciences, had never challenged him, but now, he understood, he had to explain his strategy, detail his results, and project his credibility to many holders.[16]

Legend Breaks Out of China

During the late 1990s and early 2000s, Liu attempted to diversify Legend beyond the manufacturing and selling of personal computers in China, but his initial efforts fell flat. Legend had become the premier domestic maker of PCs, but its early dominance of the Chinese market was coming under increasing attack by Dell Computer, Hewlett-Packard, and other foreign and domestic makers. Legend had held 4 percent of the Chinese PC market in 1994, and just six years later it had raised that to 29 percent, but then it began to lose market share, dropping to 26 percent by 2004. Liu and his team concluded that restoring growth could come only through international expansion, though doing so would require a name change since "Legend" was already copyrighted by companies in other countries. Liu also concluded that he and his top team would have to master multinational management despite zero experience in it.

At the time, however the renamed Lenovo had no foothold outside greater China on which to generate that experience. By coincidence, IBM approached Lenovo regarding the possibility of acquiring IBM's Personal Computer Division. The purchase would be daunting since the IBM PC Division drew revenue four times greater than that of Lenovo itself. Moreover, the division had been losing money at IBM, but on detailed analysis, Liu and his team found that a major fraction of that loss came from the overhead charges that IBM imposed on its division. Given Lenovo's far lower overhead and leaner manufacturing methods, Liu estimated that it could assemble the same personal computer in China for $4 that IBM had been assembling in America for $24.

Liu negotiated a purchase price of $1.75 billion for the IBM division, and its acquisition in 2005 moved Lenovo overnight into the global market. The company rose from eighth-largest to third-largest computer maker worldwide. It doubled its workforce to 20,000, quadrupled its revenue to $12 billion, and reduced its sales dependency on greater China from 100 percent to 36 percent, as shown in Table 2.3.

TABLE 2.3 Lenovo's Regional Sales Before and After Its Purchase of the IBM Personal Computer Division in 2005

Lenovo Sales by Region	2004 (%)	2006 (%)
Greater China	100	36
Americas	0	30
Europe, Middle East, and Africa	0	21
Asia Pacific	0	13

Sources: Lenovo Annual Report, 2004–2005, 2005–2006, and 2006–2007.

TABLE 2.4 Lenovo's Ownership Before and After Its Purchase of the IBM Personal Computer Division in 2005

Lenovo Ownership	2003 (%)	2005 (%)
Legend Holdings Limited	57.8	57.0
Public shares	39.9	20.4
Private-equity companies	0	9.5
IBM	0	12.3
Directors	0.3	0.8

Source: Report of the Directors for the years ending March 31, 2003, and March 31, 2005.

In the immediate wake of the IBM Division purchase, Lenovo also diversified its ownership, as detailed in Table 2.4. The Chinese Academy of Sciences had been the majority holder through Lenovo's parent, Legend Holdings, but after the acquisition, IBM held a significant stake in Lenovo, as did three American-based private-equity companies with a combined stake of $350 million: Texas Pacific Group (TPG), General Atlantic (GA), and Newbridge Capital, an affiliate of TPG.

When Liu announced the IBM PC purchase at a Beijing news conference in December 2004, there were five hundred reporters present in the hotel room, reminding him that his country was taking a keen interest in his overnight expansion of a purely Chinese enterprise into a global market. He realized not only that failure would be very costly but also that he would have to learn to run a multinational from scratch. To that end, he created a strategy committee, charged with vetting the expanded company's mid- and long-term decisions. Liu placed himself and his second-ranking executive, Yang Yuanqing, on that committee but also two outsiders, James Coulter and William Grabe, who represented the private-equity investors TPG and GA (Coulter as the founding partner of TPG, Grabe as managing director of GA) and held seats on Lenovo's governing board.

Liu and Yang had concluded that another key to transforming the IBM operations from money-losing to money-making would be the effective "world-sourcing" of its supply chain. "We have been relentless in trying to squeeze every penny out of this process," reported non-executive director Shan Weijian, for "making the process as efficient as possible." Here Liu and Yang turned to Coulter and Grabe, both well familiar with Asian sourcing, to fill their experience gap.

Liu also learned that his risky foray into international waters required extra steps if he was to retain the confidence of Lenovo's largest shareholder, the Chinese Academy of Sciences, from which Lenovo had originally spun off. Liu foresaw three main risks: Would IBM customers now want to buy from a Chinese company, would its American employees work well under Chinese management, and could he reconcile the professional differences between his Chinese and Western executives?

Prior to the IBM PC purchase, Liu had personally managed his firm's ties with the Chinese Academy of Sciences, but in the wake of the acquisition he concluded that more was needed to sustain the Academy's confidence in the wake of those risks. Liu had no familiarity with an international merger on the scale of the IBM takeover, nor with integrating global sourcing and manufacturing. For that reason, he arranged for Coulter and Grabe to come onto the board and to serve on the strategy committee. Their engagement, reported Yang, was important "for us to convince our large shareholder" that he and Liu could indeed learn to master "the snake-swallowing-an-elephant acquisition."

Reflecting on his lifelong experience in building Lenovo, Liu Chuanzhi offered a summary of his self-directed mastery of his management and market. "In the US, most managers are MBA trained," he said, and "in China, company founders did not get an MBA." As a result, he continued, most American "managers are very scientific," following "standard menus" in their company decisions. "But Chinese companies are in a distinctive context compared with Western companies, and Chinese managers learn and do it their own ways. So it is very difficult to directly apply the US business model in the Chinese business environment. Chinese entrepreneurs must continuously summarize their own management style from their experience and practice." They thus "should follow a Chinese menu and run companies according to Chinese practices."

In running Lenovo with his Chinese practices, Liu transformed it from a start-up with fewer than a dozen employees into the world's largest computer maker in less than three decades, building a workforce of more than 60,000 employees. Its share price had grown twice as fast over the past decade as the S&P 500, up by 170 percent compared to the S&P 500's 63 percent, giving Lenovo a market value in 2016 that exceeded $5 billion. Liu also inherited a great deal of Western management practice and brought in US business leaders to help guide the company. So whatever is distinctive about the Lenovo approach, it entails more of an adaptation than a refutation of Western practices.[17]

Wang Shi Starts Vanke

Another example of learning one's own way can be seen in the path taken by the founder of Vanke, China's largest residential property development company. Along this path Wang Shi took many abrupt turns, and his personal mastery of these without a driver's manual is similar to what we have seen in Liu Chuanzhi's navigation at Lenovo.

To appreciate this mastery, consider the landscape facing well-known American entrepreneurs such as Phil Knight at Nike, Steve Jobs at Apple, Sergey Brin and Larry Page at Google, and Travis Kalanick and Garrett Camp at Uber. Though creators of new products, these entrepreneurs could nevertheless draw on time-honored norms and business wisdom in working with their analysts, bankers, directors, employees, executives, investors, sellers, and suppliers.

In the case of Jobs at Apple, for instance, his lead director, Edgar S. Woolard, Jr., had been board chair and chief executive of DuPont, director of Citigroup, IBM, and the New York Stock Exchange, and chair of the Business Council, a premier assemblage of corporate leaders. On decision after decision at Apple, Woolard provided informed counsel based on his years of company experience, ranging from whether Apple should break its contracts with clone makers to whether it should reorganize staff, dismiss engineers, hire executives like Timothy Cook, or open retail stores.[18]

The entrepreneurial pathways in China's early opening proved more lonely, and they often began with a trading company, a brokerage service that linked customers and suppliers in a given market, facilitating exchanges and reducing transaction costs. Trading-company founders developed new ways of organizing transactions in markets that were increasingly in a kind of institutional limbo. Central planning was no longer so dominant—but market rules were yet to prevail.

With the introduction of Deng's reforms, the state cautiously sanctioned the formation of private enterprises. Deng had urged "reform" through decentralization and modernization, "opening up to the outside world," and a yet to be defined—and ironic—combination of communism and capitalism. In Deng's famous formulation, it would be "socialism with Chinese characteristics," expanding what was allowed to allow what would work, including private enterprise.

With China's abolition of communes in 1982, the tiny workshops and stores that dotted the countryside became independent enterprises under the authority of villages and towns. The hamlet and township enterprises could market their products anywhere and provide employee benefits ranging from health care to housing. Just four years earlier, some 28 million people had been employed in commune enterprises and they produced ¥49 billion in value. A decade later, the township and village enterprises employed 106 million people and produced ¥1,798 billion in value, a nearly fifty-fold increase.[19]

Extending the reform path, the Chinese government in 1984 dropped its policy of assigning production targets to factories and pre-designating their prices, which had left factory managers little incentive to streamline their work systems. In its place, the state now gave managers responsibility for their own profits and losses—and the right to retain their after-tax profits. As managers learned to run more efficient production, they would retain the difference, creating their own capital for expansion, and the amount of capital would be determined by their own ingenuity rather than by a state planner. For the first several years, managers were slow to absorb this new regimen, but in time they did learn and taxes did grow—a gain for both the nascent private sector and the prevailing public sector.[20]

Yet China still clung to vestiges of the command-and-control mindset that had long been antithetical to private enterprise. The central government did not abolish food rationing until 1985, and family enterprises could not hire more than seven people until 1987. It even deemed "price arbitrage" a capital crime until 1997, and it retained controls on a large swath of products, ranging from fertilizers to medications, until 2015.[21]

Still, the uneasy coexistence of central-planning rules with the new-market opening presented lucrative opportunities to the trading-minded, though not without perils. It was common for a trading-company entrepreneur to land a windfall in one deal and go bankrupt in the next. Worse, because the concept of private property was still in its infancy, much of the ownership of new firms was still held by a provincial government or local authority. State agencies furnished cash and protection for start-ups that could not be readily formed on their own, but being on one's own remained hazardous. It was on this evolving but shaky landscape that Wang Shi founded his trading company.

A Trading Company

Wang Shi was born just two years after the People's Republic of China finally triumphed in 1949, following years of civil war and revolution. As with most people raised in that era, Wang's life and career were profoundly shaped by the historic transformation unfolding around him.

In 1983, at the age of thirty-two, Wang joined the Shenzhen Regional Development Company (SRDC), a quasi-government entity with the authority to engage in imports and exports—a right denied most Chinese firms at that time. The company provided Wang with a bank account and a license to do business, but with neither staff nor capital to conduct the business. He was on his own, holding a warrant to be commercial, but otherwise he had to create his own commerce.

Two of the best-selling imports at the time were foldable umbrellas from Taiwan and food seasoning from Japan. Though these products were alluring, Wang reasoned that the demand for them would soon be saturated, and casting his gaze elsewhere, he stumbled upon an anomaly. America's Continental Grain Corporation and Thailand's Zhengda Group were both importing corn into southern China at high cost at a time when plenty of corn was under cultivation in northern China. Wang soon discovered why: there was simply no shipping route between the north, where legions of corn growers were based, and the Guangdong region in the south, where masses of chicken farmers were located. Without a market infrastructure to enable a transaction, the chicken farmers could not communicate their needs to the corn suppliers. Wang spotted gold.

Wang Shi ambitiously decided to build a national corn-trading market himself. He first contacted the multinational importers with a promise of securing corn for them more cheaply from within China. He then extracted letters of credit, guaranteeing payment to the sellers in the north once their corn had reached the south. With those commitments on the supply side, he turned to the logistics side, persuading officials of Shenzhen Port, Guangzhou Marine Administration Bureau, and the Guangzhou Marine Shipping Lines to open a shipping route from the seaport of Dalian in northeast China to coastal Shenzhen near Guangdong in the southeast.

Wang knew little about accounting rules or payment protocols at the time. When he delivered his first order of thirty tons of corn to the south, he carried a bag with him to collect what he thought would be a cash payment from the client. Instead, the client came with a check, which Wang had never seen before, and the client demanded a receipt, another first for Wang. Stimulated by necessity, Wang devoted evenings to poring over accounting manuals with their introductions to balance sheets, cash flows, and income statements.

As his corn-trading expanded, the Shenzhen Regional Development Company created a trading unit for animal feed, with Wang Shi as its director. Unconstrained by his initial charter, Wang began trading adjacent products, expanding from feeding chickens into swapping chickens and then nourishing pigs. Coming to appreciate that trading rather than knowledge of corn or chickens or pigs was his real forte, Wang turned to trading wholly unrelated products ranging from textiles and electronics to chemicals and medical devices—or "whatever is profitable," in the words of one company executive. When Wang's fast-growing trading unit reached 150 staff members, the SRDC spun it off in 1984 as the Modern Scientific and Educational Exhibition Center, with Wang as chairman and general manager.

The spin-off came at a fortuitous time, as the Chinese economy was growing at a double-digit clip in the late 1980s and early 1990s. Trading opportunities exploded. Wang chased deals nearly everywhere, entering a host of markets from printing and jewelry making to department-store retailing, power distribution, residential and mixed-use real estate, entertainment and advertising, and even film production. The company was renamed Vanke in 1988. By 1991 Wang was looking abroad for instructive guidance, and he decided to model his burgeoning enterprise after Japanese trading companies such as Mitsubishi, Mitsui, and Sumitomo. To that end, Vanke issued all employees a two-hundred-page booklet, "Japan's General Trading Companies." This decision is a good example of the borrowing in these early years that did not come solely from the West. By 1992, Vanke presided over fifty-five fully or jointly owned firms operating across ten industries in twelve cities.

Making the Transition

Wang's building of Vanke came at a moment when he foresaw two alternatives to prosperity. One was rent seeking, taking advantage of loopholes in the emerging markets or even bribes to state officials who still controlled much of the market. The other was more conventional business management, focusing on the fundamentals of product innovation and cost reduction. Rent seeking had become the path for many entrepreneurs, but value creation was now emerging as the more enduring avenue.

Company leaders who had not readied themselves for that transition found themselves in trouble during the 1990s. Prominent entrepreneur Mou Qizhong, for instance, had early organized a burgeoning barter trade between Russia and China, arranging for the exchange of truckloads of consumer goods for Russian commercial aircraft, making him a nationally recognized figure.

Yet when he sought to replicate his early trading successes by engaging in a series of increasingly speculative bets, most failed, and the state sentenced him in 2000 to life in prison for credit fraud. A *New York Times* reporter characterized his failure to make the transition to value creation by saying that "Mr. Mou was more a symbol of how far an opportunist can get on China's political favoritism and lack of transparency" than a symbol of "capitalistic entrepreneurship"—yet another reminder of the unprecedented personal risks that Chinese business leaders took in establishing their companies.[22]

Wang Shi was among the first to appreciate the danger of continuing down the opportunistic route on which he had initially sent Vanke. Wang invited a team of investment bankers in 1992 from Standard Chartered, a British financial-services company, to assist Vanke's initial public offering of its B-shares—those traded in foreign currencies—on the stock exchange in Hong Kong. After reviewing the company's business model, the investment bankers challenged its trading scheme. Although trading had driven Vanke's growth, its business had become extremely diverse, scale-inefficient, and without an enduring customer base. What then, the bankers pressed, was Vanke's core competency?

Prompted by this question, Wang asked his finance staff to review all of Vanke's trading records from 1984 to 1992 with an eye to their profitability. To drill down on the basics, the finance managers denoted profitable deals with black ink and losing deals with red. The resulting color coding shocked both Wang and his staff: red prevailed and, even worse, Vanke had lost more than it made in its trading businesses. Although trading accounted for most of its revenue, company profits actually came from its nascent non-trading businesses. Responding to this wake-up call, Wang concluded that his markets had changed under his feet and that he would have to refocus on value creation somewhere else.

Wang directed his strategic planning group to take a close look at the US residential market. Based on this analysis, he came to believe that the burgeoning Chinese residential market alone would be large enough to support his company's continued growth—if he focused on China's largest cities where the market infrastructure was already more developed, especially Shenzhen.

At the time, most of Vanke's revenue came from retail and trading, with less than 4 percent from real estate. Concentrating entirely on real estate would be a risky bet for the company, one that required a wrenching unwinding or even a walking away from much of what Wang had built. Vanke had formed many joint ventures and alliances, and it had usually taken primary responsibility for them. Divesting meant that Vanke would have to dissolve a number of its partnerships, and many of Wang's allies predictably resisted the separation, resulting in costly valuation and distributional disputes. Many of his own executives fought the divestiture plans, not only because Vanke's conglomerate scheme had seemingly served the company so well for a decade but also because their personal livelihoods seemed at stake.

But Wang Shi was determined to make the transition, however vexing. Over the next nine years, he disentangled Vanke from dozens of partnerships, let dozens of executives go, and sold off Vanke's other assets, including China Resources Vanguard Shop, the largest retail chain in China at the time. By 2001, Vanke had become focused on residential real estate, and by 2003 it had emerged as the largest residential home developer in sales revenue in China. By 2011, property development constituted more than 98 percent of its revenue and 99 percent of its profit—remarkable numbers for a company that had started in chicken feed.

Wang Shi's New Architecture

Divesting from speculative trading was only one side of Wang Shi's rebuilding of the company. The other was a reconstitution of the firm's architecture to serve its residential-housing aspirations.

During the trading years, Vanke's businesses were largely deal-focused in stand-alone divisions, unrelated trading areas that did not require sophisticated organizational charts or control systems over them. But as Wang decided to specialize in building residential housing for the mass market in many cities, his managers would be overseeing hundreds of housing projects across the country; city operations could share professional expertise, best practices, and building suppliers with one another, and Wang recognized that an orchestrating architecture would be vital.

Wang also worried that China's traditional reliance on personal connections—guanxi—for doing business would not prove compatible with the performance principles he had come to believe would be essential for Vanke's architecture for continued growth in a market economy. Many entrepreneurs had used personal ties for running their businesses at a time when employment contracts and other legal institutions critical to a well-functioning market were yet to be fully developed. But Wang did not want to follow a guanxi-fueled path.

Wang even prohibited his own relatives from joining Vanke. A case in point: during one of his long business trips, a subordinate had hired a relative of Wang's mother. A touching scenario, of course, but when Wang returned, he promptly fired the offending employee. "Traditional

Chinese values emphasize blood-based interpersonal relationships and hierarchy in organization," he explained. But "I don't want Vanke to go down that road."

Wang sought to build Vanke's architecture around professionalism and performance rather than on strong-willed individuals or loyal associates. One indicative measure was his creation of an executive rotation policy. He asked business heads to sign an agreement obligating them to rotate and relocate according to company needs. His stricture met with overt resistance, especially in Shanghai and Beijing, when he asked the general managers of each to swap their positions as a way of transferring expertise. As China's two greatest metropolitan regions, both markets were critical to Vanke, and both general managers had been outstanding performers. The Shanghai manager was so adamantly against the move that he offered to take a lesser position in Shanghai if doing so meant he did not have to relocate to Beijing. His counterpart in Beijing fought back as well, but Wang insisted, neither relented, and both managers were soon let go. As these decisions demonstrate, the principle of loyalty in Chinese companies went only so far. It appears that employees who challenged a founder's vision were as often fired as rehabilitated.

Was not the cost of losing two top executives, we asked, too high a price to pay for Wang's rotation policy? Could he not have found a middle way? "It was painful to lose talented top executives in a time when they were badly needed," he explained. "However, if we make exceptions in this case, where do we draw the line? If our policy can be bent by the boss in charge, would Vanke ever be able to have truly effective systems and processes? If we give in to such resistance, Vanke may risk becoming a company dominated by local warlords. That could not be allowed to happen."

Despite the departures of two star performers, the two cities' operations finished the year in the pink, reaffirming Wang's confidence in operating principles over individual personalities. That "showed that our business in Beijing and Shanghai did not suffer much," he concluded, and thus we know that the "system is more important than individuals, no matter how talented they are." Vanke's number-two executive, Yu Lang, alluded to the same working precept: "Vanke does not cultivate individual stars," he said. "We develop a system that enables ordinary people to do great things. That is why we do not give large sums of bonus to individuals, nor do we rely on an individual-responsibility contract system."

Whether decisions like these also meant that there was room for only one star in companies like Vanke—the big boss—is an open question.

China Vanke Co., Ltd., as it is formally known, became one of the world's largest residential-property developers and managers. Its revenue in 2014 totaled $23.9 billion (¥146.6 billion), four times greater than that of the largest US residential builder, PulteGroup, whose revenue was $5.9 billion in the same year. Beginning in 2013 it added operations abroad in Hong Kong, New York, and San Francisco, and as of 2014 Vanke employed more than 40,000 people in sixty-five Chinese cities. Since its initial public offering in 1991, investors have seen their stock price rise by more than 12,000 percent.

What About China's Other Billionaires?

The business leaders we have profiled from China's largest private companies are notable in many ways. But their success is also a product of risks that they could not control. No doubt they all would have been successful even under quite different circumstances, but the fact that they became so remarkably powerful, influential, and rich is at least in part the result of being in the right place at the right time and other elements of good fortune.

We might learn something, therefore, from looking at those executives who were a little less successful but, under slightly different circumstances, would themselves have been at the very top of China's new business elite. Some estimates suggest that there are now several hundred billionaires in China, many only slightly less rich and slightly less influential than those we profile here. China has become one of the world's fastest-growing sources of new billionaires. When *Forbes* magazine compiled its first list of "international billionaires" in 1987, it found none in China; by 2015 it counted 213.[23]

The *Financial Times* has offered a detailed look at one of them, Li Yonghui, as representative of this larger group of new billionaires.[24] Li is an entrepreneur, having started his own companies, but unlike his better-known peers featured in this book, he has not had the single "home run," the start-up that burst onto the scene to become a household name, at least in China. Nor has he experienced the kind of busts with early start-ups that make the contrasts with later success seem so striking.

Like many of the business leaders referenced here, Li was a university graduate, though in this case his field of study, optical physics, is not where he invested. Instead, he ended up in a truck factory and, as with most entrepreneurs, that initial experience provided a learning platform for his subsequent entrepreneurial work.

Li visited Canada in 1994 and discovered a business practice that had yet to reach China: business managers in the West routinely borrowed money to buy trucks for shipping and delivering their products. He knew that the demand for trucks to service the booming manufacturing sector was very strong in China, but also that small firms were unable to fund the purchase of trucks out of their operating budgets. Li returned to China and set up Auto China International, a financing and leasing company for truck purchases.

It proved enormously successful, but unlike his peers in many other areas of the economy, Li was eventually forced out of the market by state-owned banks that began to offer financing at more attractive rates. In the early 2000s he moved into real-estate development, another booming industry, and made more money. But then government regulations and a more difficult environment for property construction pushed him out of development and back into truck leasing, a market that state banks had by then abandoned. That market soon became crowded again, however, and in 2015, although he retained some of his real-estate operations, he shifted his business strategy yet again, providing short-term financing that truck owners needed to fund their day-to-day needs and furnishing it through the Internet. Li consolidated his offerings under the name Fincera, a company he had founded in 2005 to present the array of financing products he intended to offer.

What we see in Li is a successful Chinese entrepreneur with an ability to identify business opportunities adjacent to their current markets. In part because start-ups are lean and agile—one leader, few executives, no complicated organizational charts—it is easier for them than for large companies to pull out of declining markets and move into new ones. The ability to deploy their capital in those new opportunities, to redirect their staff to the new projects, and to achieve these goals quickly is another vital capacity. Among the skills for moving rapidly in China are an understanding of state regulators and gatekeepers, an ability to recruit talent to run the new enterprises, and a capacity to rebound from downside risks that cannot be controlled.[25]

TABLE 2.5 Disgraced Private-Company Entrepreneurs

Executive	Company	Industry	Tenure	Outcome
Bu Xin Sheng	Haiyan Shirt Co.	Garment	1981–1988	Forced out of firm
Dai Guo Fang	Jiangsu Tieben Steel	Steel	1996–2003	Imprisoned
Gu Chu Jun	Greencool Co.	Investment/Electronics	1995–2005	Imprisoned
Huang Guang Yu	Gome Group	Retail/Real Estate	1987–2007	Imprisoned
Huang Hong Sheng	Skyworth Group	Home Electronics	1989–2006	Imprisoned
Lai Chang Xing	Yuanhua Group	Trade/Transportation	1991–1999	Fugitive
Mu Qi Zhong	Nande Group	Trade/Manufacturing	1980–1999	Imprisoned
Nian Guang Jiu	Dumb Melon Seeds	Snack	1978–1997	Forced out of firm
Shen Taifu	Great Wall	Manufacturing	1989–1993	Executed
Sun Da Wu	Da Wu Group	Agriculture	1985–2003	Imprisoned
Wan Run Nan	Beijing Stone Co.	Information Tech.	1984–1989	Forced to leave China
Yu Zuo Min	Daqiuzhuang Co.	Manufacturing	1974–1993	Imprisoned
Zhou Zhengyi	Nongkai Group	Investment/Misc.	1997–2003	Imprisoned

Source: Ma, Lin, and Liang, 2012.

The uncertain terrains that Chinese business leaders have had to navigate entail both upsides and downsides. When company executives bet right, they can become super-rich overnight, but when they bet wrong, prosecution, conviction, and even execution may result. In Table 2.5 we list a number of prominent Chinese entrepreneurs who had been hailed as business entrepreneurs at one point but were later vilified or imprisoned or worse.

With Hanergy, Li Hejun Makes Himself China's Richest Business Founder

A fourth instructive illustration of mapping one's own path forward can be seen in the business byways of Li Hejun, but with a different twist in terms of the founder's accumulation and display of his personal fortune. In contrast to the self-effacing grace of Vanke's Wang Shi is the personal panache of Li Hejun, who prefers to let the world know of his triumphs. Though not directly from the business playbook of American billionaire Donald J. Trump, a parallel comes to mind.

Born of a modest family in 1967 in Heyuan, a city some 100 miles north of Hong Kong, Li earned an engineering degree at Beijing Jiaotong University, and in 1994 he founded a toy and electronics company. But then, sensing better prospects in a different arena, he abruptly and ambitiously entered the energy market, founding Hanergy Holding Group to acquire and build hydroelectric dams in southwest China.

During the time he was ramping up his power company, Li visited Cambridge University to learn about alternative energy sources, a direction advocated by the Chinese government. He soon turned toward a promising new approach to solar power generation—thin-film technology—and to that end he acquired four companies already active in the field and integrated them into a new subsidiary, Hanergy Thin Film Power (HTFP), to manufacture and sell the technology. He took the subsidiary public on the Hong Kong Stock Exchange in 2013 and became a tireless advocate of "clean energy," authoring a book and lecturing widely.[26]

Reports in the *Financial Times* and other media in 2015 referenced investor concerns about the trading patterns and relationships between Hanergy Thin Film Power and the Hanergy Group—virtually all of HTFP's sales were going to the parent or its other subsidiaries. Other concerns accumulated as well, including accounting irregularities, according to *Forbes,* and novel ways of borrowing money through a form of private trusts (somewhat like bonds) that did not trade on official markets, according to the *Financial Times.* Much of that borrowing had been backed by shares in the company and Li's personal guarantee. HTFP's share price sharply declined, followed by company losses and layoffs; then, on May 20, 2015, its trading was suspended by Hong Kong's Securities and Futures Commission.[27]

Throughout it all, Li Hejun had crowed about his own holdings, in stark contrast to both Liu Chuanzhi and Wang Shi. He had retained the maximum amount of the company's ownership permitted by the Hong Kong Exchange, just under 75 percent, creating an extraordinary personal fortune as the company's stock soared. Not shy about his wealth, Li cited on his company's website a *Forbes* magazine ranking of the richest people in China—a list that included Alibaba's Jack Ma, Dalian Wanda Group's

Wang Jianlin, and Li himself, who, at one point, was the richest of all. While many Chinese executives disclose as little as possible about their personal wealth, Li took the opposite tack. To prove and proclaim his worth, his company provided his audited bank accounts to *Forbes,* and his firm's website detailed the scope of his personal fortune. Much of that wealth, however, proved evanescent, as the suspension of the company's trading in 2015 led to a precipitous decline in Li's own fortune. HTFP's shares plunged 50 percent just before regulators suspended its stock from trading, resulting in a paper loss to Li of $14 billion in a single day.

As noted, Li's overt display of his personal assets—regardless of the rise or fall or magnitude of his billions—contrasts sharply with Liu Chuanzhi's public disinterest in his own assets and Wang Shi's personal bypassing of any such display. The divergent paths that these founding CEOs have followed suggest that business norms are not yet well formed on the question of flashy display versus self-effacement. Still, the fact that they all plotted their own ways forward indicates that Chinese business leaders have had to learn more from their own wits than from established models for building their enterprises. Whether to seek and reveal personal wealth, or to pass up or hide one's riches, is one of those secondary precepts for which shared values may later develop but on which personal latitude remains prevalent.[28]

Counterpoint

While so much company leadership has been mastered from the ground up, a learn-by-doing formula, most of the executives we interviewed had indeed borrowed at least some elements from the West. A prominent example is the founder of Huawei Technologies, China's premier maker of web hardware, telecommunications equipment, and smartphones.

After a stint as an engineer in the People's Liberation Army, Ren Zhengfei founded Huawei in 1987 to make telephone switches. In the early years, he and his staff successfully designed much of their equipment by reverse-engineering a host of foreign technologies, borrowing liberally from the West. But in those same years, he managed the business on his own—resulting, in the founder's own words, in organizational "chaos." And for a remedy he again turned to the West, asking in 1997 for counsel from one of America's premier technology makers, IBM. Ren insisted that his employees not only hear what the American icon had to offer but also fully embrace it, however ill-fitting it might seem. In an oft-cited assertion, Ren baldly declared that "you had to cut off your feet to wear the shoe"—in this case, an American shoe.

After utilizing reverse architectural engineering from the West, Ren reported that "chaos was removed and structure entered Huawei," and by 2015 his company's annual revenue had reached ¥390 billion ($60.1 billion), ranking Huawei among the dozen largest non-state-owned companies in China. It had turned to the outside in pursuit of people know-how but to the inside for its technical know-how. By 2015, more than 70,000 of its 170,000 employees were working in research and development, and the company had become the world's number-one applicant for international patents.[29]

Executives at other companies, too, have been looking over their shoulders at the West. For instance, a research team headed by Zhi-Xu Zhang of Peking University interviewed business leaders of nine state-owned and twenty-six privately owned enterprises, each with at least a hundred employees. Though the investigators did not break down the results by company ownership or size, they did find that twenty-five of the thirty-five interviewed executives cited the influence of Western management books on their leadership styles. Their list of examples was topped by Jim Collins and Jerry Porras's *Built to Last,* and several of the executives singled out Max Weber's *The Protestant Ethic and the Spirit of Capitalism.*[30]

Conclusion

Business leaders in China have of necessity learned to build and lead their enterprises through trial and error. At least initially, with no models to emulate, no successful prototypes to learn from, no veterans to study, no Peter Drucker to read, those who founded and scaled-up companies like Lenovo and Vanke had to so on their own. And that meant repeated cycles of doing, analyzing, and revising. The chair of a leading software enterprise voiced the abiding posture of many: "We learn as we go." Later on, most of these executives borrowed heavily from established foreign competitors, but the borrowing was rarely wholesale. Picking and choosing what to copy and when to go their own way created the distinctiveness of the Chinese model.

Of course, that model has required a career-long willingness to learn—a mindset that was much in evidence among the seventy-two chief executives we interviewed. The founder of one of China's largest information-technology firms with more than 20,000 employees in 2016 had worked with many "successful business leaders" in his twenty-five years since the firm's founding, and in his experience, "what the truly successful leaders have in common is that they are all very humble and eager to learn."

Certainly Liu Chuanzhi displayed that mindset when he started Lenovo in 1984, conducting weekly after-action reviews with his staff to inductively learn what would be required to build his enterprise into the global player that it has become. His learning devices ranged from trial-and-error product offerings to the placement of two private-equity directors on the company's strategy committee.

We saw the same mindset in Wang Shi at Vanke as he evolved his enterprise by testing, retreating, and morphing from chicken feed into home building. Still other executives have embraced learning methods that include the simple mechanics of disciplined notetaking, regular reading, and diverse networking.

Though mapping their own way forward was a necessity, all of these Chinese business leaders now benefit, we believe, from an unanticipated virtue in it. Research scholars and strategy consultants who focus on organizational change in the West have long noted that a company's traditions can serve as a powerful flywheel, propelling the company on a steady path forward—but also discouraging deviations from it. Unburdened by a business past—since there was none—Chinese managers, by contrast to their Western counterparts, have been freer to adopt unfettered measures in the market and to focus on where customer demand is going, not just where it has been.[31]

The self-reliant mapping of the China Way forward is generational, however, and as private-sector companies increasingly come into their own in China, the next cohort of company leaders will have the benefit of far more received wisdom for piloting its way forward. Consider just one bellwether, master's degree holders in business administration. The first

MBA programs in China were founded in 1991 for a handful of students at nine institutions, including Beijing's premier universities: Peking, Renmin, and Tsinghua. Fast-forwarding to the time of this writing, in 2016, we find that more than 235 MBA programs are up and running, graduating some 30,000 students annually. And the quality of these programs is increasingly meeting global benchmarks. Seven Chinese MBA programs stood among the top one hundred programs worldwide in a 2016 ranking by the *Financial Times*. While management training will no doubt help the rising generation take a great leap beyond what their forbears knew when they were building the private firms that have come to dominate much of the Chinese economy, they will also be more informed—and encumbered—by the past.[32]

How will the new MBAs fit into companies where the leaders explicitly eschew MBA models? That question points to one of many tensions that these companies will wrestle with going forward. We close this chapter, and subsequent ones, with observations from the fortune makers themselves—allowing their own words to speak for them and their counterparts at other major companies in China. These executive commentaries reflect the thinking of many of the business leaders whom we interviewed.

Their Own Way Forward in the Words of the Fortune Makers

I am the kind of person that can focus on one thing and become the best in doing it. . . . Once we decided to do something, we will have very high standards and expectations. Unlike the normal capital markets who think making money is a success, we have higher expectations and I do not think the professional managers can fully meet my requirements and expectations. That's why I think it's a good idea to do just one thing in my life.

—Mao Zhongqun, Chair, Ningbo Fotile Kitchen Ware

If an industry makes its profits not through its own capabilities and contributions but rather by resorting to windfalls, connections, and even illegal means, it will not be welcomed and respected by the society. Only when profits drop to the normal level through the real market competition mechanism can all the enterprises in the industry win consumers' respect and get rid of a bad reputation. This may take a long time, but it's a rational choice and it delivers better economic return in the long run.

—Chair, real-estate and financial-services company

Compared to the excellent foreign companies, Chinese private enterprises still have much room to improve. But the momentum and passion of those young entrepreneurs are really impressive. Every young man I know is full of energy and eager to launch his new start-up. I really feel becoming old after listening to their ideas and seeing what they do. [When starting] private business was still not clearly mandated in law as legal or illegal, we had to rely on ourselves and make step-by-step progress each day, and warn ourselves never to be greedy.

—Chair, electrical equipment and power transmission company

I did not come to Shenzhen to make money. It happened that a special economic zone was created in Shenzhen where one can venture with something new. It offered a new opportunity for me. But I first had to break all the constraints and obstacles to really test what I could do there.

—Wang Shi, Chair, China Vanke Co., Ltd.

CHAPTER 3

The Learning Company

Learning is embedded in everything I do.

Chinese business leaders differ from their Western counterparts in many ways, but perhaps the most important one is the extent to which they are taking learning seriously, especially their own learning. Whether it is because they are more able to control their work schedules or simply because they make learning a priority, Chinese business leaders recognize that their own learning is crucial to the success of their businesses, and they spend a great deal of time on it. Central to their approach is an appreciation for what they don't know. And the emphasis on learning extends to the requirement that their direct reports (managers reporting directly to them) always be learning as well—and, ultimately, that the organization itself learns by experience.

Knowledge management refers to the awareness that learning and acquiring knowledge are crucial to business competitiveness. *Organizational learning* is the related idea that it is possible for the firm as a whole to learn how to do things that create competencies, which in turn can bolster competitiveness. Both ideas reflect the old notion that a business succeeds in large measure by being able to do things that others could not, and that this ability results from practices and principles that it discovered itself. Good illustrations of knowledge management come from consulting firms that learn from the experience of working with one client and then leverage this wisdom to service other clients in the same industry. Toyota's lean production system may be the most famous example of organizational learning: years of tinkering have taught the company a system for assembling cars that beats everyone else.

It is often said that Chinese culture esteems traditional education and knowledge, but company executives did not necessarily translate these values into organizational learning and knowledge management in their business operations. More practical considerations did. Private companies starting out in the last several decades soon understood just how far behind their global competitors they were. They experienced a profound, pragmatic need to learn and to learn fast. They were jumping into a world they had never seen before, a world of free markets, private capital, company earnings, and worker mobility. Soon after starting out, they began to bump up against veteran international companies operating not just for decades but in some cases with a head start of a century or more.

The fact that the new Chinese enterprises were woefully unprepared for operating in China, let alone against international competitors like General Electric or Siemens, was not lost on the founders. Playing catch-up with Western businesses was initially a humbling experience, but one pursued with energy. The executives at these companies needed to learn the basics about how to designate divisions and sell products. As a direct extension of their own path of mastery, they pressed managers to learn from their own experience, too.

Self-Directed Learning

Similar to firms in the West, the most successful Chinese companies learn about leadership in three ways: *self-directed learning,* the private, self-conscious study of the leadership of others in action; *instructive experience,* learning cumulatively from one's varied engagements; and *leadership coaching,* one-on-one guidance and feedback from veteran executives. It may seem hard to argue against learning and introspection as important attributes, but they are not the foremost ones we typically see in our models of executives in the West, where the priority is often more centered on being decisive than on keenly observing.[1]

Chinese business leaders overwhelmingly pressed for self-directed learning. That is not too surprising given that most of them began their careers by starting up a company, and there was no one to learn from in the form of mentoring. Nor was there work-based learning of the kind that large Western corporations offer through their management development programs.

The chair of one of our companies began his career as a middle school teacher, so perhaps it is no surprise that for him the key attribute that anyone succeeding him should have is "the capability of continuous learning. As the external environment changes quickly, a successful company may find itself in a dead end in a new environment. Hence my successor must have the will and passion to learn new things and keen observation of external changes." The founder and chair of a real-estate developer offered much the same advice: "Introspection: I think every successful business leader has a strong inclination for self-reflection. They try to find the root cause of the problem themselves."

The self-directed development of leadership from practical experience is exemplified by an executive who presided over an enterprise employing 10,000 people and servicing industries ranging from aviation transport to information technology and financial investments. He ranked "learning ability" at the top of his list of the most important leadership capabilities when it came to building his firm's talent. "As there is no established and tested business model to follow in China, all of us have to figure out the right business models by trying different approaches," he explained. "In most cases, it simply will not work if we merely copy a business model from foreign countries. We need to find out how to adapt and localize foreign practice and experience to fit the China market." One of his enterprises, for instance, had pioneered its own way to growth in the aviation industry by offering better inflight experiences and passenger pampering. And for him and his fellow managers, reflecting on his personal experience proved to be the primary learning vehicle: "We should not take the existing theory for granted," he said, "and simply accept its conclusions." Rather, you should build a business model from your "personal working experience, apply it to your environment, and then come up with your own ideas."

Other executives singled out other devices for building on personal experience. The chair of a real-estate development company built on his personal experience to help solve his challenges by recording real-time emergent thoughts in a small notebook. "Every day I take some time to think and try to understand the reason why we have some unsolved long-term problems."

The chairman of Sanpower, a diversified high-technology group, methodically divided his calendar across four domains to diversify his learning experience. As founder of the enterprise, now with more than 50,000 employees in manufacturing, logistics, import-export, investment management, and real estate, he opted to devote only a quarter of his time to headquarters matters and spent the rest of his time meeting with multinational company leaders abroad, government officials in Beijing, and "local talents" in Shanghai. He had also retained a master's-degree student from Peking University to read the premier books in many different fields and to condense their highlights for him. For his own quiet reflection, he allocated an additional two hours every day.

The Sanpower chair's willingness to devote only one-quarter of his time to what we in the West would think of as carrying out his job responsibilities and the other three-quarters on learning is a remarkable exercise in setting priorities. In fairness to executives in the West, being the founder and principal shareholder of his company gives this executive freedom from the time demands of stakeholders that can bog down Western CEOs. There is no doubt, though, that he is focused on the company and its overall, strategic challenges: "I think about the people I meet and the books I read," he said, and he can then "summarize my own understanding" to evolve Sanpower's "management philosophies."

The chair of a department store operator with some 10,000 employees also explicitly allocates his time to optimize learning, with a third going to the company's strategy, a third to managing the company, and a third to studying and outside engagements. "Spectators see the chess game better than the players," he explained, and he thus wanted to witness his own business "from the perspective of an outsider" to avoid "losing sight of the traps and dangers ahead."

Self-directed learning among the business leaders was not limited to their experience within China. Some reported looking outside for whatever they might bring inside. They spent time and money to learn from Western companies—for instance, hiring Chinese expatriates, mainly from Taiwan and then Singapore; arranging joint ventures; engaging consulting firms to introduce Western practices; and, more recently, sending managers to Western business schools and mid-career executive-education programs.

Knowing what to borrow in management and from whom is a bit of an art form. The chairman of a medical-device maker, for instance, explained that he had retained Western consulting firms to create some of the basics for his firm, including its structure, many of its operating systems, and even its corporate culture. The chair of a major food-products company, who had a more focused need, learned how to develop business strategy from employees she had hired from Coca-Cola. Shenzhen Geely Holdings vice-president and Geely Volvo's CEO Shen Freeman learned about running the company they had just acquired—Volvo—by bringing in American and European managers who had been with Volvo when it was owned by the Ford Motor Company. The chair of a power management firm had learned Western management practices as an employee at General Electric. But the main goal of this art form, as the executive of an industrial services firm put it, speaking for most of the others, is not to copy Western practices but "to find out how to adapt and localize foreign practice and experience to fit the China market."

Some companies created their own universities to increase the learning of people below the C-suite level—that is, two or more tiers below the CEO. These schools are not, however, simply amalgamations of existing training programs into American-style "corporate universities," which often involve an upgraded renaming of firms' training departments. Rather, they offer comprehensive programs ranging from general education to basic-skills and firm-specific job training. The chair of a marine engineering firm, for example, explained that the lack of managerial talent had been a bottleneck for his expansion plans, so his company created its own internal business school that teaches everything from business basics to advanced topics, and now enrolls some 3,000 employee-students. The chair of a major industrial enterprise reported that his firm provides employees with an incentivized "learning platform," paying employees for completing courses.

Private companies in China instituted these and other practices to overcome a dearth of basic business skills in the market, a bottleneck for expansion. But the companies are also spending on the high end as well. The Wharton School at one point had senior managers coming from a different

Chinese company almost every week to enroll in our management-development programs in Philadelphia, and especially prominent in those programs was a focus on leadership capabilities. A home-furnishing company dispatches a thousand employees a year overseas for business coursework. A real-estate development group decided to grow all of its talent from within, with no outside hiring beyond the entry level, and for that, it sent employees to business schools to learn a range of professional skills.

Instructive Experience for Lieutenants

Many of the top executives we interviewed required their lieutenants to master their own way forward based on their own personal experiences, in much the same way that the founding CEOs had done in building the firm. Consider the mindset of the executive of a computer and electronic-products maker. In building his enterprise, he insisted that his managers eschew deferential behavior toward him since this would inhibit their willingness to learn to make their own decisions, and he imposed a nominal "fine" of ¥10 (about $1.50) when they backslid into using his formal title. Similarly, he opted not to attend many of his own senior-staff meetings to encourage his direct reports to learn to make and accept responsibility for their own management decisions. "Employees should figure out how to do things" was his summary prescription. More simply put, "they should not go to their boss for permission" to make decisions. This approach was in stark contrast to traditional operating practices in China.

A direct corollary of this learning principle is that first-time mistakes in many of these companies are celebrated rather than castigated. The chair of one of China's largest makers of electrical equipment for industry well characterized the precept. "A good team is crucial to the steady development of a company," he said, "so you have to find the right people to do the right jobs by incorporating them with a good vision." And for that purpose, he had found it preferable to "accept" their mistakes and better "to talk to them than to severely criticize them." The underlying agenda, he explained, was "to incorporate their talents and bring them into full play," an agenda that would be difficult to fulfill if they too acutely feared failure.

Liu Chuanzhi and Yang Yuanqing had followed a path similar to this at Lenovo. They pressed their managers to see themselves as company owners, not hired guns, and to take their own initiatives and make their own decisions. A widely circulated Lenovo metaphor to that effect: employees were the engines of the company, not cogs in a machine. This was quite a departure from the ways in which previous-generation employees in China were treated and still are in some companies. To reinforce this principle, Yang at one point initiated a "first-name-only" campaign to make employees less deferential. By traditional Chinese norms, subordinates would normally address superiors with their titles, as in "CEO Yang" or "Chairman Liu." Yang insisted that everybody skip the title and instead call him by his first name only, though that proved challenging for many employees since it conveyed a far less traditional relationship. Yet that was the main point of the exercise. Undaunted by the resistance he met, Yang at one point required his staff to face an office wall and repeatedly shout his first name: "Yuanqing, Yuanqing, Yuanqing." He also obliged his deputies to stand at the company's entryway in the morning and greet each incoming employee by saying "I am [X, with no title]; please call me by my first name."

The chair of a shipping, engineering, mining, and logistics company with more than 25,000 employees argued that all of his managers should be building their part of the enterprise "from scratch." He pressed his lieutenants to avoid emulating others and instead to learn from their own mistakes. Among his own learnings from experience was avoidance of kinship in hiring: "We are like a family," he explained, "but we are not a family company." And later, as company chair, he reported: "I try not to be the CEO, and I spend more time as a teacher."

The founder and chair of a real-estate and financial-services firm had come to be known by his rank and file as "the schoolmaster." Having founded his property-management company in the early 2000s, he now presided over the construction of more than ten thousand homes in China annually, emphasizing green technologies, and he has taken property development into both Germany and the United States. He explained his nickname:

> I spend most of my time learning. I read books, study various subjects, meet successful entrepreneurs from different industries, and participate in all kinds of social activities. Learning is embedded in everything I do. This takes most of my time [and] it's very

important to be a keen thinker to really absorb all received information and transform it into one's own guiding principle and methodology in work after contemplation. Most of the time, we are all too busy with daily routines and cannot find the time for thinking. They call me "schoolmaster" mainly because I emphasize study for all staff in the company and passionately turn the company into a virtual military academy or a training school.

Driving the executive's own leadership and its devolvement was the worrisome belief that with accumulating experience, one's learning curve goes down and one's confidence level goes up. By the time managers reach their forties, they should have the confidence of achievement, he said, but that, alas, can come with a diminished interest in learning things new. And then, "to make things even worse, successful people will usually show an upward trend in the confidence curve," culminating in a refusal of advice from others. The necessary solution, he concluded, is to urge his executives to "stay humble and stay hungry," devoting more time to learning from younger managers and others.

Sources of Company Learning

Many of the Chinese executives secured business knowledge by initially hiring expatriate Chinese managers and executives from abroad. Some companies brought in entire executive teams from Western companies just to mentor their Chinese leaders. For instance, the chair of a maker of power supplies and green technologies was hired into his company from America's General Electric. He views his role as helping the company make the transition from the more personal style of leadership and governance associated with Chinese entrepreneurs to the systems we think of as characteristic of Western companies. China's automaker Geely had a special opportunity to learn from foreign competitors when it acquired the passenger-car business from Volvo. The typical takeover model would have been for Geely to move Volvo's headquarters operations to China or at least send Chinese leaders to run Volvo's headquarters in Sweden. Shen Freeman, Geely's head of Volvo Car Corporation told us that they had been doing the opposite—bringing Volvo executives from Sweden and the United States to China to learn from them.

The fastest transfer of Western practices, though, resulted from the far-reaching use of premier management consultant firms, such as McKinsey, BCG, and the consulting arms of the big accounting firms. It is difficult to think of any Western consulting company that does not have extensive operations in China, and estimates of the volume of business of these firms in China are in the range of $14 billion per year. Ed Tse, founder of the Chinese management consulting firm Gao Feng Advisors, noted that "[t]wenty years ago, there was no notion of what management was," but now many principles come from large consultancies.[2]

Other companies secured business knowledge through joint ventures with Western companies. Despite having no formal relationship with Walmart, the chair of a diversified enterprise copied substantial aspects of Walmart's operating model for his own retail operations. He also hired former investment bankers to develop the company's strategic plan.[3]

Given the extensive borrowing of Western business practices, it is no surprise that many aspects of these Chinese companies look familiar. But Chinese business leaders are quick to reject the idea that their companies could be run using a Western model. Liu Chuanzhi, founder and chairman of Legend Holdings, is one of many who eschewed what he saw as the homogenizing experience that American managers have in MBA programs: "Most Chinese entrepreneurs have no such educational background," he said. "US business leaders have a standardized and systematic methodology to manage their company. It's just like cooking dishes based on the standard recipe." By contrast, "Chinese entrepreneurs must continuously summarize their own management style from their experience and practice. So they must learn to cook from both a US recipe and a Chinese recipe."

How can Chinese businesses have their own model when they seem to borrow so much from Western companies? No doubt some of the complaints about the standardization associated with Western models might be defensiveness. But because they are starting from scratch, they could appropriate a great deal and still be inventing much of their operation themselves. When the Chinese companies go borrowing, they pick and choose what they use rather than copying everything from a single source. Even if all aspects of a business were borrowed from someplace else, when each part comes from a different origin, the resulting model is likely to be unique.

Where do most of the distinctive parts come from? The chief executive of an industrial services firm asserted that the single most important attribute for business success in roles like his own was to learn from experience, because there was no standard model to copy or best place to borrow: "As there is no established and tested business model to follow in China, all of us have to figure out the right business models by trying different approaches. In most of the cases, it simply will not work if we merely copy a business model from foreign countries. We need to find out how to adapt and localize foreign practice and experience to fit the China market."

What is extraordinary about these leaders and their companies is the extent to which they see the task of organizational learning as resting on what they themselves have learned—a logical extension of the big-boss model of leadership, which we examine further in a later chapter. The founder and chair of a manufacturing firm describes how that task applied to him. "After establishing this business, I have been studying in many universities, including Nanjing University, Jiangnan University, Tsinghua University, Peking University, Cheung Kong Graduate School of Business, and CEIBS [China Europe International Business School], for many years. Learning is the most important way for me to broaden my horizons and improve my analytic skills. In addition, it helps me to be aware of my own shortcomings, which urges me to learn even more. Along the road, I also make good friends with outstanding businesspeople, who can really be textbooks for me." All of these experiences strengthened his capacities to guide the enterprise—in part by helping him find models to emulate and in part by allowing him to learn from the mistakes of others so that he could avoid them.

The chair of a company active in energy, real estate, and asset management applied what worked for him to the rest of the company: "I decided to build the company into a learning organization since its start-up." Accordingly, "we provide employees with a learning platform as we have developed various plans to motivate our employees to study, including an incentive plan based on the education. We also established [a university] inside the company. And I serve as the president of the university. I spend one-third of my time on learning, training, forum exchanges, and public relations, which benefits me a lot." What is important about the founder and CEO of a company also being the head of its internal university, seen in other Chinese companies as well, is its signal from the top of the singular importance of learning.

The founder and managing director of a venture-capital firm with more than $1.5 billion under management reported that priority given to learning is a key predictor of business success. His decisions to invest in particular companies are based on that priority: "We'd like to invest in those entrepreneurs with strong learning capabilities." He also believes that entrepreneurs in China need to have knowledge bases and learning interests that are different from those associated with the US stereotype of the technology genius or even just someone with a great idea: "You have to be good at everything—dealing with the government, the media, customers, and handling internal stuff as well. Therefore, from the entrepreneurs' perspective, quick learning ability is a must."

Leadership Coaching

Leadership development in these Chinese companies happens in ways quite unlike those seen in the West. More so than in Western companies, the founder calls the shots on how senior-level managers are performing and the ways in which they need to improve, often extending deeply into their character. Criticisms can be brutal and public. Some observers liken them to political trials that forced the condemned to confess their reported transgressions in public.

David Wei came into Alibaba's B2B Division as the CEO from the West in 2006. He shared what he had learned three years later with four hundred senior leaders in the company, much of it about how he personally learned to change. "I missed a good opportunity to change myself in 2007," he explained, "when I only got the score of 75 [out of 100] from Jack Ma. Instead of analyzing the root causes and adjusting accordingly, I was caught by the eagerness to prove myself next year with better performance."[4] Wei explained:

One day when the organization department meeting ended, Jack asked some twenty B2B colleagues to stay and later more from [the] B2B Division were invited to the continued meeting. [Jack] said, "Meetings like the one of tonight were held only for two times in the nine-year history of Alibaba. The first time was when the eighteen founders discussed all the critical questions that make Alibaba the company we see today. The second one is the meeting we are having now." Jack's words instantly reminded me of the Lushan Conference in the Chinese Communist Party history.[5]

At the Lushan Conference of the Communist Party's Central Committee in 1959, Minister of Defense Peng Dehuai was criticized and denounced by Chairman Mao and other top party leaders for his outspoken opposition to Mao's policies. "Jack then asked everyone to give his own candid comments on me," Wei said. "Frankly speaking, I felt very sad from 20:30 to 21:00 during the meeting as a quarter of the participants stood up to throw stones at me, criticizing my management. Then in the next two hours, half of them finished airing their views and no one stood by my side."

It is difficult to imagine any Western manager being subjected to or tolerating this kind of public collective criticism. But Wei explained why he could tolerate it. "Alibaba gives you a sense of safety more than any other companies and in such a safe and sound environment, you do not need to worry, no matter how harsh the fault-finding meeting can be. Furthermore, I also realized the meeting would not happen if Jack decided to dismiss me. What's the purpose, then, to have this eight-hours-long meeting? It could only occur when the 'party' and 'organization' still try to save one colleague with such huge efforts."

David Wei described what we might call an extended coaching session with Jack Ma, during which Ma told Wei that "you are still trying to prove yourself." Wei reported that this session "plunged me into more than three months of contemplation and only recently could I start to understand the deep meaning. I seemed to grasp the 'Tao' [universal truth and way] finally. It's believing in our mission and values, in doing things that would make me happy and make the team and organization happy."

To Westerners, the public denouncement of the mistakes of a leader, followed by an equally public confession and apology, might look like a show trial. Organizational values rather than political ideology are at issue in Wei's case, but the pressure on the individual to reform one's way of thinking is intense both here and in the political context. Wei makes it clear that he believes Jack Ma was right in criticizing him (largely for still being too much of an American-style manager), that he himself was mistaken in resisting the criticism, and that accepting the way of thinking that Ma put forward improved his entire life. The coaching in this instance did not prove sufficient, however, as Ma pushed Wei out a few years later for still not embracing the right values.

Accountability for Learning

The chief executive at many companies holds his or her senior managers accountable for learning how to lead and personally directs that mastery. A high-tech manufacturing chief executive told us, for example, that all of his senior executives must prepare a report on themselves each month, disclosing mistakes they had made and what they had learned, not unlike the self-criticism historically required in the Communist Party. Similarly, the chairman of a food-products company requires senior executives to prepare written commentaries on their ideas and thinking about leadership and change management, each to be reviewed by her.

Several of the business leaders we interviewed who emphasize the importance of making the entire firm a learning organization noted that coaching or personal instruction of other executives was key. The chief executive of an industrial group explained how he and others do so for top talent: "Our chairman and I launched a formal mentorship program in 2013. We recruited nine mentees—i.e., high-potential employees. The chairman, the VP of operations, and I form the mentoring team. Each of us is responsible to coach three mentees. We also organize internal training programs. Both the chairman and I serve as internal training program lecturers."

The founder and chief executive of one of China's largest furniture retailers requires all managers to read at least five books each year and "to share their views after the reading during management team meetings." Their choice of books and what they report learning from them are part of their performance appraisal for the year, as assessed by their superiors. "The path to growth and success for Chinese entrepreneurs is through learning," the CEO said. Though only finishing primary school himself, he returned to school after founding his company to complete an MBA degree.[6]

The chair of a food producer and the chair of a high-tech enterprise require each of their senior managers to prepare reports on their own learning about their experiences in the company—that is, about what is working and what is not. The first takes this a step further with a program that she calls the "Heart to Heart Talk," in which she sits with the senior leaders and, as she notes, "we can lead them to realize any complacency, identify new market trends and changes, and discuss how to keep the company competitive." The idea of trying to get leaders to change what they think and even their way of thinking reflects the consensus approach associated with Japanese management. How similar this is to another Japanese practice—one that relies on peer pressure rather than on the formal authority of the boss—is not so clear, however. A medical-device maker CEO told us that he used to fire employees who opposed company priorities and projects, but now he works to keep and promote them. A real-estate investment company founder and chair noted that skills are much easier to acquire than are values and attitudes, so his training program is designed to convey company values to employees. "The process is like making pickles," he explained. "You keep vegetables in the salty solution for some months and then they turn sour in flavor to become pickles."

As private Chinese companies have increasingly invested and acquired companies abroad, the learning-organization mindset has been carried along with them. This can be seen in the experience of the Golden Dragon Precise Copper Tube Group after it built a $120 million factory in the United States to manufacture pipes for air-conditioning machinery. The company hired 290 employees for its new Alabama factory but also imported 70 Chinese employees to help run the facility, including its president. However, in applying their own methods from China, the offshore managers gave offense to many of the plant's American employees, seeming to undertrain, overwork, and sometimes hector them. In this mostly non-union region of the country, the American workers voted in a chapter of the United Steelworkers Union.

The head of human resources belatedly came to realize, he reported, that if "you give them respect," which until then had not been in ample supply, "they appreciate that better than money." The firm's Chinese managers learned to come to terms with both the union and the local mindset. When Japanese firms invested in the United States, observed one consultant, they imposed their well-honed procedures; Chinese companies, by contrast, worked more by trial and error and learned adaptively.[7]

Replay-the-Game

The shift from focusing on individual learning to collective improvement can be more of a challenge. Peter Senge's influential book *The Fifth Discipline* provides illuminating examples of how organizations skilled at creating, acquiring, and transferring knowledge, and given to open discussion and holistic thinking, can adapt to market changes more quickly than others. In fast-evolving economies like China, that capacity can prove especially important.

Lenovo again provides an instructive example. Lenovo Founder Liu Chuanzhi had come to value organizational learning from his own experience, and in the process, he developed a unique methodology—what he termed "replay-the-game." The concept originated in the early days of Lenovo when Liu's managers would come into his then-tiny office, one by one, to discuss an urgent issue with him. A conversation with one manager was often unfinished when another manager arrived, Liu explained, and his days at work were fast becoming an endless succession of incomplete conversations. Upon arriving home in the evening and reflecting on the day, he lamented the inefficient use of his time and, worse, the focus on problems that seemed to have little bearing on his start-up's profitability. He resolved that he would no longer allow his days to be so fractured and undisciplined. He would set clear goals, prioritize time, and improve in doing so.

From his research scientist background, Liu realized that reviewing his daily experience could serve as an important vehicle for improving, and he self-consciously worked to build it as a learning methodology not only for himself but also for those around him and those around them. At first, the process was simply termed a review. When a major initiative was completed, whether the launch of a new product, the installation of a resource-planning system, or the introduction of a mandatory corporate indoctrination program for new staff, Liu would gather together the key people involved and conduct a closed-door review session, pressing for frank and constructive appraisals of what had been done, reassessing the original objectives, reviewing the actions, pinpointing the causes of both successes and failures, and drawing out management implications.

As Liu's after-action reviews took on a life of their own, he borrowed a method, "replay-the-game," from Weiqi (also known as Go), the traditional board game widespread in East Asia. The phrase refers to a practice in which players reprise each step after a game for the purposes of self-improvement. The formalization of the practice in Lenovo came over many years, in itself a capacity refined from experience. Liu officially adopted the phrase in 2001, and Lenovo explicitly designated it a core building block of its culture in 2006. By 2012, replay-the-game was being promoted throughout the Lenovo group worldwide, and it has been applied to companies in which Lenovo has invested as well.

Lenovo's replay-the-game scheme requires a four-step review cycle: (1) recall the original objectives and expected outcomes; (2) compare the results against original objectives and expected outcomes to identify effective and ineffective measures and actions; (3) analyze the root causes for the success or failure from a host of perspectives; and (4) summarize and extract the general management principles from the experience, and specify actions for improvement.

Liu Chuanzhi's English-language interpreter offered a concise framing of the main issue here: "We often see a phenomenon in business as described in a Chinese proverb saying, 'Flowers do not blossom where one intently plants the seeds while willows flourish even though the seeds are accidentally sowed.'" Lenovo asks whether its own flowers should have given way to more willows. Was the goal of planting flowers wrong? Maybe the flowers were not planted correctly? Or was it the wrong place to grow them?

Company leaders, including Liu Chuanzhi himself, subject themselves to the management criticisms that often emerge from replay-the-game. When shortfalls are deemed their fault, they are required to reflect on and correct their own behavior. For instance, in his early years Liu had been short-tempered and quick to pound a desk, but on learning that his behavior was stoking office tensions, he became more patient.

Consider how Lenovo's executives learned from their own strategic redirections. The company's first commercial success came from developing a proprietary device—the Han-card—allowing IBM and Apple computers to process Chinese characters. The card proved profitable and generated most of Lenovo's early revenue, but Lenovo soon expanded into the PC-distribution business, and thanks to that, it was able to survive a collapse in demand for the card when personal computers no longer required the additional hardware. The company subsequently moved from the distribution of PCs made by others to its own PC manufacturing and sales.

Drawing on the four steps of replay-the-game, the Lenovo executives concluded that both transitions were well premised on Lenovo's original objective of continuously seeking market opportunities and exploring new business models so that the company could survive market disruptions. For this start-up with little capital (less than $25,000 at first), no business experience, and thus little margin for error, the objective of seeking and exploring rather than seeing itself as a hardware maker proved company-saving.

The second step of replay-the-game is to compare results with the original objectives. On reviewing the strategic redirections, Liu Chuanzhi concluded that the results exceeded his expectations, helping the firm avoid a fatal "heart attack" that might otherwise have come from the disruptive technologies. The objective of seeking and exploring new technologies had led its move into PC distribution just in time. But by 1990 the "Wintel" system had become the dominant standard, and competition in the PC industry was moving from product innovation to cost control. Believing it could undercut the costs of making PCs that IBM, HP, and other makers were then incurring, and consistent with its goal of seeking new markets and exploring fresh models, Lenovo decided to manufacture its own PCs. The bet paid off, and by the year 2000 the company's own products dominated the Chinese market, with a 27 percent share—far higher than Liu's original expectations and once again reaffirming the firm's original objective.

The third step in Lenovo's replay-the-game is to analyze the critical factors for success or failure. Here Liu and his colleagues concluded that their active monitoring of technology trends and commitment to being ahead of the wave proved prescient. From their review, Liu found that three factors had proven critical and thus should be applied in the future: (1) close monitoring of the market and informed identification of the next target for expansion; (2) deep understanding from systematic study of technology trends, supply-chain management, and quality and cost controls; and (3) personal determination to prevail even if competing against global leaders like IBM.

The fourth step in replay-the-game is to summarize the experience and extract the emergent principles. For Liu, this step paid off significantly. In short, he had learned to look to the next move beyond the firm's present success. Borrowing from agricultural aphorisms, said Liu, the company leader must first "eat the rice from the bowl already in your hand" and "set your eyes on the rice still in the pan," but also remember to "plant crops in the farm field." It is too late to start new crops if your bowl is empty, and thus one must develop far-sighted plans while still taking care of current business.

The notion of after-incident reviews as represented by the replay-the-game model at Lenovo was well known in the West before it was widely used in China. What was innovative at Lenovo was the willingness to actually take this model seriously, to follow it continuously, and to change based on the results.

A take-charge attitude is also critical. When Lenovo started in 1984, China was still a planned economy, and start-ups like Lenovo could count on few resources, even such basics as a license to manufacture computers. But rather than yield to such barriers, Liu worked around them, initially partnering with a PC maker in Hong Kong. Finally, Liu learned that as the leader of the company he had to step back from his daily chores to appreciate the larger picture.

As Lenovo repeatedly applied the method, it accumulated a host of guidelines for optimizing its application. It now asks of managers that they be open-minded, candid in communication, and self-reflective. Similarly, for each of the four steps in replay-the-game, Lenovo sets forward principles for optimal learning:

Recall the original objectives or expected results:

- Distinguish objectives from goals. Objectives give direction in setting goals, while clear and staged goals can help to achieve objectives in a step-by-step manner.
- Besides pinpointing objectives, quantitative goals or milestone targets must be specified. Without quantitative or measurable goals, it's hard to hit the objectives and also difficult to evaluate the results.

- If the original objectives and goals are not clear enough, then try to specify them when conducting replay-the-game to facilitate the review process. This will also improve the setting up of objectives and goals in the future.

Compare the result to the original objectives:

- First, compare the outcome to the original goals and objectives, and then analyze any unexpected gains and losses.
- Identify both strengths and weaknesses and what's behind wins and losses. Do not understate the importance of understanding wins; too much humbleness is regrettable and one should not overlook one's own strength.
- Include related external cases in the discussion to put the review process in a broader context to ensure an objective conclusion.

Analyze the critical factors for success or failure:

- When analyzing factors of success, pay more attention to objective causes and be critical in evaluating the organization's own competence.
- When reviewing the causes for failure, spend more time in examining the weaknesses of the team. Carefully review whether there were obvious mistakes in setting up those objectives and goals that led to the final failure. Otherwise, the whole review process could have centered on the wrong objectives and goals, making it a meaningless endeavor.
- When reviewing the experience of success or best practice, try to step out of the discussion and look for universal patterns without narrowly focusing on the subject matter.

Summarize experience and principles:

- Be very cautious when extracting summary conclusions. Always think about the issues in a dynamic and broader context. Never mistakenly treat any single observation from a concrete experience as a universal law.

Conclusion

In mastering their own personal way forward in an unfamiliar business landscape, the private-company Chinese executives we interviewed projected their own learning experiences onto the firm. They of necessity invented their own "learning organization," a precept that Western management had also embraced some years earlier, and they did so unself-consciously, not borrowing but erecting it on their own. But, again of necessity, they took it a step further, insisting that their company learn to be a learning organization with greater zeal than is common in the West.

The executives built a learning-company mindset through three channels already well familiar to the West: self-directed learning, instructive experience, and personal coaching. For the first channel, self-directed learning, some set aside daily time to attack unresolved management problems, while others divided their time across a host of domains to optimize their understanding. They pressed their lieutenants to do the same. Still others, not letting national pride get in the way, brought in Western consultants and hired Western expatriates to share their wisdom. Some executives launched their own universities inside the enterprise to reach as many managers as possible.

For the second channel, instructive experience, the executives asked their lieutenants to make decisions, reflect on their outcomes, and draw from these outcomes to improve subsequent decisions. And for the third channel, leadership coaching, company executives pressed their subordinates to eschew hierarchic deference, act like owners, and learn to take charge.

The Learning Company in the Words of the Fortune Makers

The strength of Chinese enterprises is that we are still young, [and] compared to the excellent foreign companies, Chinese private enterprises still have much room to improve. . . . Therefore we must always keep a humble and learning attitude no matter how strong our momentum is, how energetic our passion is, and how big our goal is. . . . I believe we will have a bright future, and I have no doubt that one day Chinese enterprises will pay big roles in global competition.

—Chair, electric equipment and power transmission corporation

Great leaders must be able to understand both the future and [themselves]. In fact, understanding oneself is the more difficult task, especially for those who are in [a] leadership position. . . . I have seen many successful business leaders in my career [and what] the truly successful leaders have in common is that they are all very humble, and eager to learn.

—Chair, information technology services company

We'd like to invest in those entrepreneurs with strong learning capabilities. Chinese entrepreneurs and American entrepreneurs are different. American entrepreneurs may be a specialist, but Chinese entrepreneurs are required to be an all-rounder.

—Chief executive, venture-capital firm

The first [leadership principle] is the learning capability. As there is no established and mature business model to follow in China, all of us are trying to figure out the right business models by risking different approaches. Also, most of the time it will not work by simply copying a business model from foreign countries.

—Executive, industrial services enterprise

As we started up this business from scratch, we [didn't] know what is the most effective way to sell our product and all the experience came from our practice. For example, to sell a new product, you cannot just place it in the store. You need the promoters to demonstrate how to use the product and also to let the consumers . . . taste the food like soymilk. To some extent, we are forced to learn how to do the marketing and then summarize our practice to theory including experiential marketing. Once we have confirmed its effectiveness, then we will promote it on both offline and online channels. Eventually, it becomes our core competitive advantage.

—Wang Xuning, Chair, Joyoung Co.

CHAPTER 4

Strategic Agility
for the Long Game

I am a crocodile in the Yangtze River.

The strategies of successful companies have long served as templates for budding entrepreneurs in the United States. Executives of American organizations can study how Estée Lauder, General Electric, and Southwest Airlines built competitive ways forward. Chinese prototypes were, however, nonexistent when China began to open its economy in the 1980s.

Chinese executives, even those who built Fortune 500 equivalents, have had to navigate their own way forward by discovering which strategies work and how to benefit from experience rather than learning from the proven models of other firms in their markets. With so little guidance for building enterprises, business leaders in China, unlike their counterparts in the West, have learned by testing more than by emulating. Accordingly, Chinese business leaders have drawn on agility—that is, on the capacity to nimbly change their strategies for growth as they progressively learn how to achieve it. These entrepreneurs by necessity have looked to their own experience, adopting trial-and-error, experience-based learning in the face of political uncertainty and rapid change.

Company strategy is usually seen as a matter of setting the firm's general direction and then identifying what best creates sustainable value and advantage. Underpinning strategy is a central idea and an enduring vision for the enterprise, providing both an overarching trajectory for the firm and an inspiration for thousands of employees to achieve it. That said,

China's rapidly evolving marketplace has rewarded firms that are able to adapt fluidly. While central ideas could thus remain relatively fixed, company strategies could hardly remain so.

In his classic work *Strategy and Structure,* business historian Alfred Chandler argued that US corporations in the first half of the twentieth century followed a practice of letting business strategy drive company structure. Chandler found that structural change in the firm's organization and leadership would generally follow strategic change. However, his famous formulation for the United States has been put to a stress test in China, where rapid-fire changes in strategy have been essential for survival and growth, which in turn have often required fast and recurrent redirections of the strategies themselves.

As we will see in this chapter, the growth of Alibaba from tiny start-up to New York Stock Exchange darling depended on its strategic agility above all else. Chief executive Jack Ma repeatedly redirected Alibaba's strategy in response to his fast-evolving market, and in doing so he successfully toppled the better established but less adaptable business of America's eBay in China.

Much the same had occurred when a fleet-footed Didi Chuxing Technology Co., China's leading ride-hailing service, defeated America's Uber Technologies in China in 2016. Two years earlier, Uber chief executive Travis Kalanick had offered to buy Didi, but the latter declined, CEO Wei Cheng warning that "there will be a day when we will surpass you." And indeed Didi did. After two years of fierce competition, Didi had attracted 42.1 million active users compared to Uber's 10.1 million. Throwing in the towel, Uber CEO Kalanick opted to sell Uber China to Didi, taking a 20 percent stake in his Chinese nemesis, a company already valued at $35 billion.[1]

Whether in China or the West, setting company strategy requires that company leaders focus on several questions. First, how are we positioned in our markets? Here the time-proven concepts associated with competitive strategy—including the influence of suppliers, the likelihood of new entrants, and the threat of substitutes—are of primary concern. Second, which of the company's features, specifically those subject to a manager's discretion, create superior value? Third, given those external and internal factors, what decisions by a manager can create additional advantage for the enterprise in the market? At the center of all three of these questions is the issue of how best to create and sustain a superior-value proposition—that combination of product features and costs which most appeals to customers.

Whatever the business strategy, the management principle of strategic fit calls for ensuring a close match between the leadership skill set of its top executives and the specific strategic challenges facing a company. A firm's strategy thus defines the kind of leadership it requires, and by way of a well-honored practice in the United States, governing boards of firms facing financial challenges are more likely to move their chief financial officer into the corner office; boards of companies tackling marketing challenges are more prone to bring up an executive from sales; and directors of companies looking to enter international waters are more likely to promote a manager with global experience.[2]

That causal arrow has, however, often been flipped in China. Company leaders, without well-established and clear pathways, time and again have had to decide that their enterprise required a new direction as they learned what worked, or did not work, based on their own evolving experience with the market.

Given the uncertain ways ahead in the Chinese market, devising and revising company strategy have proven of great importance for its private company executives. This was evident when we asked the executives to identify the three most important roles for them as chief executive or executive chair during the past five years, and also the areas where they devoted the greatest amount of time. More executives singled out the role of setting business strategy than any other role, as shown in Figure 4.1, and more identified setting strategy as the area of their greatest time commitment, as shown in Figure 4.2. Of special note is the fact that owner and investor relations received little attention, consistent with the scant consideration that business leaders give shareholders in China.

Agility at Alibaba

To appreciate the value of strategic agility, we followed Jack Ma, the founder and chief executive of Alibaba from its beginning in 1999 to its dominance of the Chinese online retail market. We witnessed how his repeated redirections of the firm led it to become one of the largest online retailers, auction sites, and payment portals in the world.

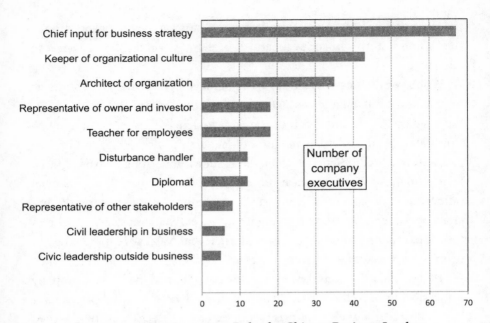

FIGURE 4.1 Most Important Roles for Chinese Business Leaders
Question: "What are your three most important roles as CEO or chair in the past five years?"
Number of CEOs/Chairs = 72.

Jack Ma was born as Ma Yun in 1964 in Hangzhou, a provincial capital some 120 miles southwest of Shanghai. Though his parents were musicians, speaking English from an early age became more of a personal passion than mastering scores. Over a period of eight years, he rode his bike for forty minutes to a downtown hotel to engage foreigners in English conversation. In addition, he enrolled in a college to study English and taught English for five years. The new language opened his global horizons. "What I learned from my teachers and books was different from what the foreigners told us," he said. "Those eight years really changed me. I started to become more globalized than most Chinese."[3]

When Ma visited the United States in 1995, the Internet's commercial potential was just being discovered. Jeff Bezos had founded Amazon.com the year before, and Pierre Omidyar was creating eBay. A friend guided Ma online, but when Ma tested the Internet's reach by searching his home country for a beer maker, any brewery, none popped up even though he knew that hundreds were on the ground. The Internet promised extraordinary access, he realized, yet it offered the barest visibility into one of the

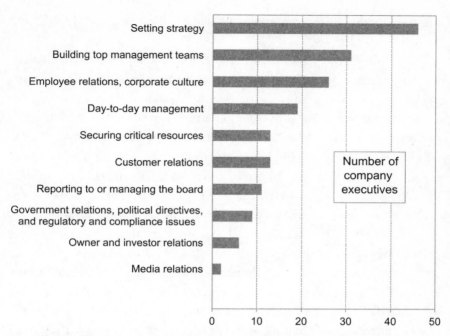

FIGURE 4.2 Most Time-Consuming Activities of Chinese Business Leaders
Question: "What are your three most time-consuming activities?" Number of CEOs/Chairs = 72.

largest commercial markets in the world. "This is something interesting," he said. "If we can take companies in China and make a home page for them, this could be something big." Its potential was virtually untapped. "I felt like a blind man," he recalled, "riding on the back of a tiger."[4]

Despite zero experience in webpage development, Ma returned to China and raised $20,000 to create a website for consumer access to small-business catalogs, analogous to an online Yellow Pages that he had spotted in the United States. He mainly attracted small regional companies that were starved for visibility, but he also drew the attention of Hangzhou Telecommunication, the local telecom that had started a competing service of its own. Facing a deep-pockets player, Ma opted to merge rather than to contest, but strategic differences emerged, and Ma exited with $800,000 in walk-away money. He joined the payroll of a company under the Ministry of Foreign Trade and Economic Cooperation, but there, too, a mismatch became apparent. "My boss wanted to use the Internet to control small businesses," he said, "but I wanted to use the Internet to power small businesses. We had a totally different philosophy."[5]

With the Internet rapidly gaining traction in China, Ma invited seventeen friends in 1999 to his apartment in Hangzhou, to consider a web-based service beyond showcasing beer and catalogs. Brainstorming for days, he and his coterie converged on a platform for small merchants to promote their wares. Ma adopted the name of Alibaba to invoke Ali Baba's fabled access to the hidden treasures of forty thieves. When he later asked a waitress in a San Francisco coffee shop, his focus group of one, what the name connoted to her, she responded with "Open Sesame!"—exactly the metaphor for what Ma was hoping his plan would achieve.

At first, Ma's Alibaba.com mostly featured products of smaller enterprises, offering exporters a vehicle through which customers worldwide could order products directly. Though he started small, Ma's vision for the enterprise was big. In meeting with some of his customers at the opening of a Shanghai office, he ambitiously declared, "We want Alibaba to be one of the top ten websites in the world. We want Alibaba to be a partner to all businesspeople. And we want to build a company that lasts 80 years!"[6]

Ma's aspirational goals seemed utterly unrealistic. With reserves of only $10 million, Alibaba was burning through cash at the rate of $2 million per month. But he experimented with a fee-based product enabling exporters to connect directly with Western buyers—in effect, making the world their market—and it clicked. By 2002, the company had become profitable and continued to expand as Ma and his lieutenants increasingly tailored their services to what they were hearing from their customers.[7] Ma had started with the simple service of listing catalogs of medium-sized and smaller merchants, but soon added services to attract more traffic on his sites. In response to customer mistrust of arm's-length purchases, he allowed them to inspect shipped goods prior to payment.

When eBay, by then not only an auction site but also a shopping venue, successfully entered the Chinese market three years later through a local partner, EachNet, Ma believed that its rapid growth posed a mortal threat to his still-small online business. In response, in 2003 he created Taobao ("search for treasure") to link both individual and commercial buyers and sellers via the web—for free. Executives at eBay scoffed at the concept of a costless service. The company's approach to China was to adapt but not fundamentally alter its US model, and it initially secured good traction by charging sellers a listing fee and then collecting a transaction fee when their items sold. The eBay executives saw Taobao as a modest local player with neither the financial clout nor the professionalism to challenge a company that had already achieved so much success in the United States.

Under Ma's leadership, Taobao billed neither sellers nor buyers, opting instead to charge sellers for use of an advertising platform. Ma also concluded that the facilitation of web-based transactions constituted the kernel of his strategy, and he accordingly outsourced most else, including logistics, warehousing, inventory management, and even order fulfillment, making Alibaba an "asset-lite" enterprise and allowing executive attention to concentrate on customers. eBay's executives had been less attentive to those customer demands, and Alibaba increasingly cut into eBay's market share in the now burgeoning e-commerce market in China.

From his accumulating experience, Jack Ma came to believe that a critical stumbling block for Internet commerce in China was a deep distrust among buyers and sellers who did not know one another in a culture that still placed a premium on personal familiarity. He and his team sought innovative ways to narrow the trust gap, such as hosting e-mail communication between prospective buyers and sellers. But the biggest single strategic redirection was the creation in 2004 of Alipay, an escrow service to facilitate web-based transactions, allowing customers to inspect purchased goods with a money-back guarantee while protecting sellers against defaulting buyers. The model allowed sellers to confidently ship, assured of payment once the buyer had inspected the goods. Alipay proved such an attractive service that eBay suggested a merger.

Ma declined eBay's offer and instead opened discussion with CEO Jerry Yang of America's Yahoo. Ma was looking for an infusion of capital to scale up both Alibaba and Taobao, and in the summer of 2005 they met at a conference in Pebble Beach, California. By now, Yahoo had become a global giant though it was still stumbling badly in China. Working with a succession of local partners, including a search-engine player with the intriguing name of Beijing 3721, Yahoo had failed to make substantial inroads in China, and Yang was eager to find a better partner. Yang agreed to invest $1 billion in Alibaba in return for 40 percent of its stock and 35 percent of its voting shares. Alibaba would take over Yahoo China, gain capital for expansion, and acquire instant scale and credibility.

The Yahoo investment allowed Taobao to open access on its site for free to all customers for three years, a direct threat to eBay's fee-laden model. "We call on eBay," said Ma provocatively, "to do what's right for this phase of e-commerce development in China and make your services free for all buyers and sellers"—which eBay of course could not. "Free is not a business model," an eBay spokesperson responded defensively. "It speaks volumes for the strength of eBay's business in China that Taobao announced that it is unable to charge for its products for the next three years. We are very proud that eBay has created a sustainable business model in China." But Taobao and Alibaba vaulted ahead, and it proved eBay's denouement. After entering the market in 2002, eBay had reached 70 percent of China's e-commerce market at its peak, but just four years later it was forced to shutter its operations, defeated by an agile competitor. "eBay may be a shark in the ocean," said Ma, "but I am a crocodile in the Yangtze River," and "if we fight in the river, we win."[8] Jack Ma learned that many customers were ready to pay more for extra bells and whistles, and it proved a gold mine. Alibaba began offering a subscription-based premium that allowed sellers to display more detailed product information and certification from an independent credit agency that confirmed the legal registration of the company and its financial condition.

By 2007, 70 percent of Alibaba's revenues were coming from its premium services. Later, Ma created Taobao Mall—TMall.com—as a platform for branded retailers to sell their products on the web at no cost. In 2015, Alibaba invested $4.6 billion in electronic retailer Suning Commerce Group to gain access to Suning's vast supply chain and its five thousand physical stores.

While Yahoo's investment was a much-needed cash infusion for Alibaba, when Yahoo later faltered, it was Alibaba that returned the favor. By 2016, Alibaba's success had raised the value of Yahoo's holdings in the company to $28 billion, essentially equivalent to the entire market value of Yahoo itself.

Jack Ma changed Alibaba's strategy repeatedly as technologies emerged and customers evolved, symptomatic of the nimbleness required by fast-growing Chinese markets. He responded to eBay's Chinese entry with an online model based on different principles, bridging the distrust inherent between remotely connected buyers and sellers, and brought branded merchants into a web marketplace. In the face of customer challenges that

TABLE 4.1 Alibaba's Group Revenue and Earnings, 2011–2016

Year	Revenue ¥ Millions	Operating Income ¥ Millions	Number of Employees
2011	11,903	1,608	12,878
2012	20,025	4,665	21,930
2013	34,517	8,649	20,674
2014	52,514	23,402	22,072
2015	76,204	24,320	34,985
2016	101,143	29,102	46,228

Sources: Alibaba company reports; YCharts, 2016.

could have destroyed Alibaba if he did not quickly respond, Ma recurrently revised what had been the company's business model since its founding. In nimbly revising the firm's value proposition, outmaneuvering proven successes like eBay, he led his company to annual growth rates of more than 45 percent in revenue and 75 percent in earnings. Alibaba's extraordinary expansion proved compelling to Western investors, and the company raised $25 billion in its US initial public offering in 2014, exceeding Facebook's $16 billion IPO two years earlier. By 2016, Alibaba employed over 46,000 people and realized income of more than ¥100 billion (see Table 4.1). Its market capitalization had soared to more than $250 billion in September 2016, placing it among the top ten companies worldwide and giving it a market value more than twice that of eBay and Yahoo combined.[9]

Decentralized Structure

As Jack Ma repeatedly redirected Alibaba's strategy, he also built an architecture to support that agility. He placed great emphasis, for instance, on fostering a strong team around him who could exercise the same dexterity. "I think leadership is about the team," he told us. "A leader is never a lone person; it's about a team. Nobody is great enough, smart enough to do everything. A great leader should always think about and believe that other people are smarter than you are." Find the best people, he urged, and "and then you have a chance to win." And it was vital to mold them into a team through direct engagement. "I look at your eyes, you look in my eyes," he explained, and then "I can easily tell if there is something wrong with you, whether family problem, work problem, or whatever. Trust building is a big job"—and once in place, it gave his lieutenants a license to make their own quick decisions.

To further enable Alibaba's agility, Jack Ma preferred not to set a single driving agenda from the corporate center but, rather, had each subsidiary fix its own strategy under his general directive that they would each have to become a major player in their market. Ma explained that "business unit presidents must have the freedom to do what is right for their business," and going further, he declared that their units should feel free to compete with one another, all with the purpose of "being the best in their business." Alipay's primary objective, for instance, was to be a leader in payment processing. Toward this end, it had to build its own client base of online merchants, yet that included taking some clients from Taobao, another Alibaba company.

For his devolved strategy-setting, Ma built a decentralized architecture. Alibaba established separate governing boards and executive teams for each of its subsidiaries, and it extended the decentralization down to operating systems, allowing each subsidiary to choose its own IT infrastructure. When internal competition led to conflicts among Alibaba businesses, Ma pressed his divisional executives to optimize their own interests, whatever the impact on the group. If internal competition resulted in net disadvantages for the subsidiaries, he held their presidents responsible for resolving the issues among themselves.

We have seen in Jack Ma a readiness to repeatedly alter the company's strategy in a decentralized structure that facilitated such shifts, even as Alibaba became a well-established player, reversing the causal arrow that normally defines strategic fit. Leaders are recruited to positions for which their experience and temperament are congruent with the strategic challenges facing large firms in the West. But not constrained by that fit, Jack Ma repeatedly redirected his firm's strategy to fit the market, and he did so in ways that archrivals eBay and Yahoo could not. Jack Ma's strategy and leadership in building Alibaba are briefly itemized in Table 4.2.

Underlying Alibaba's strategic agility, however, is a continuity in general purpose, a shared "central idea" that the company is creating an invaluable foundation on which companies and consumers, buyers and sellers, can meet in the virtual marketplace. David Wei, who served as the

TABLE 4.2 Jack Ma's Strategy and Leadership at Alibaba

Year	Leadership Decision	Action
1995	Started an Internet company, "China Yellow Pages," that created websites for company catalogs	Perceived commercial potential in China after testing the Internet in the United States
1999	Founded Alibaba in his apartment with seventeen friends	Developed a business strategy adapted to Chinese customers with a subscription-based model
2003	Created Taobao, an e-commerce platform for small and medium-sized Chinese firms	Watched eBay import its US model into China, but developed his own model for China
2004	Founded Alipay, an escrow service to facilitate web-based transactions	Added web service to overcome distrust between buyers and sellers
2005	Secured $1 billion from Yahoo for 40 percent stake; declined eBay offer to acquire	Had high growth plans but low capital; secured capital to vault ahead of eBay
2014	Raised $25 billion in IPO on the New York Stock Exchange	Secured the capital and visibility to build global enterprise

company's chief executive from 2006 to 2011, argued that the company's agility was made possible by the fixity of this central idea. "We believe only a company with soul can be called a great company. Like a man, strategy is like the skeleton while execution power can be seen as the muscle. But for a company to succeed, it always needs to have soul first, then followed by skeleton and lastly the muscles."[10]

We have seen a close and mutually influential linkage between agile strategy and agile leadership at Alibaba—two sides of the same coin. Jack Ma brought both to his steerage of Alibaba, setting direction and building the team and the architecture to achieve it. This integrated exercise of strategy and leadership is increasingly important among private enterprises, for three major reasons. First, Chinese companies are becoming more globally interdependent, and shortcomings in either their strategy or their leadership are likely to have greater downsides than would be the case in a less connected world. Second, the contracting life cycles for products and the rapidly increasing change rates for markets place a greater premium on having an appropriate strategy in place *and* an executive team than can execute it in timely fashion. Third, firms are increasingly contending not just with their direct competitors but also with disruptive innovators and changing customers, and this, too, has placed a greater premium on more vigilant company leaders with a greater readiness to redirect their strategy. All of these factors point to the unique features of agility, which has been necessitated by rapid changes in market conditions and growing market opportunities as domestic populations have flooded into online shopping.

Far Horizons at Vanke

While a leadership capacity to quickly shift strategic gears has helped drive the growth of many Chinese companies, we also see evidence that company executives look well beyond the next market shift at the same time. Turning on a dime is a distinctive feature of business leadership and strategy at many Chinese companies (or perhaps we should say, turning on a yuan), but so too is a more deep-lying long-term agenda. Less constrained by unrelenting Wall Street demands for steady growth in quarterly earnings and annual dividends, Chinese companies have felt greater latitude for swinging at the fence.

In a fast-growing transitional economy like China, company leaders face markets that are perpetually evolving. Few would deny the importance of building on a long-term vision for a company's place in that world, but in practice the prospects of securing windfall profits from repeatedly presented opportunistic openings are hard to resist—the dark side of an agile mindset. Immediate boons can bring short-term bonanzas but also dim long-term prospects.

What we see in China, however, is a combination of both. The joining of near-term flexibility with a distant-vista fixity was evident in many of the companies in which we have interviewed, including Vanke. We have already described its chief executive Wang Shi agilely moving his enterprise along an uncertain path as it morphed from a commodities trading company into a property-management company. What we also witnessed is a chief executive focused as well on the far horizon.

25 Percent

Vanke entered the residential housing industry at a time when demand for both residential and commercial property was fast growing. Should

Vanke pursue both, Wang Shi wondered? And if he opted to focus on the residential market, should he go for the high-margin luxury-villa market or the low-margin mass-apartment market? And then, should he pursue a land-bank strategy of acquiring large tracts of land, constructing nearly finished residences but holding on to them until the heated economy brought windfall appreciation? Or, alternatively, is a fast-cycle strategy preferable, building small finished units for near-term sale to people who would actually occupy them?

The key for the speculative land-bank strategy was to acquire land at low cost—and for that, government connections proved an invaluable advantage. With the right relations and a willingness to pay under-the-table, returns could be high. The core of the fast-cycle strategy, on the other hand, was an ability to meet tangible buyer needs and to impose cost controls, neither of which could be achieved in the near term. The fast-cycle strategy commanded a lower profit margin but would also come with lower capital requirements, more predictable demand, and less vulnerability to market bubbles.

To help resolve the strategic questions, Wang declared that his company would not go after any line of business that promised a profit margin greater than 25 percent. Initially, his inner circle did not understand what seemed to be an arbitrary restraint on their profit-seeking instincts. Others in the property industry were shocked. Why, they asked, should one not seek higher profits? The incremental reform and "dual price track" system had brought windfall opportunities, and for entrepreneurs willing to take advantage of them, making large bets on uncertain policy changes, sometimes with under-the-table assistance, abnormally high returns were not only possible but often easier than the old-fashioned way of serving customers and making money by earning it.

But the "market is fair," Wang explained, and "you cannot consistently outsmart the market and build a sustainable foundation." Eventually, market discipline would prevail, and when that happened, product innovation and operational efficiency would be essential for company growth. Accordingly, Wang opted for the lower-margin but also more enduring "buy-to-live-in" market. His 1992 decision defined how Vanke would operate for years. Two decades later, 80 percent of its units had been finished and sold, and 90 percent were targeted to buyers of modest means, offering space of 140 square meters (1,500 square feet) or less.

Quality Growth

Vanke's determination to pursue a long-term strategy was also evident in its focus on quality control from the beginning. Because of growing demand and still limited supply in the early years of real-estate development in China, some builders learned that they could cut corners without losing sales, the resulting quality shortfall just one collateral but acceptable consequence.

Wang Shi instead committed Vanke to quality construction from the start. This was partially a consequence of Vanke's "no bribery" policy, which often forced it to acquire less preferable tracts. In Shanghai, for instance, Vanke purchased land adjacent to an airport where noisy take-offs and landings occurred every few minutes. In the western city of Chengdu, Vanke purchased land next to a cremation site where traditional superstitions forecast bad luck for nearby residents. Vanke would have to make up for those evident drawbacks with superior homes and services.

To that end, Vanke declared 1996 to be its "year of quality." Wang Shi set forward a vision of "growth with quality" and asserted that when construction speed conflicted with product quality, the latter would prevail. Likewise, when cost controls conflicted with quality, quality would prevail. And property quality would have to be defined by the buyers rather than by the builders. Vanke retained independent survey firms to poll its customers, and it introduced an online chatroom—"Complaining to Vanke"—where buyers could register their grievances for all to see.

In 2001, Wang Shi introduced the goal of "building houses with zero defects," stressing continuous improvement; he also launched a program, "Anchoring Rock," to work with suppliers to improve the quality of their components. In 2010, he initiated a program of dispatching a thousand of his construction engineers to study quality control in Japan, another example of a learning organization. He declared that Vanke had to improve quality at all costs, even if this meant slower growth, and in 2011 he set forward a three-year initiative that came to be known as the "Vanke quality dream." In 2012, Vanke adopted the millimeter rather than the centimeter as a baseline for tolerance in home designs. In 2014, China's main property-management association accorded Vanke its top rating for the quality of its residential services.

Grow with Partners

In the classic strategy framework of Michael Porter, companies work to enhance their bargaining power with suppliers and buyers—again, a compelling step for the near term, but in Wang Shi's view, costly in the far term. He believed that sustained expansion could be achieved only if business partners grew with his own company. One of his driving values was thus "to grow together," treating land suppliers as allies even when Vanke found itself in a superior bargaining position. This approach of holding suppliers close borrowed from Japanese practices in manufacturing, rejecting the "arm's-length" approach of US companies.

The city of Chengdu had offered, for example, to reduce the price of a parcel of land by ¥30,000 per "mu"—about one-fifteenth of an acre—and the city oddly requested in return that Wang Shi personally join the final negotiation. The government was seeking to attract other developers in to the region, and it reasoned that his visible presence at this negotiation would signal the city's credibility. The informal understanding before the meeting was for Wang to request a price reduction and for the city manager to accept the price cut. But Wang instead asked for ¥50,000 to be added to the price per mu, explaining that he wanted Chengdu to adequately compensate those who would be displaced by the project. Vanke was beginning to be viewed as a fair partner; when it later asked to acquire another piece of land for housing development, Chengdu set a price that was considered more generous than demand might have dictated.

Wang Shi also extended his fair partnership rather than an arm's-length posture to those he hired to construct his properties. He reasoned that those building residences would care more for their construction if they were treated well by their employer. Most construction workers in China were poor migrants from the countryside with little education. With limited bargaining power, they often encountered poor sanitation, payroll delays, and dangerous venues. Vanke required construction contractors to place mobile toilets on construction sites, refused to pay contractors on time if they had not paid their own employees on time, and adopted a practice of withholding year-end bonuses from its own managers of worksites that had experienced a fatality even though worksite safety was technically the contractor's responsibility. During its monthly executive meeting, Vanke reported construction-site safety statistics, and if a construction worker had died during the past month, all executives mourned the loss. The idea of paying contractors more than one has to would be unthinkable to most US businesses, as would the notion of interfering in the relationships those contractors had with their own employees.

Lead with Integrity

Wang Shi also wove his far-horizon precepts into Vanke's corporate culture, leading his executives to embrace what he termed the "right way" of doing business. This extended to integrity in transactions. Reflecting the mores of the time, when Wang Shi challenged those attending a real-estate conference—"for those who dare to say that you never bribe government officials, please raise your hand"—few hands shot up. It was widely believed that it was impossible to prosper in real estate without illicit deals. But Wang Shi prohibited bribery in any of his company's dealings, and this, too, proved a long-term advantage.

Because of its squeaky-clean posture, Vanke had difficulty at first in acquiring prime development sites and often fell back on undesirable or remote tracts that other developers would not consider. Even when it purchased more propitious venues, its practice had the effect of delaying construction permits for years. Yet, if more costly in the short term, the no-bribery rule brought long-term advantage. For example, Vanke often acquired rural sites that were completely undeveloped, with no water, sewage, power, transportation, schools, or hospitals. As a result, it was forced to institute its own infrastructure, and that would later yield valuable advantage with local governments when contracting for regional development. Given its reputation for integrity, Vanke executives also found themselves freed from illicit demands by local officials as well as demands after the fact. Wang summed up the long-term benefit for his sixty-five operating subsidiaries in our interview with him: in the anti-corruption campaign launched by the Chinese government during the last few years, none of his executives had been implicated, even though many officials in the cities where Vanke operated were found guilty of taking bribes, a product of his no-bribery policy.

To reduce costs in the industry, Wang established a research center in 1999 to develop less expensive prefabricated home components including

TABLE 4.3 Wang Shi's Long-Game Leadership at Vanke

Year	Practice	Application
1992	Stated that profit margins must not exceed 25 percent for a "sustainable foundation"; prohibited bribery	Constructed low-margin built-to-live-in residences rather than speculating on unoccupied high-margin luxury villas
1996	Declared "year of quality"	Worked with suppliers to improve components and with construction engineers to increase quality control
2001	Campaign to build houses with no defects	Focused on continuous improvement
2012	Introduced greater precision in home construction	Adopted millimeter in place of centimeter in defining home-design tolerance

walls, balconies, and bathrooms. By producing these components in a factory and assembling them on site, Vanke shortened the construction cycle, lowered its costs, improved home quality, reduced solid waste, and cut energy consumption. By 2014, 100 percent of its residences' internal walls came pre-made, not even requiring a coat of paint.

Finally, Wang Shi became an ardent proponent of environmental protection, including forest preservation. He asked Greenpeace in 2008 for advice on combatting the use of illegally logged timber in the China construction industry. Vanke adopted the use of metal rather than wood molding in the construction of high-rise buildings, and it worked with industry to create a labeling system for imported timber. Wang also collaborated with the World Wildlife Fund in its campaign against climate change, and he even attended the 2009 Copenhagen summit on climate change.

We have seen in Wang Shi a focus on the far horizon, even when costly in the short run. He declared that his company's profit margin would not exceed 25 percent since windfalls were not sustainable and could result in lasting downsides. He gave up location in favor of reputation, focusing on quality construction and on growing with partners, not at their expense. He emphasized building homes with no defects and the "right way" of doing business. Wang Shi's long-game leadership, an agility anchored in enduring principles, is summarized in Table 4.3.

Risk and Failure

One implication of the learning-company executive mindset along with a plotting of one's own way is a greater willingness to take chances with less received wisdom on how to manage the associated risks. Consistent with this, the hazards of starting up a business are higher in China than in the United States, as we saw in Chapter 2. And consistent with the importance of self-directed executive learning for devising a way forward, analyses of survey data from China's industrial firms reveal that a company's age is a better predictor of its eventual survival than its productivity.[11]

The researchers who performed these analyses inferred from their findings that prospering in the Chinese market is much dependent on executive learning about the market. Knowledge and market experience, they concluded, are drivers of survival in China. Because of the greater hazards that come with inventing one's own path forward, the average age of Chinese companies is relatively low. Among the surveyed private industrial companies, their average annual age in the period 1998–2007 ranged from eight to eleven years.

On the affirmative side, China's uncertain terrains have led business leaders to build company cultures that embrace a readiness for quick redirection. For instance, agility enabled by a loyal team and strong corporate culture was evident in a diversified conglomerate whose founder and chair we interviewed. With more than half a dozen business lines, ranging from steel making and auto parts to aviation services and beverages, the company is at the ready to enter new and unrelated markets. For that to work, according to the founder and chair, he had to build a loyal team at the top but then swiftly recruit the next tier from outside, with grounding in the new arenas.

To enter the aeronautics business, for instance, the company's chief executive hired people with prior experience in aviation; to enter the steel-making industry, he formed a joint venture with a European partner to learn from face-to-face contact with seasoned steel makers. "I believe we need to build different management teams based on the situation," he explained. "So my criteria for selecting the management team are flexible and depend on a lot of factors including industry, business maturity level, and time frame." The ability to move swiftly by hiring or allying has proven beneficial to the company. As he put it: "I think our first competitive advantage is our management system design" and its "flexibility." The projects his steel makers have supplied include some of China's most iconic buildings as well as international airports in China and abroad. "We can make important business decisions quickly since we don't have an overcomplicated decision process. This is the most important thing if you want to stand out [from] the fierce competition," he said. "If we have a problem, we will act quickly at all levels of the organization and solve it efficiently. This is the atmosphere we created in the company. It's related to our corporate culture. We can gather the whole company's resource to solve a problem."

Conclusion

As we have seen at Alibaba, founding executive Jack Ma repeatedly redirected its strategy. Each new course of action was a direct product of necessity. Without proven models to build from, he constructed his company around what he believed was a promising service, only to learn from his own direct experience that other customer services were more promising. This had the effect of reversing what we know to be a classic formulation in the West, expressed as well as anywhere in Alfred Chandler's *Strategy and Structure*—namely, that a company's strategy dictates its leadership, with top executives selected to fit the strategy. Yet in private Chinese businesses the opposite has often prevailed, with company leaders frequently redefining the strategy. Given the fast-evolving market in which they have operated, a good watchword has been agility, a leadership capacity to change direction nimbly.

As we have also seen, with a more dexterous leadership and thus flexible strategy in place, Chinese firms have reached for more enduring principles—not only to undergird their immediate growth but also to sustain that growth in the years ahead. Alibaba's Jack Ma declared that he was building his company to last eighty years at least. Vanke's Wang Shi sought to make his company an enduring mainstay of the Chinese economy through constrained returns, a focus on reputation over location, growth with partners, and a code of integrity.

Underpinning agile leadership and strategies is a relatively unchanging central idea: the enduring concept of market and purpose. This concept is the animating kernel from which operational details emanate, the defining conception of the firm that shapes the firm's strategies but also transcends them. It is why a firm exists, whom it serves, what it produces, how it should grow, and where it must be going. It is akin to a company's identity, its raison d'être, or what business-school professors Hamid Bouchikhi and John R. Kimberly have called "the soul of the corporation." Company agility then, born of necessity, rests at the same time on a more enduring focus, as we shall see in the chapter ahead on talent and growth.[12]

Strategic Agility in the Words of the Fortune Makers

By learning the latest knowledge and practice, Chinese commercial leaders are able to develop business visions to quickly adapt themselves in today's volatile global market. The quest for continuous self-growth among leaders is a great competitive advantage for Chinese companies.

—Chair, real-estate investment firm

The only thing that helps us to grow is the government's open reform policy, which allows private business to exist. But it was still a period of ambiguity as the policy was not clear and everyone could only tentatively try this or that. No one knew what would come ahead, and there were no official documents and laws.

—Chair, electrical equipment and power transmission group

It's very important that you have your own understanding of the industry through real working experience. As a matter of fact, we can say that lots of critical strategies are naturally developed based on a unique understanding of and insights into the competitive environment of our own industry.

—Chair, consumer products company

CHAPTER 5

Talent Management

We will make it because we are young and we never, never give up.

Chinese executives place great emphasis on trust and transparency, reducing the need for internal control systems. At the same time, they believe that managing people is one of their fundamental challenges, and they are thus prepared to invest in training their own talent. Engaging schools and universities in preparing the next generation has proven difficult, and growing talent within the firm has become paramount. But managing talent remains one of their biggest challenges, especially looking to the changing generations in the years ahead.

Management Development in the Communist Party

So far at least, most Chinese companies do not have very sophisticated programs for developing and directing the careers of their managers and executives. One institution that does, however, is the Communist Party. There are a surprising number of similarities between the way the party and US-based "Academy" corporations like General Electric and Procter & Gamble known for people development and talent management.

The world's most powerful human resources department—nothing else even comes close—is the Central Organization Department (COD) of the Chinese Communist Party. It controls appointments to the key jobs in government, business and, indeed, the entire society.

The COD keeps detailed tabs on promising leaders—both within and outside government—following their career achievements. A promising young administrator might be given an assignment to run a small agency in a remote area to see how well it can perform. Imagine this as the equivalent of Jack Welch's "popcorn stands" at General Electric, the small profit-and-loss centers used like a farm team in sports to test junior executives. Among the most important of these test assignments is turning around a failing agency or region. Party leaders are also assessed against a series of metrics that measure the overall achievements of the organization they have been running.

In deciding which leaders should get promotions to bigger roles, the COD uses many of the techniques employed by search consultants and sophisticated talent managers: extensive background checks to look for problems in their private lives that might become issues in a bigger role, psychological tests on factors such as temperament, 360-degree evaluations from peers, and an elaborate set of metrics to measure objective aspects of performance.

The COD routinely makes use of developmental assignments for leaders, including job rotations to different agencies or indeed from government jobs into business and vice versa. That is easy to do because the biggest business operations in China, by far, are state-owned enterprises. The idea behind these rotational assignments, as in big corporations, is to provide exposure to new contexts and the opportunity to learn from them.

Succession planning is the ultimate mission of the Central Organization Department. To get a feel for how important succession is, note that the successor to the president of China is decided on a decade before the individual takes office. The term of office is ten years, and a new successor is appointed each time a new president assumes office.

The best guess is that the Central Organization Department controls roughly five thousand of the most important positions in the country, from university presidencies and state-enterprise CEOs to party secretaries in each province. Anyone who wants to reach one of those key jobs has to stay in the good graces of the COD and therefore the party. That means taking assignments when given—just as corporations require executives to move to new jobs—and performing well in each position. If you get into trouble in your personal life, if you fail to show commitment to the Communist Party, if you did not perform well in your last job, you will never receive the next promotion.

It is perhaps not surprising that the Central Organization Department exists. Its roots arguably can be traced back to the Han Dynasty and the

Civil Service Ministry, which set exams for entry into government jobs and then advised on promotions. The Soviet Union had a similar organization, and China borrowed from that model in the 1930s. The move to a market economy created new, powerful institutions in the form of businesses and new, powerful jobs for the people who run them. If the United States has a revolving door for leaders who sometimes move between business and government jobs, from running industries to regulating them and back again, China has much the same thing—except that it is all done intentionally.[1]

The Communist Origins of Talent Management

One of the surprising aspects of employee management at private companies in China is that their practices evolved quite a bit even in the early years, through the 1980s, when the government controlled everything about business operations. Management scholar Malcolm Warner describes the changes from the inception of communism through the early 1990s as oscillating between "suffocating centralization and decentralized anarchy." Modern China has been remarkably pragmatic in its approaches to running enterprises, something that can be traced in an earlier period to the regime's interest in the work of American thinker John Dewey on the importance of being pragmatic, but it certainly accelerated after Deng Xiaoping assumed control and gave priority to making economic progress even at the expense of ideological purity.[2]

We might assume that decisions about factories and production operations were dictated by ideology, but concerns about productivity and economic performance were often the driving factors, albeit supported by Marxist precepts. In the early years of Communist Party control, just after World War II, China copied many of its practices from the Soviet Union. These included centralized authority governing all employment decisions across the country, a wage system based on the labor theory of value—where pay varied little across jobs and the highest-paid managers earned only three times as much as the lowest paid—and arrangements for designing and supervising jobs straight out of Frederick Taylor's scientific management, including elements of piecework. Vice-Chairman of the Communist Party Liu Shao-Chi, who headed China's industrialization policy from the mid-1950s through 1966, described those arrangements and how they mapped onto topics like education and social policy, with the simple phrase "brains for the brain work and hands for the manual work." Rates of pay were similar for brain work and manual work, but it was clear that government and party officials were to be the brains.[3]

The more grassroots nature of the Chinese revolution softened the top-down approach of the Soviet model, however. "Production leaders," whom we might think of as shop stewards in a Western context, were elected by the workers and played a role in influencing the decisions of managers. The "Workers Congress," created in 1950, was something like a European-style works council where workers elected representatives to a formal structure that gave the workers an official voice in management decisions.

The poor performance of the economy in those early years, especially compared to the Soviet Union, led to an official rebellion against top-down organizing principles. The Great Leap Forward from 1958 to 1961 pushed China to decentralize the economy and seek better solutions for production at the local level. Its best-known and least successful aspect was the collectivization of agriculture, which led to the death by famine of tens of millions, but it also gave local officials more control over what local factories did and how they did it.

The Cultural Revolution in 1966, as it played out in the workplace, further extended the principle of local control, shifting more power to the workers in the plants. Liu Shao-Chi was purged along with his top-down practices. "Revolutionary committees" run by the production workers now became the formal authority in factories, and managers reported to them.

This exercise in decentralized, shop-floor democracy retreated initially with the return of the All-China Federation of Trade Unions as a power in local factories. Although the federation began in the 1920s, it was an arm of the Communist Party. In contrast to the Workers Congress, it was run from the top down, and it usurped much of the congress's influence.[4] The Cultural Revolution and many of its innovations were surely put to rest in the wake of Mao Zedung's death in 1976 and the rise of Liu Shao-Chi's deputy, Deng Xiaoping, to power. Deng brought back more of the top-down practices of the earlier era. Most of the plant-level democratic practices ended, and all worker strikes or other interferences with local managers were banned. Financial incentives to encourage production returned, and formal authority with technical experts assumed management of factories. The role that the Workers Congress played in influencing local management ended, and it was reduced to just another monitoring mechanism for the Communist Party.[5]

The 1980s in China were a period of intensive inquiry into the best practices for running the economy and production operations efficiently. The search for international lessons shifted sharply away from the Soviet Union toward the West, especially to production and management experts from the United States. From the perspective of the employee, however, little changed. The Iron Rice Bowl, the employment system in which workers effectively could not be dismissed or look for jobs elsewhere and in which individual initiative and performance mattered little, remained firmly in place.

By the early 1990s, however, changes had become obvious. It was less the deliberate imposition of new practices and more the taking down of old ones that caused market-based alternatives to appear by default. One of the new practices was permission for foreign companies to set up businesses. Ninety percent of the foreign operations were without unions, which helped signal that their operations would be different. Even in the massive state-owned enterprises, one-fifth of the workers were now governed by individual labor contracts that allowed the enterprise to drop them at the end of the contract, effectively signaling the end of the Iron Rice Bowl.[6]

But rather than move directly into uninhibited free-labor markets, the government passed a new labor law in 1994 that outlined the responsibilities that management had acquired in return for greater freedom to hire and fire. These included labor protections that go beyond those seen in the United States, such as maternity leave, as well as requirements that are standard in the West, such as minimum-wage laws, eight-hour workdays, and equal opportunities for women. The law also created a new system of individual contracts between employees and the employer that set out the terms and conditions of work. Except in periods of grave difficulty, workers were to keep their jobs until their contracts expired, typically for three years. Even then, the arrangements for dismissing employees had to be worked out with them, sometimes through local unions. Their agreement on those arrangements was required before they could be dismissed, something that goes well beyond worker protections in the United States and most other industrialized countries.

An example of requiring agreement about layoffs is perhaps the best workplace illustration of what is distinctive about Chinese talent management. In the United States, it may seem hard to imagine a more dysfunctional arrangement than to require that workers concur with the terms on which they would lose their jobs—just as it is hard to imagine that they would ever agree to this. Observers of union-management relationships in the United States know that worker-say on dismissals do happen here occasionally, though not routinely, and only when the alternative is complete failure of the business, in which case the workers receive nothing. It also happens in the European Union, where required Works Councils play a similar role in negotiating the terms of layoffs. Of course, no one would argue that such negotiations in the United States or the European Union are models of effectiveness, especially for employers who see the European model in particular as an enormous drag on business.

The difference in China is that the unions have been and are an arm of either the Communist Party or the government, depending on the period of time, and of course the leadership of state-owned enterprises also reports directly to the state. Even private-sector leaders are accountable to the government. With two groups both accountable to the same bosses, expecting disputes between the two to be resolved through negotiations makes much more sense.

The most famous of the disputes over layoffs in China arguably involved Walmart. That the conflicts with the local workers continued so long and played out in so many different places was no doubt influenced by the fact that Walmart is not accountable to the Chinese government in the same way that Chinese firms are. The company's decision to close twenty stores in 2013 led to protests across the country that, in turn, led to pressure on the company to improve its offer to the laid-off employees. The government also pressured local workers to accept the company's improved offer and blocked their efforts to take more militant action. Eventually, both parties accepted an arbitrator's ruling—reminding us that in China, even foreign companies are accountable to the government in terms of how they execute the most basic employment decisions.[7]

Job Merit and Work Security

By the end of the 1990s, workplace management practices in the private sector had changed dramatically. They had far more in common with those in the United States than with those in the China of a decade earlier.

Professional managers were in charge, merit-based hiring and layoffs were common, most workers were governed by the new contracts, and the institutions that let the government and the Communist Party keep track of operations—the trade unions and the workers councils—were gone. So were any vestiges of democratic practices and employee influence on management decisions.[8]

Talent practices through the 2000s were dominated, on the one hand, by the extraordinary growth of the Chinese economy and, on the other, by the equally extraordinary supply of semi-skilled labor available for factory work. Estimates of the number of individuals, typically poor peasant farmers, who were brought into factory jobs ranged from 300 million to 600 million. Some factories moved west to take advantage of the larger supply of cheap labor, but the more common practice was to build dormitories and bring workers east, much like American textile companies had done in Massachusetts in the nineteenth century.

Given the abundant labor supply, employment practices did not have to be either sophisticated or effective to meet the needs of the factories. The new workers were motivated by the opportunity to get a job and to keep it. Managers of these factories generally followed the precepts of Douglas McGregor's famous Theory X, which said that employees are motivated by incentives and fear: engineers used techniques from scientific management to design and structure jobs, and supervisors used the threat of dismissal to keep current workers motivated. A lack of government oversight meant that the terms of the 1994 labor law were routinely ignored. By one estimate, about 40 percent of the workforce through the 2000s held jobs with low wages, little job security, and no employer benefits.[9]

Just as their counterparts in Europe found ways around restrictions on laying off full-time workers, Chinese businesses have done so, too—in both cases, by hiring contract labor and temporary help as a substitute for regular employees. Some 13 percent of the Chinese workforce is employed as temporary help, a figure three times greater than in the United States.[10] Despite the apparent protections of labor law, a survey of employment practices across private companies in China found little evidence—even from the employers—that their employees had any substantial job security.[11]

A detailed study of employment practices in Chinese companies describes how these arrangements work. In an auto manufacturing company, for example, 80 percent of the workforce was actually engaged under contract through a labor-hire company. Those workers have one-year contracts, as opposed to the three-year contracts for actual employees of the auto company. In some ways the contract workers are treated like regular employees, especially with respect to training, but they are typically paid less, and of course they have much less job security.[12]

In white-collar jobs such as banking, the arrangements are more complicated still. There are headcount limits and individual labor contracts. We might think of white-collar workers as longer-term employees of the company, and they are typically college graduates. There is "informal" labor, regular employees who have no assigned jobs; these are workers in lower-level jobs, typically vocational-school completers, who are not expected to advance and who have less job security. Finally, there is temporary help contracted through labor-hire companies and moved around the bank to meet short-term variations in demand. Here, too, the employers have developed arrangements that get around the protections that employees believe are guaranteed by the government.[13]

Workplace Education and Training

Where the Chinese companies do better for their employees than job security, albeit by necessity, is in training. Another detailed study of the practices of individual companies, this time in the booming electronics sector, found that employers engaged in a variety of practices to improve the skills of their workers. Although the vocational-education sector is well developed in China compared to countries elsewhere, including the United States, companies nevertheless engaged with local schools to fine-tune the training of the type of graduates they needed. This simple practice is one that the United States still struggles to put in place. Chinese employers uniformly had training programs for their employees, focusing on technical skills and understanding manufacturing operations—in other words, training for production workers. Not surprisingly, employers do the most training when they have difficulty hiring.[14]

The notion, widespread among many American employers, that "we cannot afford to train workers for fear we will lose them to competitors" is not accepted in China. In fact, the opposite is true: Chinese employers actually responded to poaching of their employees by increasing training.[15] One sees a similar practice in India, where poaching is also a huge

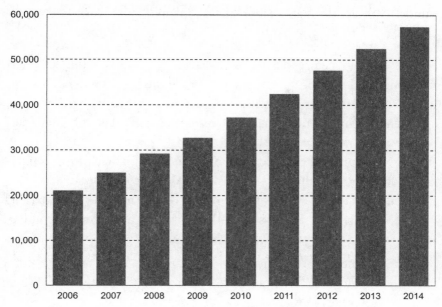

FIGURE 5.1 **Average Annual Wages in China, in Yuan**
Source: Trading Economics, 2016.

concern for employers. Perhaps the United States is the outlier here. If companies in China can train their employees, despite not having any historical experience as to how to do it and despite levels of job-hopping that dwarf those in the United States, the resistance to doing so in America is hard to understand. Our interviews suggested, though, that management and supervisory training remains something of an afterthought.

As noted earlier, employers in China benefited enormously from the hundreds of millions of disciplined workers who poured into their factories from the 1980s through the mid-2000s. That supply has been exhausted, and with that, wages are rising. Average annual wages in China almost tripled from ¥21,001 in 2006 to ¥57,361 in 2014 (see Figure 5.1), a period over which US wages rose by just a quarter (from $16.4 per hour in 2006 to $21.4 per hour in 2014). Accounts of wages for Chinese production workers rising by 50 percent per year were common after 2011, and workers job-hopped from employer to employer, sometimes weekly.

In one of our executive classes, the owner of a factory in eastern China offered us an account of how the job-hopping works: when the employees go back to their home villages and families for the New Year's break, the company sends them gifts, typically money and, in recent years, larger sums—in an effort to entice them to come back after the break. Most workers do so, but not before touring nearby factories to see what they are offering in pay and starting stipends, known as "switching bonuses." Then, a day or so after returning to their employer when the factory has started up again and when vacancies are very costly, they negotiate a higher wage based on their comparative research.

If production workers in China have been having a field day with tightening labor markets, that has not been the case for college graduates, who, surprisingly, face a very poor job market—one that gets considerably worse the more education a student has. School leavers from secondary school seem to be able to find jobs, but the "official" unemployment rates for new college graduates are well up into the double digits, compared to about 4 percent for those with less education.[16]

Why is this? Like parents in the West, those in China want their children to attend college. Thus more go, including those whose grades are poor. Perhaps, then, the quality of graduates is not as stellar on average as it was in the past. The Chinese also value education for its own sake, so many young people go on to college without giving much thought to whether there will be a job for them when they are finished. There apparently are just too many young people graduating to fill the number of managerial and professional jobs available. While the services orientation of Western economies generates a large number of white-collar jobs, China is still focused on production and factories where the number of white-collar positions remains small compared to production jobs.

Unlike in the United States and to some extent in Europe, unemployed Chinese college graduates are not stepping down the hierarchy to take the kind of jobs that require only high school degrees. That explains why their unemployment rate is so much greater. What kind of jobs do college graduates in China seek? A conversation with students at Peking University, thought by many to be the best school in China, offered some surprising contradictions of the notion of China as an entrepreneurial hotbed. The number-one job for those asked is working for the government. Despite the fact that it does not pay nearly as well as the private sector, these are prestigious, influential positions that are also stable and offer a secure future. The number-two choice is working for a state-run enterprise. Stability is the key attribute there as well, and pay is better than in government jobs—though prestige is lower. Number three is the Chinese private sector, where the money is considerable, but so are the risks of instability. Last on the list is Western enterprises, especially US firms. The general perception about those enterprises, as one student told us, is that they "chew you up and spit you out," offering neither stability nor long-term careers.[17] Jobs for new college graduates do not pay especially well, about $1,000 per month, which is less than the rent for even a small apartment anywhere near the center of Beijing. The monthly minimum wage in Beijing is roughly $220. Most college-completers are happy to stay close to Beijing, however, even if this means commuting long distances to reach their work sites. On the other hand, if they can get a regular job with an employment contract, they receive forty-five days of vacation per year, similar to the arrangement in the European Union but unheard of in the United States, along with training and a three-year employment contract whereby the employer will not lay them off and it is difficult to fire them. A small percentage of new grads do, however, get jobs like that every year.

Rising labor costs represent a huge challenge for the competitiveness of businesses in China and also for the operating models of many of its companies. A report by the Boston Consulting Group (BCG) concluded that the cost of manufacturing in China as of 2014 was almost the same as in the United States. Competing based on low wages will soon have to be replaced by some other strategy.[18]

A Cultural Underpinning

Workplace practices reflect societal norms, but in no country are they simply a product of those norms. In the case of China, a great deal of ink has been spilled trying to draw the connection between Chinese culture and Chinese business practices.[19] The appeal of the link begins with China's ancient civilization. The notion that "China is a civilization pretending to be a state" reflects the idea that national culture is more persistent and more important in understanding China than even the government institutions. Other countries have civilizations as old—in the Middle East, for example—but nowhere else does the idea that national culture drives business practices seem as strong as in China.[20]

It is easy to see matches between social values and the nature of business practices in any country. The importance of private property in the US business system, for example, seems closely aligned with the prominence of individualism as an American norm. But establishing whether practices actually resulted from these norms is quite difficult, and it is easy to overlook instances where there is no obvious association.

There are two challenges associated with the argument that Chinese business practices stem from national culture. The first is that establishing what the true Chinese norms are is difficult because, as in any country, they are always in flux, and no other nation in modern times has had the lives of so many of its citizens changed so profoundly in such a short period of time as has China. It is a country of more than a billion people that in less than a generation went from being dominated by agriculture to domination by factories; it is a country where standards of living have risen dramatically in just a matter of years. By some measures, half the population rose out of poverty this past generation alone. It is also a country that transformed from a stark form of communism to consumerism, as experienced by the average citizen—again, within a generation.

It is impossible to believe that these transformations have not also affected social values. For example, a study in the mid-1990s among middle-aged Communist Party members found that loyalty to the organization trumped all other personal values, yet the contemporary view is that there is now little if any loyalty to organizations, including the government and the party.[21] Another study comparing Chinese employees who were raised after the opening of China to capitalism with their older peers found much greater individualism among the younger generation.[22] Still another study of biographical information on two hundred Chinese business leaders in the 2000s found evidence for strands of both Confucianism and Maoist thought in their actions, and other research has reported still other cultural sources.[23]

The second and related challenge is that it is difficult to define the true nature of business practices, because those practices are also in flux. Observers of early private-sector business in China reported something similar to the Iron Rice Bowl, a system of mutual obligations between workers and bosses whereby the company, not the government, was the provider. As we saw earlier, however, arm's-length, transactional relations seem widespread in most Chinese companies, at least among production and frontline workers.

A common view among China observers in the West is that Chinese business practices are based on Confucianism, a set of beliefs and practices created by Confucius in the fifth century BC. Confucius wrote about a wide range of topics, and his views are complex and subtle, but their essence often boiled down to two ideas: *Jen,* the goodness and benevolence toward others as the essence of humanity and a virtue worth dying for, and *Li,* the notion that there is a proper way to behave that involves a series of obligations and that resists individualism. Among the practices most distinctive of Confucianism are respect for age and the belief that there are rules or at least norms governing every aspect of life.

Authority, hierarchy, and respect are still important values. Guanxi and networking remain prevalent in business life. But of course that is true for virtually every society. A puzzling fact for those who believe that Confucianism is the foundation of contemporary business practices in China is that there was a systematic campaign over several decades to root out the influence of Confucius and his ideas from Chinese society. Beginning with the Cultural Revolution, Confucian ideas were denounced, temples devoted to Confucius destroyed, and even his grave defiled. There was no equivalent of priests to carry on the teachings of Confucianism, nor monasteries to protect those ideas. Most of the founders of the private companies in China grew up during this period or shortly after, when Confucianism was out of official favor. There are overlaps between the values of Communism and the values of Confucianism, including the importance of order and rules, loyalty to leaders, and the harmfulness of individualism. Those values existed under Soviet communism as well, so it is difficult to see Confucianism as the primary source of such values in China now.[24]

The Communist Party began to resuscitate Confucius after the Tiananmen Square protest in 1989 as an additional source of influence for promoting social stability. Aspects of Confucianism have become popular, although whether they actually correspond to traditional versions of Confucianism is another question.[25] Public pronouncements of virtue are common among all leaders, including some that directly reflect Confucianism.[26] Confucianism is today being promoted as a handmaiden to the party's current ideology of the "harmonious society," and perhaps a brake against the fast pace of social change and especially rising individualism.[27]

Another place where cultural norms do not correspond to practice is the notion of "face," the idea that Chinese society works hard to avoid situations where individuals are embarrassed. One often hears, for example, that issues of performance management are especially difficult in China for that reason: performance feedback is not honest and performance appraisals are superficial. Yet at the same time, the practice of public shaming—the antithesis of face-saving—became prominent in China under communism. This is most obvious in public confessions of those who have been accused of crimes or disloyalty, but it occurs in everyday life as well.[28] A 2016 video showing a bank's management consultant spank underperforming trainees on a stage in front of all the employees caused a sensation when it went viral. But what happened just before, making the trainees confess their failure and personal defects, passed without much criticism.

The basic day-to-day management of employees in these private companies sounds similar to that in most any Western company: employees are recruited from schools or college campuses, and current employees are sources of new hires through extensive networks of job boards and personal connections. Many companies use traditional performance appraisals to award pay increases and to drive advancement. As noted earlier, training programs seem to be more prevalent in China than in the United States, although perhaps not more common than in Japan or Europe. Bonuses are widespread but stock options are less so, except for very top executives in a few listed companies. Poor performers are dismissed, albeit with some difficulty if the employee is protected by the initial three-year employment contract. Employee benefits vary across employers—especially private health insurance to supplement the bare-bones government plan, which is available to about half of the employees.

The variation in work practices across the economy is vast, however, depending on the nature of the work. The conditions in manufacturing companies like Foxconn (Hon Hai Precision Industry Co.) are truly Dickensian; reports of employee suicides from the stress of overwork had been common, and management jobs in major cities on the east coast of China would not look dissimilar to those in the West. Yet there are distinct practices, too, in many of the private companies. For example, in keeping with the paternalistic traditions of Chinese employers, companies in big cities often furnish housing to their employees. The chairman of a resort and real-estate development company provides residences for employees once they have been with the company for twenty years or more, and he has also made it a practice to fill all but entry-level openings from within. The director of human resources for a large paper and forest-pulp product maker with some 10,000 employees reported that his company not only offers housing for employees but arranges sports teams and social events for them.[29]

Yang Shaopeng, chair of SITC International Holdings, a shipping and logistics company, reports that his firm has adopted the US practice of bidding and posting, whereby current employees can nominate themselves for any job. The company assesses all candidates based on their emotional intelligence as well as their IQ. He allows managers to remain in jobs designated as important for no more than five years to avoid blocking promotions and new ideas.

The fact that these companies are new, all having started after the advent of open-market capitalism, and that they have been created by founders who have followed very different learning pathways, has meant that they are often quite different from one another. Initial differences have been magnified as the companies have grown larger and succeeded in different ways, but a common thread among them is that their management practices fit together and align with their business strategies in sensible ways. We see this below in our discussion of two very different but also very successful enterprises.

The Company's Own Culture

Alibaba is the company most often held up as a model of the new China, in part because of its success and the fact that it touches so many people and so many businesses through the Internet, but mainly because its operations—especially its management of people—are so different from those of traditional Chinese organizations, with its own distinctive culture as the central unifying strand.[30]

A mix of East and West, Alibaba is a blend between the large American company and the Silicon Valley start-up, in the Chinese context. If Alibaba was not the first enterprise to bring the architecture of a Silicon Valley start-up to China, it was certainly the most prominent one. The borrowing of US practices across Chinese businesses has become more common among companies in technology not only because American companies have been so dominant but also because there were no existing Chinese models to copy.

As we have seen, Jack Ma's inspiration for Alibaba began after a 1995 visit to the United States that exposed him to the budding Internet market. He realized that there was no way at that time to connect the booming Chinese supplier community to prospective business customers, especially in the United States. His first company, China Pages, was an abortive effort to do that, and in 1999 he tried again with Alibaba. As a first sign that its human talent would be managed differently, Jack Ma gave the seventeen friends who helped get the firm off the ground a stake in the company.

What made Alibaba so influential was Jack Ma himself, who became the first Chinese celebrity CEO. The child of theatrical performers, Ma is a charismatic executive with a flair for the dramatic and memorable. It is also fair to say that he had little competition in that regard, since Chinese business leaders keep relatively low public profiles. Alibaba bears the unmistakable footprint of its founder. From the social events he holds for employees to his willingness to perform characters in those events—often in costume—he easily stands apart from his low-key contemporaries.

Ma's decisions and declarations early on created the culture for the company as it operates today. He early offered, for instance, a statement that is now oft-repeated—namely, our brains are as good as theirs, where *theirs* refers to Silicon Valley innovators. Part of what motivated Alibaba employees from the first day was pride, an eagerness to show the world that China could beat those elsewhere, including the Valley.

The most public example of this posture came with Alibaba's creation of Taobao, an online marketplace for individuals that was established to compete with eBay. Taobao played up the fact that it was a Chinese company, in contrast to eBay, and that it was intended to help the Chinese business community compete on the world stage. Echoing his counterparts in the Indian business community, Jack Ma put forth a social agenda, not just a commercial purpose, in building the enterprise: helping the many businesses in his country reach out to the global market, win in the global economy, and rebuild the leadership position many Chinese believe their country should have in world affairs. In the appraisal by Zhang Yichi, a professor at Peking University, the building of Alibaba was stimulated in part because of Jack Ma's "appealing to the noble call in an employee's heart to help small companies."[31]

Fast growth, especially internationally, left Alibaba overextended during the 2001 downturn, and the restructuring that followed created an even more purpose-driven organization and management structure. The rebuilding plan was called "Back2China," reflecting a shift toward a more modest, China-focused strategy, part and parcel of which is a more Chinese-focused organizational mindset. Ma called his approach "Hupan culture" after the name of the apartment building in Hangzhou where the company began, and his articulation of the new ideals drew on the framework of a Kung Fu novel: his "Six Vein Spirit Sword" denoted the company values of customer first, teamwork, embrace change, integrity, passion, and commitment.

The effort to cement these values was launched in the company as the equivalent of a military campaign, with Ma as the general and Alibaba employees the troops of the Red Army. The first wave of the campaign was a deliberate effort to create the common set of values with public pronouncements and the company events that became legendary. Only after that would the focus shift to building the skills of employees.

Flat hierarchy became an important part of Alibaba's culture, along with employees whose priority was commitment to the company first before thinking about their own contributions as individuals. One of Jack Ma's more quotable principles was that he did not need many individual contributors as heroes because his goals called for collective achievements. Company hiring initially focused on attitude: the ability to get along with others, to be committed to tasks and to organizations, and to exhibit loyalty. It was possible to keep that focus in part because Alibaba was pioneering an industry and it was not clear initially which competencies would be required. A novel tool for keeping the sense of hierarchy low was asking all new hires to give themselves a nickname, usually from Chinese literature. Even top executives are thus referred to by their nicknames. It proved difficult for, say, Mr. Hou to stay perched on a pedestal since he was widely known as "little bird."

Ma told us that one of the key reasons for keeping the entrepreneurial feel of a start-up is to make the company feel small so that trust among the employees is easier. From its first days, Ma described the company as a fighter taking on bigger opponents. Porter Erisman, an American who joined Alibaba as an executive in 2000, created a documentary about the early days of Alibaba that showed Ma's charismatic side. In it we see him telling employees "We will make it because we are young and we never, never give up." Ma rallies employees around an attribute they shared, albeit one not universally admired in a culture that respected age.[32]

Jack Ma is also a demanding leader who pushes his employees hard. Erisman described how a "manager would set a goal and then he [Ma] would triple it. Everyone would push back and say 'That's impossible!' but he'd tell them that it *was* possible, and that they could find a way. He has this reality distortion field where he can make you think that something is possible that you would never have imagined." This is a description that is more or less identical to what people routinely said about Steve Jobs, Apple's founder. Employees work long hours at Alibaba as they do in many companies in the developed economies, and they push themselves hard. A difference here might be that many say they do it because they do not want to disappoint Jack Ma, a classic example of a charismatic leader.[33]

For many business leaders in China, the relative absence of hierarchy and the ambiance of openness and fun grated against the norm. What arguably got Ma the most attention within China, however, and represented the biggest challenge to the older business leaders, is his personal showmanship. He makes bold predictions, especially about the company's future. In an echo of IBM chief executive Lou Gerstner's pledge to wear a dress to a holiday function if one of the company's division achieved aggressive targets, Ma routinely shows up to celebratory events in outlandish garb—one year as a punk rocker and another as Snow White, often singing and performing on stage. Ma gave employees Silly String to help celebrate the launch of the company's IPO. Alifest, the company's annual gathering, is a day of entertainment and activities for employees and their families now held in a stadium—a festival of all things Alibaba, featuring inspiring speeches from Ma. To further burnish his image as the personal leader, he officiated at a mass wedding of 102 couples, all Alibaba employees. Ma has said that it is sometimes necessary to say and perhaps do outlandish things to attract attention, but his actions have also been targeted at building a culture where employees feel committed to Alibaba and its goals.[34]

Culture also drives compensation at Alibaba. One of the more surprising aspects of Alibaba for those who see it as a unique Chinese creation is that Ma in 2001 appointed Silvio Kwan as his president and chief operating officer. Recruited from General Electric, Kwan brought with him many of GE's practices, especially its compensation system, whereby half of one's annual performance appraisal score is based on how well the individual models the company's values. In 2004, Kwan moved to become the company's chief people officer and remained in that role until 2012. Another American practice, stock options, was added to the compensation mix when the company began making plans for its 2014 initial public offering. The company's most unusual compensation benefit is providing interest-free mortgages to help its employees buy homes. Stock options and home loans have proven powerful retention devices.

Ma knows that not all of Alibaba's employees will buy into the company's values. The key, he told us, is that the top eighty people in the company, the ones with operational roles, believe in it. They shape the important actions of the company, and it is crucial for those actions to remain in step with the company's overall goals, especially at a firm that wants to operate in a decentralized fashion and where leaders are given autonomy. Hence Ma's emphasis on culture and values to make that happen.

The most innovative practice at Alibaba is how employees make use of the company's intranet communications platform called Aliway. Employees are allowed, indeed encouraged, to note problems and concerns about the company's products. The teams that developed the products often dispute those challenges, and the arguments can rage back and forth for some time. Some insiders say that employees can also dispute official evaluations of their work, asking for public opinion to support their positions. A further nod toward decentralization—a foundation on which swift responses can be made to market changes—is Alibaba's allocation of resources on a project basis. When a project is completed, the employees and their budget are redeployed within the company.

Managing Through People

If Alibaba's own culture has become an aligning and animating force, so too is its way of directly managing its workforce. CEO Jack Ma views and treats his employees as a source of sustainable advantage, and in return they take the extra steps to deliver that advantage.

Very little about Alibaba might seem uniquely Chinese. It may appear more like a mash-up of a traditional US corporation and a Silicon Valley company, where the focus on flexibility, lack of hierarchy, and audacious goals reflect the latter while the emphasis on organizational culture reflects the former. In fact, Jack Ma had learned much from Silicon Valley companies like Oracle and Google.

Yet important differences from American companies are evident. The first is the much greater focus on employees as the source of the company's competitive advantage. Jack Ma says that while customers are the first priority of the company, employees are the second, ahead of shareholders. Few US executives would dare say that the interests of their shareholders were not their top priority. And few American companies have a CEO who is as charismatic as Jack Ma, or one who spends as much time managing the culture of their organization. But a more fundamental difference is the loyalty that the company shows its own employees. Except for a restructuring in 2001, Alibaba has imposed no layoffs. Employees are moved elsewhere in the company when projects finish or strategies change. Nor are employees routinely fired, though there are exceptions, as we will later see in Ma's dismissal of his CEO, David Wei. There are even accounts suggesting that when executives have committed fraud, they are allowed to quietly resign and retain their stock options.

What the company receives in return for its loyalty to employees is their loyalty. That translates into trust, especially the willingness to tell the truth about what is going on. Ma's top seven executives have his trust, and because of that, they know they will not be punished if they face up to problems and do so sooner rather than later. The job of his seven top reports is, in turn, to manage their top seven reports the same way. As a result, and this is true in many of the Chinese companies, the need for elaborate systems of accountability and control, internal auditing practices, and complicated compliance rules goes away.

Is this Alibaba model temporary? The company has been around now for less than two decades, and its market value in 2016 was already larger than 490 of the Fortune 500 companies, many of which go back many decades. It is well past the point where large size can strangle start-up culture.

One reason the model has continued is because of Jack Ma's relentless efforts to keep it that way, in part by relying on culture—particularly internal transparency instead of rules—and in part by openly attacking the roots of bureaucracy whenever they appear. Whether the company will survive the exit of Jack Ma is a much more difficult question.[35]

Managing Through Innovation

Many of the most influential private companies in China have been around for a least a dozen years and have benefited either from close alliances with state-owned enterprises or from Western multinational companies. Xiaomi sits at the other end of the spectrum. Started in 2010, it epitomized one model for Chinese company-building: take a successful product selling at premium prices in the West and find a way to make a knock-off at a fraction of the price. Its spectacular growth, now in a global context, sets it apart even in a country where hurried growth has been the norm.[36]

Xiaomi makes cellphones, a product that was already ubiquitous even in the developing world. Xiaomi's approach was to avoid China's domestic competition in its bare-bones market and instead compete directly with Apple and Samsung, the prestige smartphone brands that Chinese consumers were buying from Western companies. As with Alibaba, Xiaomi's initial focus was the Chinese market, which it knew well. In just three years after launching its first smartphone in 2011, Xiaomi had become the fourth-largest smartphone manufacturer in the world and number one in China, selling phones of Apple quality at half the price. By 2015, it was one of the most valuable start-ups in the technology world, and in 2016 it sold 70 million mobile phones.[37]

Xiaomi achieved this success in part through clever negotiations with the suppliers that provide quality components to its mobile telephone phone competitors. But its distinctiveness also rests on its ability to incorporate innovative features, something it does by leveraging the ideas of key customers who act like users in open software systems. How the company is able to do that relies on customer input, and that, in turn, depends on the way it manages its employees.

Xiaomi leveraged its brand to build its internal management system. Many of the customers who were initially willing to buy a technologically sophisticated product from an unknown company were techies, a group that was also likely to be product evangelists in online communities. Company co-founder Liu De reported that most of the early employees in the company were customers who visited the company and were hired in the process. The others were hired through referrals from those initial employees.

The operating system for the Xiaomi smartphones is something that the users—assuming they are computer programmers!—could adapt themselves. The very first employees of the company came from that user community, so it was not a challenge for them to remain plugged into it once employed. The company reports that product managers spend as much as half their time monitoring company user forums. Hugo Barra, a Brazilian who headed the company's expansion outside China, noted that a useful idea from that community "gets picked up by a product manager within hours. Within a few more hours it can be at an engineer's desk." That might be a software enhancement, to allow users to switch from one application to another more quickly, or something about improving the appearance of the phone. Users, not just employees, compete to have their innovations adopted by Xiaomi and get recognition for it.[38]

Getting product ideas from users is one thing; turning them into actual innovations is another. That happened, in part, simply because the company had no alternative system for generating innovations. Xiaomi did not have departments in charge of innovating or strategic plans for sorting and prioritizing possible improvements in its products. It could not afford them, at least initially.

A second, more important factor driving the user-led innovation model was empowerment, delegating action down to those product managers. Initially there were only two levels in the organization chart: "partners" who were the company founders and "engineers" who did all the technical work. The engineers were all deemed peers, and thus there was little hierarchy to overcome in making decisions, though the company has since added a third layer of professional managers. Company founder and CEO Lei Jun set up an organization structure for Xiaomi based around teams of ten people who held great autonomy over what they did. This structure was designed to make accountability stronger, as it was easier to see who did what in small teams, but it was also instituted to make innovations faster. When the partners saw a good idea, they could jump on it without waiting for it to be approved or expecting that all useful ideas would come from some innovation department in the organization.

One of the challenges such a decentralized approach introduces is quality control: How do we prevent bad innovations from being introduced? Here the company was protected by its flexible, almost open-sourced products. Most of the innovations had already been tried by users, but if they failed after Xiaomi introduced them, it was easy to undo them. Customer-user groups let the company know quickly if a feature was faulty.

How could the company get employees to operate in this very decentralized—we might even say "un-Chinese"—manner? One way was to hire employees who had no prior work experience. As the company became more successful, it also became well known on university campuses as a technology innovator, in part through its user community, and this made it easier to hire the best and brightest from among the country's software and mobile-application graduates. The average age of the company's workforce is still only twenty-six.

The other approach to hiring was to reach outside, including well beyond China, to hire managerial talent from companies that already operated more or less as Xiaomi wanted to operate. One reason it seems very much like a Silicon Valley company is that so many of its leaders have been hired from the Valley: Google, Qualcomm, and Spotify are among those firms Xiaomi raided for talent. Xiaomi's fast growth meant that it could not develop enough leaders internally to meet demand, and its rapid international expansion required expertise that could most quickly be met through outside recruitment. Hugo Barra, who had been hired from Google, noted that the "culture here is very similar [to the culture at Google]—this notion of having a company formed by a large number of small teams that move very quickly, have a sense of ownership, and are somewhat autonomous and independent." The fast turnaround time for innovations at Xiaomi—mobile phone updates are released almost weekly—also means that employees can see the immediate consequences of their actions in the marketplace. That, in turn, makes it easier for them to keep their focus on customers. Employees receive sales figures in real time.[39]

As Xiaomi became more successful in an industry first dominated by companies from other countries, it became even easier to hire the best Chinese talent. Whether pride in the ability to hire the best has gone too far for its brand is an open question; we were told of one Xiaomi executive who publicly ridiculed employees of another smartphone company, saying they were not good enough to be hired by Xiaomi. Other aspects of employee life at Xiaomi also look like Silicon Valley, including free perks (food and massages) and long work hours. On any given workday, some 80 percent of the company's employees are still at work at 11 p.m.[40]

It is always tempting to ask whether the way companies operate when they are less than a decade old, as Xiaomi is, will remain that way in the future. The usual concern is that as they get bigger, systems and rules take over, and the rigidities and stultifying aspects of bureaucracies take hold. Xiaomi by one ranking had by 2016 become the fifth-largest cellphone company in the world, though. In contrast to Alibaba, it does not have a charismatic founder who orchestrates the company through a unique culture. But it does have a set of practices that support innovation and a brand that attracts engineers who are eager to lead in technology.

Conclusion

Business leaders in China have learned to manage large workforces, sometimes very large ones. Many of the CEOs now preside over firms with thousands of workers, up from none three decades ago. As of 2016, Xiaomi employed more than 8,000 people, Alibaba more than 46,000, and Foxconn more than a million, even though the first two formed in 2010 and 1999, respectively, and Foxconn had only entered mainland China in 1988.

As labor markets have tightened, it is not surprising that managing employees has become the biggest issue for CEOs and other business leaders. A survey of CEOs found that employee issues were by far the biggest concern for them—50 percent more important than the next most important issue. When asked what they were doing about it, though, the attention and resources devoted to managing people were far down the list of priorities.[41]

A study of human resource practices among Chinese companies found that older CEOs were less likely to use more sophisticated practices in their firms, relying mainly on pay and the fear of dismissal to manage performance and tolerating high levels of turnover. Younger CEOs and those with experience outside China were more likely to utilize sophisticated practices. More generally, firms that pursued a low-cost strategy as the source of their competitive advantage maintained a simple, Theory-X relationship with employees. Managing employees, and human resource systems in general, is the least sophisticated and developed aspect of the Chinese businesses we studied.[42]

Most Western companies have well-established architectures for organizing work, appraising performance, and rewarding success. Sometimes these practices become bureaucratic, especially when layered on the legal protections of the European Union and other regions, leading to employment contracts that are "thicker than a Bible." There is much less of that architecture among Chinese companies. What they do instead, in many cases, is rely heavily on the charismatic leadership of the founding CEO—an observation well illustrated by the high-profile actions and even antics of Alibaba's Jack Ma—as well as on a clan-like corporate culture. Almost without exception, they also rely on a culture of company purpose and personal engagement, as seen at upstart Xiaomi, which vaulted to the top of its mobile-phone market in just five years, and at Alibaba, where Ma has emphasized how his enterprise would allow Chinese business to reach a global market and demonstrate to the world that Chinese companies are as innovative as any, including his cross-Pacific competitors in Silicon Valley.

A crucial question for these Chinese companies, perhaps the most pressing one of all, is what they will do about the tightening labor market and the challenges involved in managing employees. Will strong company cultures continue to be enough to manage a new generation of employees who have grown up with capitalism, who did not experience the material deprivation of the years before the market economy, and who have many more choices regarding where to work? It is difficult to conclude that the current arrangements will continue to be sufficient, but aside from training, we do not see the CEOs we interviewed innovating on the employee management side.

Will Chinese companies change their approach? It is worth noting that the entrepreneurs who started the great US companies were not big fans

of sophisticated employee management practices. They had to be forced
by government pressure and unions to move away from the simple "drive"
model of employee management, which relied heavily on pushing employees hard through punishments. One explanation for their lack of interest in such practices, which may translate to China as well, is that few
entrepreneurs are motivated by employee management. Instead, they
tend to be more customer-focused, with interests and expertise in product
development or finance.

Talent Management in the Words of the Fortune Makers

I believe we need to build different management teams based on the
situation. So my criteria for selecting the management team are flexible and depend on a lot of factors including industry experience,
business maturity level, and time frame. Generally, my philosophy
is openness. After they join us, I will trust them and give them
enough authority and platform.

—Chair, steel- and equipment-making corporation

We have tried all kinds of different methods [for building the management team]. We had hired senior managers from abroad, big
multinational companies in sea freight and state-owned sea freight
companies. In the process, we have made some mistakes, and then
we finally concluded that the right way is to train and promote internal staff. Internal staff has high identification with our culture
and is willing to devote itself to our course. . . . Most with our management team has a service period of over ten or even fifteen years,
although the company is only twenty years old. Some of them
joined us when the company started. Through years of selection
based on the principle of survival of the fittest, we finally came up
with our current management team.

—Yang Shaopeng, Chair, SITC International Holdings

I think it's very important that the leader and the core management
team of a company have to keep learning new knowledge to catch
up with the latest social and technological developments and

trends. Only in this way can the leader and company figure out the new goals. Study is also very important to keep the company updated with the social change and demand. In our company, the core management team often gathers together and studies the relevant trends of the world to find out our gaps and shortcomings.

—Chief executive, commercial bank

CHAPTER 6

The Big Boss

The Chinese leader is always top down.

The role of the chief executive in shaping workplace policies is especially central in China, because so many of the CEOs there are founders as well—and also because there was no preexisting model on how to run these companies. Chinese business leaders play an outsized role in their firms, one that might aptly be termed a "big-boss" management model, where the operations and the success of the enterprise depend more on the person of the CEO than on the office of the CEO.

Compared with executives of Western firms, Chinese business leaders play an especially dominant role in the life of the firm; their hand is more evident, their style more consequential. Chinese culture values humility as a personal attribute, and company leaders display the requisite elements of self-effacement, but that does not get in the way of personal boldness, an individual readiness to define direction and execute around it. The resulting authority is both hierarchic and hands-on; the CEO is at the top of a very high chart from which directives are felt throughout. The big boss is surrounded by the usual trappings of authority, and the executive's personal charisma adds to it all.

For those working with, selling to, or relying upon large private companies in China, their chief executives loom large. Those on the front line feel the personal imprint of these CEOs, and major decisions start and stop with them. In time, the office of the CEO is likely to attract the formal staffing, scheduling, and status with which American managers are well familiar, but for the moment the occupant still defines much of that office.

Zhang Ruimin Transforms Haier

"Successful companies move with the changing times," offered Zhang Ruimin, founder and CEO of Haier Group, which makes home appliances and consumer electronics ranging from washing machines to television sets. Zhang has led his 1984 start-up to become the world's largest appliance maker, with more than $30 billion in annual sales by 2015. Despite Haier's great scale, Zhang exercises a deft and powerful hand; he transformed the firm from the large pyramid that he had constructed over three decades into something more akin to General Stanley McChrystal's "team of teams," an array of collaborating but autonomous decision centers with authority to act but not over one another.[1]

Zhang explained that he had moved his company over its thirty-year existence from one premised on the management precepts of Frederick Taylor's "scientific management" to one fashioned on Max Weber's theory of "bureaucracy." Scientific management as a model emphasizes breaking work tasks into small fragments that individuals can learn to efficiently perform, with managers then forcefully assembling the many pieces into a finished product; Weber's bureaucratic model describes a pyramid of impersonally defined reporting relations, with the more senior layers—each with six or seven sub-units reporting to them—coalescing the many pieces from below to deliver the company's finished products. Taylor's model is well exemplified by the assembly lines in the US auto industry's early decades; and Weber's model, by the original American Telephone & Telegraph, AT&T, whose nearly 1 million employees delivered telephone services across the entire country through vertical coordination. But now, Zhang has come to forge a third way, transforming his company from a very tall hierarchy and sharply delineated tasks into a host of hubs, each focused around a clutch of consumers.

In making his management model "customer-centric," Zhang had come to it from his own "trials and errors," learning what works by testing what might work better in changing times. He pressed the rank and file to innovate—"every employee can be a business creator"—and he backed the new regime with extra pay for those who created value as judged by end-users, not just inside appraisals. He also dispatched legions of sales people into the countryside to learn directly from his buyers.

As companies like Haier balloon into behemoths, Zhang believed, they become less innovative, less dynamic, and less expansive, stymied by a "big-company disease." And as boss of it all, he was determined to ward off that infection. "Overcoming obstructions instead of being overturned by obstructions" became his priority, he explained. He forced inventories down, cutting stock turnover in home appliances from thirty-two days to just three, in effect learning how to sell a product based on customer demand rather than dispensing from a warehouse inventory. He basically fractured a bureaucracy into dozens of profit-and-loss centers, giving their managers some of the value they added.

By 2015, Zhang's company had created 103 product incubators, 3,800 micro-enterprises, more than a million "micro-stores," and ¥3 billion in venture funds. By means of radical decentralization and devolution of authority, Zhang contracted his employment rolls from a peak of 110,000 to fewer than 60,000 by 2015, all despite a 6 percent compound annual growth in revenue over the previous decade. And behind it all was Zhang himself, who had forced himself and then his organization to undertake the vast remake. You have to "constantly challenge yourself," he vowed, and then, as the big boss, challenge the enterprise as well.[2]

The Power of the Big Boss

The power of the big boss to make a large personal difference is a theme that appears throughout our interviews with the private-company executives. We had not come into the interviews expecting to hear what they repeatedly referenced, but their own recurrent descriptors made for a contrasting picture with the West, where top positions have long been institutionalized, their occupants representing a nexus of relations defined by the office of the chief executive.

Most of the executives we interviewed are still the founders of their companies. As of the end of 2015, sixty of the seventy-two executives we interviewed had established the enterprise that they now run. And while they have of necessity learned to devise complex architectures, since many now employ tens of thousands of people, their companies remain remarkably founder-centric, with their own passions and preferences defining much of how their firm operates. Their personal experiences and individual penchants continue to have a substantial impact on their company's work-place practices. They still demand of themselves a personal capacity to understand most facets of the business and where the company should be directed.[3]

As the chief executive of a maker of computer hardware and information technology equipment observed: "The leader, either chairman or CEO, plays a much more important role in a Chinese company than in an American company," and "I think the leader is more important to the strategic decisions than the board in Chinese companies." The chairman of an interior design and decoration company said much the same in referencing both his own leadership and that of his compatriots:

> It's quite a common phenomenon with most Chinese companies that the leaders play a decisive role in the development of enterprises, and the culture of the boss usually defines and represents the culture of his company. Typically the leaders make all the critical and strategic decisions that determine the ups or downs of their companies. When a leader goes wrong in decision making, his company falls onto hard times.

The founder and chair of a large textile and apparel firm went even further, asserting that the top executive is the core competency itself:

> In my view, the capabilities of the founder determine the core competence of a company. . . . A company cannot survive with a lousy and incompetent leader. The core competitive competence of most old European companies is embedded in the company itself, rather than in the leader personally, because those companies are run by the fourth or fifth or even the sixth generation. For new start-ups and companies that are still run by the first generation, such as those in China, the founder or leader determines the fate of a company. . . . Besides building up the company systems, the leader has to have authoritative power over his staff. What's authoritative power? A leader has to demonstrate his strong capability in managing every aspect of the business. . . . The leader has to be the most capable among his team. . . . For us, I am the core competence and competitive advantage.

This is a large self-imposed burden and a potentially flawed perception for the longer term, since it runs the risk that the executive's competence and advantage may prove misaligned with later market shifts—with, for instance, the rise of digital commerce and international trade. But even here many of the executives viewed themselves as bringing an appreciation for such dislocations to the table and playing the driver in forcing their firm to restructure itself, as Zhang Ruimin had done at Haier, in effect doubling-down on themselves. As the chair of the textile and apparel firm explained, "Only a competent founder or a leader can ensure the long-term sustainable development of a company." At the heart of it all, he explained, was the premise that a successful big boss attracts loyalty and duty: "The reason why the team is willing to follow a boss is no mystery. [It's] absolute admiration of the boss's capabilities in always making the right decision and seizing the business opportunity at every critical moment. You can find the worship of the boss by the team in all successful Chinese companies." When asked about critical decisions, he reported that he had to make them all—and he asserted that, so far, all of his decisions have been "right." Whether his self-appraisal is accurate, it is his personal confidence in it that, he said, brings "complete trust and respect from the frontline staff." So "long as the founder develops the company in the right track," he concluded, "the employees believe in what a leader says and does," thereby affirming the leader's authority over the company.

Surveys confirm the greater dominance exhibited by Chinese CEOs than by their counterparts elsewhere. The World Economic Forum's annual cross-national survey of informed observers regarding their home country's firm structure, for example, annually reports the degree of delegation of authority inside the firm on a scale from one to seven, lowest to highest. Those from European countries scored 5.31 for delegation of authority, and Anglo-Saxon countries were not far behind at 4.87. But Chinese companies scored just 3.60 on the delegation scale. The chairman of a maker of industrial electrical equipment confirmed this point: "In American companies, many people, including many organization investors, have a stake in the companies," he said. But "here in this company, I am the first shareholder, and I have complete control in making decisions."[4]

Chinese business leaders as a result directly involve themselves in everything from strategic decisions to daily operations. Their personal mindset and temperament cast a longer shadow than is customary in the less personal world of Western leadership. They play an outsized role in both directing their operating methods in the present and reshaping their operations for future markets.

Personal Character

Given the central place of the big boss in the Chinese enterprise, the CEO's personal character becomes central as well—though character is, of course, not a precise imprint or exact replica of the boss made large. Their companies reflect much of the leader's personal journey and understandings, which is not surprising since the founding CEOs had few others from which to replicate a way forward. Without models or exemplars to mold but also limit their ways of building and running the enterprise, their own character served as a blueprint for the management methods that followed. And at the heart of what is required for leading with character is a combination of moral authority, personal behavior, and work ethic.

Mao Zhongqun, founder and chairman of Ningbo Fotile Kitchen Ware Co., a maker of kitchen cabinets and ventilators, observed:

> I have attended many classes on leadership and read many books about leadership. Most of them are Western studies and theories that tend to emphasize skills and techniques. But in Confucian and oriental culture, leadership is all about the power of character and charisma. In Lun Yu, the great work of Confucianism, there is a saying that "governing based on virtues is like taking the position of the Big Dipper with all stars circling around it."

The founder and chairman of a venture-capital firm made much the same point: "Leadership is about what kind of person you are, and what personal example you set for your staff. It is not so much what you educate them to do, than what you show them how to behave yourself. People will follow you because they admire you and like you, and enjoy working together with you."

Wang Licheng, CEO of the Holley Group, active in pharmaceuticals, manufacturing, and real estate, offered a similar formulation:

I think there is one thing different in corporate culture between Chinese and Western enterprises. In China, people believe authority. So as a business leader, you must have a very strong leadership to build your prestige and convince your employees. To build this strong leadership, you must lead by example and work harder than anyone in the organization. Then your employees will be convinced by your personality and accept your leadership.

Personal behavior becomes the broadcast medium. The chairman of a real-estate and financial-services firm offered a revealing account of his own habits. "The only way that I can influence others," he affirmed, is through "exemplary behavior," and for that he adopted a posture of giving more than anyone else in the organization. "I always work for a longer time than anyone else every day," he reported. He allowed himself just two days' respite annually—and even then, out of adherence to the Chinese tradition of being with one's family on New Year's Eve. "Nobody could be found in the office in the afternoon of the last day before Chinese Lunar New Year"—except for him, he confessed. He recounted one such evening: "I watched all my colleagues leave office for home—leaving no one in the office but myself." By the time he left and fetched his family for the forty-minute drive to his hometown, it was very late and everybody had gone out of town for the holiday, including the toll collectors on the turnpike.

After his brief holiday respite, he was back at work, with an immediate visit to a construction site and staff dinner, followed by 363 nonstop-labor days: "I continued to work day and night without weekends and holidays. I went to the office at 9 in the morning and basically arrived home around 12 midnight in the evening, working for about 15 or 16 hours a day, day in and day out" over many years. The company "was a newcomer in real-estate industry," he explained, "and no one had heard of us. The only way to succeed is to dedicate my full time and efforts in the business and lead by example."

Humble But Bold

Despite the CEO-centeredness, Chinese business leaders ironically adopt a veneer of humility that goes well beyond the normal trappings of modesty. This is particularly important for operating in China, where a humble bearing is considered a virtue in itself and employees expect executives to display at least a modicum of social self-restraint. Research confirms that relational behavior is more valued than individualism among managers in China than among those in the West, and that it has greater impact on employee behavior.[5]

National differences in leadership styles can be just that. As we noted in an earlier chapter, researchers have well documented variant country leadership preferences. For instance, managers universally applaud decisiveness and honesty in company leaders, but in some countries those with higher ranks are treated with greater deference and in turn are expected to be less self-referential. Our Chinese business leaders certainly fit that pattern, and leading an enterprise in China would be more challenging if the executives significantly deviated from their nation's prevailing norms.[6]

That said, the overt display of respect for subordinates and the apparent subordination of management ego can bring special advantage to executives who embrace them as their own behavioral way. And here the Chinese executives find special advantage: boldness and humility bring decisiveness and honesty—universally applauded—but also greater openness to the ideas of subordinates and their greater willingness to devote themselves to the enterprise.

"Respecting subordinates is embedded in every detail," offered the chief executive of a venture capital company. "My office is of the same size as everyone else's. If you have a huge office while subordinates work in 1.2 by 1.2 [meter] cubicles, if you ask them to work on weekends but you are not working yourself, what does it say about your values, and what kind of example are you setting for your staff?" He followed a practice of personally engaging with all of his second-order direct reports through one of the most status-equalizing rituals available to any. With six lieutenants and each of them with six more, the chief executive arranged to dine weekly with one of his thirty-six indirect reports. Down from his lofty perch, he shared with them not only what went on inside the corner office but also his personal concerns.

That said, an unassuming style does not diminish the power of the big boss—and, if anything, enhances it when exercised well. This can well be seen in ways that company executives more aggressively challenge a persistent barrier to growth than is evident in the West.

If a business leader fully adheres to all government regulations, he or she is unlikely to succeed in building the enterprise since remnants of the planned economy still pervade the market. Bold rule-breaking in a hazardous context is a necessary result, and some regulations will be violated. Authorities sometimes look the other way, deeming such moves as "creative solutions" or "reform innovations," but sometimes they do not, terming such violations as "anti-socialism system and anti-Communist Party."

Even for those far from politics and untouched by personal corruption, personal resolve can be vital in the face of political upheavals, reported our business leaders. The chair of a diversified manufacturing firm offered: "When I started the business, I had never thought about the difficulties ahead. No matter what lies in front of me, be it cliff or trap, I can always find the solution to resolve it. I feared nothing."

Lenovo founder Liu Chuanzhi had even prepared himself to face imprisonment as he challenged China's prohibition of what he viewed as vital for his company's growth. "My work is very difficult," he said, and that "difficulty comes mostly from the risk of political uncertainty." As he was working to build the enterprise on the elementary principle that a manager's reward should be commensurate with performance, in 1988 he ran headlong into a state constraint. For every yuan paid in performance bonus to his managers above a low threshold, Lenovo would have to pay a tax of 300 percent.

This extraordinary bonus tax derived from the fact that employee salaries at state-owned enterprises were low at the beginning of the economic reforms in the 1980s. When the liberalization brought rapid pay raises in collectively owned farms, employees at state-owned enterprises (SOEs) asked their managers to raise their compensation, and the latter resorted to bonuses for doing so. But to limit the escalating demands, the national government in 1985 imposed limits, capping bonuses at the equivalent of three months' wages. Anything above that would be taxed at 300 percent.

Liu's predicament: his company could not afford the tax, but it also could not grow without incentive pay. Perched on the horns of that dilemma, Liu opted to pay the bonuses in cash, thus bypassing the bonus regulation at enormous personal risk. "If things turn out right," he said, "everybody in Lenovo would benefit." But "if the government found out, I have to shoulder all the consequences. I was prepared to go to jail." Going beyond rhetoric, Liu and his lieutenants had provisioned for his family if he were indeed imprisoned, a form of risk management less familiar to Western executives. Liu authored a lengthy letter to the leaders of the National Academy of Science, explaining his rationale in having knowingly violated government regulations.

As feared, the government discovered Liu's bonus misdeed. Luckily, the National Academy of Science supported Liu and explained to the tax authority why Liu had committed this act. The government imposed a penalty on Lenovo rather than on Liu, fining the firm ¥3 million but leaving Liu free. Looking back on his risky challenge in the name of business, Liu said: "If you want to succeed in leading a business, you have to be willing to make major personal sacrifices."

Serving as the big boss could logically lead to being paid as the big boss, as happens in many Western firms. Indeed, studies of US executives repeatedly confirm that exceptionally powerful and long-serving chief executives are compensated exceedingly well, and some remain highly paid even during company setbacks. According to one investigation, the average compensation package for the chief executives of forty-five large manufacturing companies had reached $13.4 million in 2015, up from $10.7 million a decade earlier. And while Western disparities in income and wealth continue to expand within both the company and the society, with CEO pay packages soaring to more than three hundred times those of the average worker, the countervailing current of humility in China militates against the kind of excess to which Europeans and especially Americans have become habituated.[7]

Here, too, China's cultural heritage is felt. In the oft-cited words of Confucius, "the trouble of a society lies not in having too little, but in its unequal distribution," and while the Chinese public envies the wealthy, like publics everywhere—witness the support for a leading candidate for the US White House in 2016 when he displayed rather than downplayed his wealth—that envy had not yet morphed into unalloyed admiration in China. If anything, a still prevalent precept gives status not to those of great personal achievement but to those of great personal sacrifice, a principle still embraced by many who lead China's private companies.

Hierarchic and Hands-On

Extending the big-boss management model in still another direction, leaders of private Chinese companies have retained a seemingly odd combination of both hierarchic and hands-on people management. The idea that a founding executive is always in charge of everything is not unusual in any company where the founder is still around, in either the West or the East, but it appears to be particularly persistent among these enterprises. As company founders give way to a new generation of executives, however, the model of the big boss may give way to more collaborative concepts at the top.

In the succinct summation of the chief executive of a manufacturing firm, "the Chinese leader is always top down." And in the blunt summary of the chief executive of an interior design and decoration company, the "parenting framework of management means one has to report everything to the leader, no matter whether the issue is a major or a minor one. The leader acts like a parent." To the Western eye, this may seem ineffective or worse. If the big ideas are mainly coming from the top and subordinates can do little more than salute, Chinese companies may be missing the fresh thoughts and innovative models that often emerge from among the ranks in the United States. This could be a profound weakness of the big-boss model—one not yet much noticed in this era of fast growth, but which may be exposed when torrid expansion no longer prevails.

By extension, with the top executive in charge of everything and on top of all decisions, few rules and procedures are required to guide employees' decisions because they make none. The interior-design and decoration-company chair contrasted his own hands-on style with what he found among Western companies, with their thick employment contracts and employee handbooks to cover all eventualities. Similarly, the chair of a company in the food industry described herself as directly engaged in what every executive in her company was doing, aided by frequent "heart to heart" talks with each to keep her abreast of the facts. She probes for what is most on their mind, and in hearing their responses she listens for nascent market trends and ways to keep the company competitive. She in turn coaches her subordinates on selecting and maintaining desirable customers, and on better understanding the company's values and culture.

Without detailed rules or financial controls to monitor and align the behavior of their lieutenants, big bosses rely more upon personal loyalty than is common in the West. The chief executive of a marine engineering firm cited a Chinese proverb to make this point: "When you have difficulties, people give you a little water, and you should give back a river." If you take care of your team, they will feel obligated to take care of you. But that paternalism was sometimes extended even to a fault—for business. The chief executive for a maker of electrical equipment for industry offered: "We tend to take human relationships into consideration when we make business decisions that," as a result, "turn out not to be forceful enough." He and others would thus not fire employees who would readily have been dismissed by Western standards. The interior-design and decoration-company chair recalled a moment when his firm had promoted design engineers into management roles but found that they were unable to gain the respect of those who reported to them. They were shuffled elsewhere in the company rather than shown the door.

Balancing these extremes—the all-powerful boss on the one hand, the empowering leader on the other, the paternalistic mentor who nevertheless fires even longtime employees who resist the leader's ideas—is one of the central attributes of the Chinese leaders we talked to. As with successful politicians, we might say that they are good at managing appearances. They understand that symbolic gestures go a long way, yet they also understand that what employees see them do has a powerful effect on the firm's mindset.

Whether the Chinese CEOs will be able to remain hierarchic and hands-on as their firms continue to grow remains an open question. Most well-placed observers, including the executives whom we interviewed, believe they will not. The chair of a power and energy management enterprise viewed one of her current priorities as facilitating the transition from big boss to "big system," a formal hierarchy where titles and protocols are more defining than incumbents and their whims.

Culture as Glue

The medium that is facilitating the transformation from a big-boss model to a big-system company, report many of our executives, is a common mindset widely shared among employees. Corporate cultures in the West are just as magnetic, lining up the needles in the same direction and telling employees what is acceptable behavior even when no rules have specified it. But in more established Western firms, the precepts have been inherited, handed down from regime to regime. For private Chinese companies, by contrast, the mindset is a work in progress, newly minted, still shaky, but already important. According to our executives, self-consciously creating that mindset has come to be almost as vital as anything else they manage. When asked to name the most important roles they play in their company, the executives we interviewed identified "keeper of organizational culture" as the second most vital function after setting strategy (as earlier seen in Figure 4.1).

Mao Zhongqun, for instance, had co-founded Ningbo Fotile Kitchen Ware in 1996, and over two decades he had grown it into one of China's premier providers of high-end kitchen appliances. But with scale, this wide dispersion of his workforce had also become a premier problem. "Now we have a huge staff" of some 7,000 to 8,000 employees "spread all over the country," he explained, and "to be honest, it's a tough job to manage." With a roster dispersed across dozens of cities and with accounting shortfalls on the rise, Mao decided in 2008 to explicitly remind employees of their Confucian heritage as a way to define values and shape behavior, but that proved insufficient. He then linked the entire incentive system to support the company's culture, because "culture should be a comprehensive system"—a code of conduct, he had learned, "rather than the mere application of Confucian ideology."

As the executives built up their enterprises, they increasingly worked to sustain their emerging mindset by bringing in only new hires who would fit with it. In one of the more imaginative applications, a real-estate and financial-services firm had created the position of "chief smelling officer" (something might have been lost in translation), whose function is to evaluate a job candidate's cultural fit. As explained by its chairman, "when selecting senior executives, we first evaluate whether the candidate is aligned with Landsea values and company management mentalities before considering his professional capabilities." Although this approach may not be widespread, it is similar to what we might see in Western corporations. The difference is in the chief driver of the culture, which in most of the Chinese companies is still the CEO and his or her pronouncements. In this respect, the Chinese companies are little different from what we see in the West, but they differ in terms of the chief driver of the cultural fit. For the former, the big boss at many companies remains the primary definer of the culture; for the latter, codes, credos, and honors are more likely to define the DNA.

The chief executive of a food products company carried the precept into promotions as well (as did many other executives). "To really make culture work, it also needs to be felt and witnessed in those detailed aspects on who gets promoted and why salaries increased. Culture must be built into every aspect of business operation to demonstrate its value and power." For a real-estate-investment company chief executive, "the key is to ensure everyone is aligned in values, from executives down to frontline staff. Once a company achieves this level of consistency in staff values across the board, it would be as powerful as a religion whose believers all hold true belief in the same god and follow the same code of conduct everywhere in the world."

If the newly erected company cultures are a kind of preservative, they may also turn out to be an albatross, a glue that will not let go of the past. Corporate culture has been described as a giant flywheel, providing inertial guidance but also resisting redirection, and very strong corporate cultures strongly resist change. As our Chinese executives or their successors face dislocating technologies or new competitors, what serves them now may prove an impediment later.

Ousting the Boss

We learn the most about organizations and businesspeople, one might argue, in moments of crisis when their management model is pressed to the limit. That happened in Alibaba in 2011 when the company's then-CEO, David Wei, was pushed out of the company.[8]

It is not uncommon on websites like Alibaba, where large numbers of vendors do business, for occasional acts of malfeasance to occur. The problem at Alibaba was that the vendors were apparently defrauding customers systematically. The company acknowledged the problem, reported that it had dealt with those vendors, and business went on.

One of the first points evident from this story is how difficult it is to identify and track down unethical and even illegal behavior in Chinese companies, in large part because they do not operate like their Western counterparts. They do not have elaborate systems of rules in place, including internal accounting systems that can identify fraud relatively quickly, or oversight authority structures where someone is watching local practices. As companies like Alibaba grew large, the ability of the founder or "big boss" to police everything diminished, and as a consequence the actions of the company became more decentralized.

Jack Ma discovered that fraud had occurred at Alibaba while he was casually looking through e-mails and spotting one about a group dinner where an auditor complained that she was too busy to go out because of her work investigating other employees. Jack Ma went to her directly, diving down the organizational hierarchy, to find out what she knew.

That led to an internal company investigation, six months after the initial events, in which more than a hundred Alibaba staff members were implicated. The fraud went deep: company officials allowed fake companies not only to remain on the Alibaba website but to be registered in the most trustworthy category, "gold suppliers." They also helped these fake companies to hide the scheme from Alibaba's internal investigators. They did so in part to meet their own Alibaba performance targets. It is not clear to outsiders how far up the hierarchy the fraud went, although knowledge of it seemed to be widespread. Some 2,300 vendors were involved in the malfeasance from 2009 to 2010, when it was discovered. There had been no investigation before this, nor any indication that company employees were involved.

What should Alibaba do now? The second lesson from the story is about the extent of loyalty within these companies. It would not be surprising to find—in Western companies, especially those in the United States—that "heads would roll." People would be fired, lots of them, including executives.

In China, by contrast, such actions would contradict personal loyalty to the leaders, especially to the big boss. At Alibaba, Jack Ma had been unusually critical of the idea that executives should act like professionals with norms for behavior set from the outside. Managers, he thought, should be driven by the values of their own company, and loyalty in Alibaba mattered.

Ma went on a personal retreat to decide what to do, specifically about David Wei, the chief executive at the time. There was no evidence that Wei was personally involved in the fraud, but he was in charge of Alibaba's day-to-day management. Wei was not a founder or a longtime employee, having come into the CEO role from the outside in 2006. Nevertheless, he was perceived as an effective and loyal executive who became a central part of the inner circle—what Ma referred to as a "gold-collar," not just a white-collar, employee.

Ma described the dilemma of whether to fire Wei: "We are human beings and not God! The feeling was like chopping off one of your hands and you are going to fire one of your brothers." Ma was sure that Wei would take the blame and resign if asked, "but what can I do for his future then?" Ma deliberated for a month.

Finally, Ma allowed Wei to resign along with Chief Operating Officer Elvis Lee. Many of the implicated lower-level employees were dismissed, and one other executive—the head of human resources—was demoted. Before departing, David Wei gave a speech to the employees, taking responsibility for the problems in the company—a move not unlike the public confessions one might see in a political trial. Jack Ma praised both of the departing executives and expressed regret at their departure, but their exile proved incomplete: Wei started an investment fund with Jack Ma as one of the investors, and Elvis Lee came back into Alibaba later as chief operating officer for the Alibaba Group in the United States.

The dismissals would not have surprised any US-based business observers. Indeed, they would have been shocked that the decision to dismiss employees was not made immediately and was not more widespread. But in China, this decision reverberated in powerful ways. Many business leaders chimed in as to whether Ma's decision had been appropriate, and not all agreed with the forced resignations. Those who did concur noted that it was important to act as he had done to support the company's culture, although (as is often the case) that culture pointed in contradictory directions: responsibility versus loyalty. But whatever the external appraisal, in our view it constituted a moment when the big-boss model gave way to something different.

That moment also represented something of a turning point for Jack Ma. He had moved away from day-to-day involvement in the business in 2007, focusing instead on people issues and managing the culture. In 2011, he described his priorities as the company's chairman: "I spend most of my time in considering 'people' and basically I do not get involved in business. . . . First I try to be a qualified gatekeeper of the company's mission and values. . . . Secondly, I shall discover and develop high-potential business leaders. Lastly, it's my job to expel any 'professional managers' from the organization."

But the fraud incident suggests that the culture was not right, and Ma redoubled his efforts to define the culture of Alibaba. He sent a letter to all company employees the day Wei and Lee left, reminding them about the company's core values and specifically addressing the fact that the employees who committed fraud were doing so to book more business and meet their own performance targets: "Since the day that Alibaba was established, pursuit of profit has never been our main goal. We have no interest in turning the company into a mere money-making machine. Rather, we have long held firm to our mission of 'making it easy to do business anywhere.' When we say 'customer first,' we mean that 'we'd rather sacrifice growth than do anything that would jeopardize our customers' interests, much less be a part of any blatant fraud.'"[9]

Ma also made a personal journey to Bijia Mountain, where in 1929 Chairman Mao drove the idea that "non-proletariat" ideologies had to be pushed out of what became the People's Liberation Army, and that the Communist Party's control over the army had to increase. Rather than just focus on military goals, Mao was arguing that it was necessary to "fortify the army through political propaganda." For Jack Ma, the emphasis on appropriate ideology and not just military goals helped the army succeed, and that sounded a great deal like the distinction between organizational culture and managing through financial and other "key performance indicators." He said he was enlightened by that insight.

Conclusion

The communal always overshadows the individual in communist orthodoxy, one of the sorest of many vexing features for writer Ayn Rand and other critics, and though Chinese business still remains overshadowed by regime ideology, privately owned firms are remarkably focused on the individual at the top. Though the United States certainly went through a period of "celebrity" CEOs with attention focused on them (Michael Eisner at Disney and Jack Welch at GE come to mind), they were never as all-powerful as the Chinese leaders we studied. The big-boss management model faded in the West after founders left and scale dictated that bureaucracies and C-suites rule. Not so in China, at least not yet. If the West has become more collectivist, China remains more individualist.[10]

The special place of top executives is partly a product, we believe, of their having founded their firms—and also partly a product of having no preexisting models to suggest otherwise, even as they came to preside over tens of thousands of employees and billions in revenue. Whatever the drivers, the upshot for the moment is for Chinese firms to place a primacy on the character of the chief executive. The CEO sets the tenor for the enterprise through his or her personal behavior. If a management priority is for employees to devote long hours to the enterprise, the CEO has to work the longest hours of all.

Two psychologists who examined the leadership style of the Chinese executives in Taiwan and Hong Kong reported that "paternalism" was indeed a defining strand, calling for an adroit combination of authoritarian, benevolent, and moral actions. The first type of action is defined by an executive's display of tight control over subordinates and their unquestioning obedience. The second is marked by an executive's holistic concern for each subordinate's individual and familial well-being. And the third is delineated by an executive's display of superior character through personal integrity and selfless behavior. How close these actions are to what we see in China is an open question, but analysts who reviewed a host of research studies on Chinese leadership reached much the same conclusion, with paternalism standing out as one of the defining leadership threads.[11]

A riveting focus on the big boss, however, creates a potential anomaly since business culture still carries the traditional national value of personal modesty—a value that stresses personal sacrifice for the common good. Accordingly, Chinese business leaders have embraced a simultaneous posture of boldness and humility, stressing a willingness to take aggressive actions even if these can be personally costly. And given the lingering limits on private business to make private-business decisions, corporate executives have found that they sometimes have had to make decisions that put their own liberty at risk, as we saw at Lenovo when founder and longtime CEO Liu Chuanzhi risked imprisonment in adopting an incentive pay system—a commonplace in the West but still a dangerous frontier in China.

The big-boss management method has also led to an ironic combination of hierarchic and hands-off people management. While the company "leader acts like a parent," in the self-appraisal of one of our CEOs, Chinese chief executives are increasingly learning to work via others and through a hierarchy. This can be seen in the decision of Alibaba founder Jack Ma to dismiss the chief executive whom he had hired to run the enterprise. It proved a personal turning point as Ma took a step back from hands-on management and a step forward in the direction of system management.

Whether the humble, bold, hierarchic, hands-on, and caring leadership currently coming from these chief executives will be sustainable as their companies continue their rapid growth and overseas expansion remains to be seen. We agree here with other observers that this is one area where East will likely meet West, not the other way around.

The Big Boss in the Words of the Fortune Makers

Leading by example covers every aspect of business operation from setting the rules and disciplines to values and spiritual pursuit. Before asking employees to work hard, a leader shall work hard himself to really motivate his staff.

—Chief executive, venture-capital firm

As the boss, you have to be generous and willing to let all employees benefit from the company's success. Also, you need to be open-minded. Over time, staff will accept your leadership and follow you. Then you can lead them in the right path to success.

—Yang Shaopeng, Chair, SITC International Holdings

So there is a big difference in the quality and capability between the chairmen of [Chinese companies and those of foreign firms in China]. The latter are not comparable to their counterparts in China, as they are not at the same level of competency. In terms of starting a new business or company, innovation, and problem-solving capability, Chinese chairmen can score 100 [on a scale of 0 to 100]. Those foreign companies' chairmen are definitely below 59.

[There is] no reason to admire them as they experience many fewer problems compared to their Chinese counterparts.
        —Chair, computer and electronic products company

Leading by example is especially important as Chinese believe in the saying "Subordinates always follow the behaviors of their boss."
        —Mao Zhongqun, Chair, Ningbo Fotile Kitchen Ware

In China, the chairman or number-one guy has to stand up and personally handle lots of things, especially managing the relationship with government, media, and investors. They all want to talk to the number one. For every company leader in China, this is the obligation that must be addressed well and readily.
        —Chair, consumer-products company

I always personally lead the project if it is big enough—for example, if it accounts for a tenth of our total profit. To obtain the key resources, I will not delegate it to our employees and always do it by myself. I have the responsibility to face such challenges because I have the biggest share and highest authorization. I believe this is my duty.
        —Chair, real-estate company

CHAPTER 7

Growth as Gospel

The most important thing is to grow the cake
and let everyone take a piece from it.

To appreciate the drivers of Chinese business leadership, we return to *The Protestant Ethic and the Spirit of Capitalism*, briefly referenced in our first chapter. Sociologist Max Weber argued that the industriousness of Western company executives was driven by a religious ethos: they would find religious merit by building an enterprise and reinvesting rather than by consuming the surplus that resulted. This ethos propelled believers to discern signs of their own personal salvation in the success of their enterprise. On producing a profit, managers felt duty-bound to reinvest the surplus rather than use it for their own enjoyment and personal consumption, yielding even more surplus and thus ever more promise of salvation. Company entrepreneurs in effect served as their own angel investors, and in one of the most fortuitous coincidences of all time, what was spiritually propitious also proved commercially auspicious. Material success and personal salvation were one and the same.

Whether or not the Protestant ethic stimulated the early rise of private enterprise in the West, capitalism later came to be animated through a very different logic that dominated the thinking and actions of company leaders. By the late twentieth century and the early twenty-first century, the driving rationale behind capitalism had morphed from religious tenet to secular ethos, especially in the United States. Increasing total shareholder return—TSR—would become the defining purpose and rallying cry. For publicly traded companies, directors and executives were compelled to regularly boost their share prices and dividends on a par with—or even better than—their competitors. Institutional holders demanded strong shareholder return, equity analysts detailed it, and activist investors targeted those who failed to deliver it.

For American firms, investor capitalism has become a straightjacket. The rise of institutional stockholding in recent decades has riveted executive attention on the delivery of TSR. Executive compensation has been aligned to drive it, and governing boards have been restructured to ensure it. While this objective has been set by the institutional owners, premier holders such as Blackrock, Fidelity, and Vanguard have left it largely in the hands of company leaders to devise ways for doing so.

In recent years, that hands-off attitude has been supplemented in the West by vigilant investors who have not been shy about instructing company leaders on how to generate greater value through spin-offs and breakups. Whether the delivery of investor value is enforced more passively or more actively, however, the goal has been the same, and the resulting mindset has become a dominant ideology defined and disciplined around the goal of increasing shareholder value. It is the prevailing rationale and benchmark for critical decisions, as was evident, for instance, when two major pharmaceutical companies, Pfizer and Allergan, abandoned a $152 billion merger plan in 2016. Pfizer chief executive Ian Read explained: "We remain focused on continuing to enhance the value of our [business and] to pursue attractive business development and other shareholder friendly capital allocation opportunities." Thus, despite the dropped plan, "as always, we remain committed to enhancing shareholder value." By contrast, when China's Anbang Insurance Group abandoned an unsolicited $13.8 billion offer to acquire Starwood Hotels and Resorts in 2016 (having already acquired New York's Waldorf Astoria hotel in 2014), it simply cited "various market considerations."[1]

If the accretion of shareholder value has come to serve as a compelling driver for American executives, nothing comparable was even hinted at in our interviews with the Chinese executives. Their overall objective has centered not on assuring the company's market value or the executive's afterlife but, rather, on growing the firm's current life. Expansion has become an end unto itself, gauged by market scale rather than by shareholder return.

Forces for Growth

As leaders of private companies in China mapped their way forward, they defined the goals of their own Chinese ethic and the spirit of capitalism very differently from what we are familiar with in the West, both historically and contemporarily. We see several forces facilitating Chinese private-company leaders in an unquenchable quest for growth, just as the concentration of equity assets in institutional hands has driven American executives' insatiable quest for shareholder value. By themselves, these forces generated nothing, but they provided company executives with plenty of wind at their back for doing so.

Just Lin of Peking University, former chief economist for the World Bank, singled out China's comparative advantage as one such force for company growth. He argued that Chinese enterprises had been able to capitalize on an abundant and cheap labor force. Academics Neil Fligstein and Jianjun Zhang looked elsewhere, stressing the state's "helping hand." The government directly supported what it designated as strategic industries, such as banking and energy, and those sectors in turn facilitated growth in still other industries. The state also exercised a stronger hand in labor relations, capital allocation, and regional development than is customary in the West, and it prioritized national expansion, even allowing state-owned enterprises to run at a loss if it ensured the growth of others.[2]

Another factor, outlined by Yang Yao of the National School of Development at Peking University and Chenggang Xu of the University of Hong Kong, is what the latter has termed China's "regionally decentralized" regime. Local governments have been incentivized by the national administration to develop their region, and they did so with a strong hand, creating essential infrastructures and favorable climates for firms to prosper.[3]

Strategy scholars Zeng Ming of the French business school INSEAD and Peter Williamson of Cambridge University have added another consideration from their study of Chinese multinationals—namely, that the successful expansion abroad could be traced to executive decisions not to simply flood the world market with cheap, low-quality imitation goods but to provide quality at vastly lower prices. Zeng and Williamson dubbed this approach "cost innovation," offering more for less. For example,

Mindray, a Chinese manufacturer of medical equipment founded in 1991 in Shenzhen, supplies patient-monitoring equipment to American and European hospitals that surpasses the quality of a leading brand, Hewlett-Packard, but at a price that is 30 percent lower. After Fitbit introduced the wearable health monitor, Flex, in 2013, it dominated global sales with 24 percent of market share in 2015, but when China's Xiaomi introduced its own wearable tracker at a fifth of that price, its market share rose from 0 to 17 percent a year later.[4]

Growth for What?

The executives we interviewed generally embraced their companies' growth as the compelling agenda, and they actively chased it. The driving logic could not be more different from what we have witnessed in the West. For large companies in the United States, the central question in acquiring and spinning-off assets, adding business lines and opening stores abroad, and compensating executives and electing directors is whether these actions will add value to the companies. For large firms in China, by contrast, the primary question is whether such actions foster their expansion.

For the past several decades, the ascendance of shareholder value in the West as the arbiter of company decisions and investor allocations has sometimes led its devotees to see this form of capitalism as logically emergent everywhere. Yet our interviews with the Chinese business leaders point to a very different logic.

For chair Yang Shaopeng of SITC International Holdings, "The most important thing is to grow the cake and let everyone take a piece from it." The chair of a maker of recycling equipment, who had built his 80,000-person firm from scratch, offered much the same:

> Huahong is a poor village and a problem for both the leaders and the people. But I wanted to be a leader, and I became the leader here during the hardest times. Why? It's because I want to live up to the expectations of both the [Communist] Party and the people. I came here to be the leader twenty-five years ago [and] I wanted to build something myself, to develop the economy, to serve the public, and to make ordinary people sense the change. In the past twenty-five

years, I started from nothing to something, from small to big, from weak to strong, and I have won recognition from the people.

The principle of striving for growth infused virtually all aspects of the Chinese firms' architecture and culture. As a medical-devices company chair told us, he realized early on that without a strong team at the top he could not nurture his enterprise in the direction of growth. In the first few years, he had brought functional leaders into the upper tier, but he then came to understand that he actually needed general managers in his inner circle if his company was to optimize its growth. Toward that end, he instituted a practice of rotating his rising managers across an array of professional and operational responsibilities. "Previously," he reported, "our leaders were functional experts who [were] focusing on their functional areas. But now we [have] found [that] the all-around generalist is very important to support business growth." While Western executives also place great emphasis on the top management team and its general management, they expect that inner circle to focus on shareholder gain. The individuals brought into the upper echelons in Chinese companies are simply devoted to growing the enterprise.

A related question concerns how company executives justify the purpose of growth to themselves and explain it to others. What animates a lifetime of leadership for making a company larger rather than getting richer or some other objective? And for thousands of employees, what should justify the relentless pursuit of growth? Max Weber answered the equivalent question regarding the spirit of capitalism in the West by referencing the transcendent value of material accumulation, at least for those at the top. No strict parallel is evident here, but we do see a secular analog.

In our interviews with Chinese executives, we found that the overriding rationale for the pursuit of growth is creating a better world, albeit a very material one, by making the firm's products or services available to an ever-expanding consuming public. That may sound hackneyed or even cockeyed to executive devotees of Western-style capitalism, and even more so to their institutional shareholders. But it was a central thread in our interviews, and it makes sense when we remember how little these leaders and their communities had when they started.

For example, the chief executive of a chemical company had transformed it from a small rural enterprise into a major polyester maker—

producing 2 million tons annually—with more than 7,000 employees and a public listing, but he remained centered on his village origins and its indigenous needs. As former farmers, he and his colleagues had carried their frugal ways and practical mentalities into their operations, competing on cost controls and low prices, all with an eye toward improving "the living standard of our villagers" and sharing "the economic value with everyone."

If the Protestant ethic points toward personal redemption and investor capitalism toward market value, the China Way points toward social betterment, though with no single target or constituency in mind. It could be the community, the province, the end-user, the nation—or all at the same time. Our executives' allusions varied, but a common thread was the well-being of others on earth rather than one's merit for heaven. In the words of the founder and chair of one of China's largest agribusiness companies, "I believe we must create value for the whole society, not only for our shareholders but also for our employees and community." Achieving that "balance," he said, is very important. The chief executive of a mining and steel enterprise put it this way: "We want everyone to share in the benefits of growth" since we "want everyone to live well."

For the founder and chair of a real-estate developer, growth was ultimately a service to the region where he had long constructed residences. "I may only solve the housing problem for 1 million people in thirty years, and it's a long journey ahead," he said, but "I take it as my social responsibility to let people in [my] province live in better homes." Similarly, a chemical company chair reported: "We continuously invest in public facilities, social benefits, and support for our villagers," and to that end "our company must grow and make profits" since "our mission is to increase the income of our villagers and improve their living standard."

According to these Chinese executives, growth is a public responsibility that comes with private benefits. The chief executive of a mining and metals group, for instance, drew on the human resources rationale: "If we give employees a good life, they will work hard." Jack Ma alluded to its status value, whereby public assistance confers private acceptance. "New start-ups in China," he said, "have to engage fighting on two fronts: the market front and the legitimacy front." And "in a time when the future is uncertain, people follow leaders who make personal sacrifice because it demonstrates that the leader truly believes in the future" of the country. It should be noted, however, that not all Chinese enterprises seem especially concerned about growing the company for the benefit of their employees. In fact, many have not been particularly generous with them.[5] For some business leaders, although their companies are making a profit, the key identification is with purposefulness—the extreme end of doing well by doing good. The founder and chair of an environmental company, for instance, focuses on improving land use, including deserts. Though his parents were farmers, their high status had bequeathed a severe stigma in post-revolutionary China. His mother had been raised by the wealthiest landowner in her hometown, and his father was not only university-educated but also a prominent official in the Kuomintang Party. Deemed a counter-revolutionary family in revolutionary China, the founder nonetheless managed to join the Communist Party and then local government. When an opportunity came for the son to run a salt-works company serving several million customers in a remote area, he seized the offer. Building what became an enterprise focused on developing the desert regions of China—a third of the country's landmass—he planted trees and introduced solar technology. "We are engaged in the humble business of desertification control and developing a commercial business opportunity from the desert. . . . Even until now many people are suspicious about us and wonder how we can make any money from the damn desert!" The guiding purpose of his company, he said, "is to figure out the way to solve this problem with a new business model," and "it's not about how much money we can make. Billions or trillions in profits? The ultimate success a company can achieve is to develop a new way to resolve a big problem for the country, society, and humankind."

Still, for many of the executives whose companies are listed on one stock exchange or another—Hong Kong, New York, Shanghai—shareholder returns were of concern. But in the China Way those concerns were more of an afterthought than a driving force. The executives viewed investor value as an important collateral benefit of growth, a fortunate consequence but not a defining criterion for executive decisions—more a silent partner than an existential mark. In the words of the chair of a medical-devices enterprise: "If I am doing things right, I will automatically maintain investor interest." As founder of the company and still its majority shareholder, he acknowledged that it was his "natural responsibility to protect the interests of the shareholder even if I don't mention it."

And the fact that American executives so often do mention shareholder value was to him both understandable and indicative of the differences between them and Chinese executives. American executives "must keep reminding themselves the importance of the shareholder interest," he said. "Otherwise, they will lose their job." But he would not lose his job if he failed to so remind himself.

Market capitalization, what investors universally crave in the West, hovers in the background as a result—a useful corollary of growth but not a primary driver of it. As more Chinese executives take their companies public on international exchanges and global investors come into their shares, the era of expansion for public good more than for private value may one day reverse in priority. But for the moment, growth serves as the bigger compass for mapping one's own way forward.

The growth agenda predictably makes its way into the boardroom. When asked about the criteria for identifying new non-executive prospects for their boards, many executives singled out the prospects' ability to assist the company's expansion (including the management needed for bringing this about), with virtually no reference to their shareholder monitoring or value-generating talents. The top executive of a clothing retailer with more than seven thousand stores defined his company's director-recruitment agenda as focused first on growth, then on management: "At the early stage, we invited the people who can help us to grow the business; it was utilitarian and purposeful. But now we need competent external directors to help us improve on some management weakness."

Government for Growth

The ties that Chinese executives have with government officials have often been characterized as a kind of social glue. Personal relations are often seen as a sine qua non for doing business and, thus, as a requisite for growth. State-owned enterprises by definition are built on such ties, but non-state-owned enterprises are less so. And while the leaders of the latter acknowledge the historic importance of government connections, such relations have become less salient for growth and more impersonal in the way they are exercised.

Companies in urban property development are one exception that does not negate the general practice. Since tract acquisition and resident relocation require city sanction, preexisting informal ties are enabling, if not invaluable. But for most firms, they are less personal and less essential.[6]

The more modest view of personal relations with government was well expressed by the founding executive of an advertising agency. When it came to government contact, he neither sought nor valued personal favor. "There are so many opportunities to make money in China," he observed, and public favor did not have to be one of them. At the center of exploiting those opportunities, he found, are the care and feeding of personal relations with his customers but not the equivalent with local or national officials. "Live and let live" had become a leadership motto. "We are not much impacted by the government," he explained. "I won't break the law, the government wants our tax money, and I just hope nobody harasses me."

For the top executive of a clothing retailer with more than seven thousand stores, local government was on the radar but otherwise neither a target of special concern nor a source of special assistance. And given the uncertainties of government policy makers, it is best to keep it that way. "Frankly speaking," he explained, "we are trying not to leverage the government resources. Right now, we are trying to understand the existing government policies that are related to us—for example, the tax benefits of office building construction. We always emphasize our relationship with consumers, and I think we need to keep a reasonable distance from the government, not too far nor too close. Since we are not in the real-estate business, we do not need much support from the government, so our attitude is to respect the government, however big or small the department—and always keep a low profile."

The chief executive of a mining and metals company offered a parallel appraisal: government relations are a "double-edged sword" that comes with short-term benefits but long-term risks, and as a result he sought "to avoid reliance on government resources." The chair of an electronic-components maker had been drawing on Internet technologies to move into new markets including energy, automation, and high-end equipment. Looking over his shoulder at the experience of two of the West's largest engineering companies with similar product lines, France's Schneider Electric and Germany's Siemens, he sought to reach a similar stage of "business maturity," whereby his company would be "less vulnerable to external factors like government policies."

Many of the executives we talked to view local government as an interested but otherwise uninvolved bystander, at least when the company in question is performing well. Like institutional investors in the West who give scarce attention to companies in their portfolio when all is well but weigh in when not, provincial and town officials stayed on the sidelines if their local firms were producing what officials prized—above all, jobs and revenues. Thus, for example, the chair of a chemical corporation stayed vigilant but invested little in actively cultivating public ties. "We track government policy changes but don't spend much time on the government relationship," he explained. Local officials had recognized the company's contribution to the area's development and, accordingly, "did not make trouble" for the company. "We will contact the government about our new projects," he observed, "but for key decisions like product structure, we always rely on ourselves."

Likewise, the chief executive of a leading steel company reported that he did "not put a lot of effort in building government relationships." His company had become the largest tax payer in the region and the local government thus came to him, as often as the other way around—providing, for instance, free land for the company's industrial park. The chief executive of a retail-store and supermarket operator made a similar point:

We do have a very good relationship with government. But we keep a reasonable distance from the government. Our business is growing based on our internal capability and strategy rather than relying on the government strategy. We take [seriously] our social responsibilities like creating jobs and improving the community, which will support the local government to achieve their goal for the economic growth. Besides that, we do not have a very close relationship with local government, [and] for our own strategy, we are not influenced by government.

As with companies everywhere, the Chinese executives we interviewed were attentive to the national government's macro policies, even if they bestowed no favors on the company. Trade policies, corruption crackdowns, currency revaluations, and export subsidies were of special interest, even though all of these factors were well beyond company sway. For example, the maker and seller of branded clothing with more than ten thousand retail outlets in China benefited from state subsidies for research on high-tech fabrics that facilitated its entry into Europe and the United States, yet the founder and chair saw few partisan benefits otherwise.

More Official, Less Personal

In China, individual relations with public servants and party officials have become more institutional and less personal. Such relations are expected of company executives by virtue of their leadership role but are not expected of them personally.

The chair of a textile and apparel firm limited his formal contact with government officials to what was required for growth. "I go to government," he said, "only when I have to for company business," and "I will let the business needs be the driver." He avoided unessential relationships with government officials—otherwise, he warned, "you plant a ticking bomb"—but he also cautioned that "you cannot be far from them, as you still need to deal with them to resolve some basic problems and get work done." As the chair of a chemical company put it: "We have good balance in the government relationship. It's neither very close to ask for special policies nor very far away to alienate the government."

For an agri-business company chair, government ties represent a logical outgrowth of his pursuit of growth but not of his personal temperament. "I think [the] government relationship is very important for us because our government is very powerful." But for managing it, he explained, a guiding "principle is avoiding the special relationship with any individual government official. It may provide some special advantage in the short term if you have special relationships with government officials. But it is very risky in the long run." Accordingly, he built his relationships based not on his personality but on the company's contributions. "Our government relationship," he explained, "is based on the value we created for the local community and local government," including the taxes he paid and the jobs he created. He found that the local government reciprocated the favor as his firm helped authorities meet their targets: "We believe we can build a healthy and trusted relationship with government because of our business performance." In sticking to an institutional rather than a personal script, "we may lose some good opportunities but we maintain our core values," including those of transparency, integrity, and compliance.

One reason to eschew dependence on local or national authorities is executive recognition that public drivers are far from coterminous with company objectives. Given their separate mandates, public officials can press company leaders for investments that the executives would not otherwise make for enterprise growth. In the warning of the chair of a steel company, the state has many targets. "From the positive side," he affirmed, "the local government attaches importance to the enterprise development, which can promote local employment and increase fiscal revenues. But from the negative side," he further warned, "the local government also keeps an eye on whether the enterprise is in support of the government's work."

Maintaining an arm's-length relationship with government also helped give company executives the autonomy they believed was essential to optimize their own strategic imperatives. The CEO of a food products company employing more than 20,000 people explained: "We don't like to build too close a relationship with the government. As a private company, our core competency is developed from competition in the free market. You will ignore that capability development if you spend too much effort to get the resources and support from government." A relationship with government is thus just "not sustainable," and he consequently passed up some opportunities to bid on government food concessions.

Yang Shaopeng, the chair of SITC International Holdings, a logistics company with more than seventy ships servicing Asian ports, cited much the same rationale. His customers were primarily multinational corporations, and thus, he said, "we are lucky to be in a simple industry without too much involvement of government." Since sea freight is one of the more open and market-oriented industries in China, he observed, fortunately "we do not need to deal with banks and government in most of our business operations."

Other factors contributed to keeping one's distance from government. Given the central government's episodic crackdowns on corruption, aggressively promoted by President Xi Jinping in 2015–2016, the fewer personal relations company executives have with public officials, the less likely they are to be questioned. Social distance reduces reputational risk, and it can also enhance business stature. If the commercial market perceives that a firm has benefited from government favor, several executives reported, their brand could be compromised by the insinuation that company growth came more from personal connection than from management acumen.

The extent of the formalization of government ties depends significantly on whether a government agency had the upper hand in regulating or purchasing company products. For instance, one enterprise that manufactures fireproof telecommunication cables had grown from just 200 employees a decade before our interview to more than 80,000 employees in 150 operating subsidiaries. A government policy requiring the use of such cables was an obvious public benefit, though also costly, and one that the company's chief executive favored for self-interested reasons. The central government of China now requires that telecom companies install cables that are fireproof, and local governments are responsible for enforcement. As a result, explained the chief executive, it has proven important that she work closely with local officials.

Similarly, a company whose broad range of industrial product includes steel cables for road bridges and fiber optics for telecommunications sells to a range of local governments and state-owned enterprises along with exporting to the United States. It has become one of China's largest makers of metal products, with more than 10,000 employees. Since a close relationship with public buyers was, in the words of its chief executive, a "tangible asset for the company," he had established a team of managers dedicated to the firm's relations with the state. "Government policy has a huge impact on the industries we serve," he explained, and thus his firm's relations with government were a "foundation for survival." Contributing to the local tax base and regional development was the first measure taken to facilitate that relationship, but the CEO still sought out key individuals with ties to the local government. Though the company operates through nine business units, so critical were state relations to the enterprise that the chief executive continued to personally manage the firm's liaisons with public agencies and state-owned enterprises.

One outgrowth of institutionalization was evident when company agendas differed in key areas from those of government. When in conflict, company leaders asserted that their own priorities should prevail. "Government officials focus on short-term achievements during their tenure," observed the chair of an electrical-equipment and power company, "while we focus on long-term sustainable development." Accordingly, he said, "we need to keep a good relationship with government while keeping a clear understanding [of] the potential conflicts." And with that understanding, institutional relations have prevailed over personal relations. "When we receive some requests from government officials," he continued, "we'll try our best to accomplish them if they are legitimate. But sometimes, these requests will conflict with our business interest. It is a challenge to explain it to the government. But we should not dodge the difficulty, and we must show respect to the government while insisting on our principles."

Personal relations with public servants have thus morphed from more personal to more official, with ties that are weaker, less informal, and maintained more for company advantage than for their own sake. The evolving picture is akin to what in the West might be termed government relations. This point was emphasized by the chief executive of a technology manufacturer, who explained how his company had rapidly expanded. With his own business strategy in hand, he found, it was then vital to engage his employees, to learn through "trial and error," and to build relations with the government. The CEO of a medical-device maker summed up by saying that we "still need government support" and government relations to secure it, but the relationship is now more instrumental for the company and less a culturally favored behavior.[7]

Less ambivalent is the attitude of executives toward the power of the personal in the private market, where guanxi remains a more prevalent reagent, especially with business customers. By way of example, the chair of an advertising agency defined his company's central idea as creating value for buyers, and his strategy for doing so was a matter of both reducing costs and personalizing customer contact as much as possible. "Executives from international firms have failed with Chinese customers," he said, describing what he found in his market. "They come from the US or UK, they did not emphasize detail, and they did not personalize. You have to do business in person." And, as a result, he has come to avoid Western recruits. "We'll hire Japanese managers, but not from the US or UK," he warned, "since they are not customer focused."

The power of the personal also still extends into operating within the community. The president of an international bank stressed that a Chinese private-company manager like herself had to tend first to her family and then to the community. "You do care about your neighbors," she said. "I think that's very much embedded in the Chinese culture." And if a company manager does not fulfill these obligations, this failure so violates country norms that it can undermine the respect that is essential for enterprise leadership. "Chinese people do normally care how people look at them," said one leader, and once you "become successful, you want to be respected, too."[8]

Abroad

As Chinese business leaders search for growth, going offshore has proven irresistible. Foreign markets offer new arcades—and a hedge against the vagaries of the home market. Yet the terrain abroad can be far more treacherous than at home, with its disparate customs and unfamiliar customers. Well-crafted acquisitions, however, can lessen the uncertainties, as can organic growth.[9]

Many Chinese companies have opted for mergers and acquisitions abroad in recent years. The number of outbound mergers and acquisitions rose from less than 100 annually in the early 2000s to more than 250 in the 2010s. We witnessed such growth but also the gaps in this form of expansion when Zhejiang Geely Holding Group acquired Volvo Group from Ford Motor Company. Geely chair Li Shufu had begun his business with a photo studio, selling pictures to tourists. He later turned to making refrigerators, founding Geely—a Chinese word meaning "luck" or "auspicious"—for that purpose in 1986, and then morphed it into making motorcycle parts and motorcycles themselves by 1994. Li then turned to making autos—"four wheels and two sofas," in his own colorful phrase.[10]

Like his contemporaries, Li learned as he built, attending auto shows abroad and targeting the mid-priced segment of a burgeoning market at home with some thirty models by 2009. He learned literally from others through reverse-engineering: Geely's Maple, introduced in 2002, came with a Citroën platform and an engine that resembled a Toyota powertrain. Customers found Li's cars fuel efficient, affordably priced, and utilitarian.[11]

Li Shufu chose to expand initially in underserved regions abroad, and by 2010 Geely had entered thirty-six national markets, primarily in the Middle East, Africa, Eastern Europe, and Central and South America. In a

quest for improved technologies and designs, Li acquired a 23 percent interest in a British-based maker of London taxis, Manganese Bronze Holdings (MBH), and moved much of its production to China. Li also acquired
Drive Train Systems International, an Australian transmission producer
that was the world's second-largest independent maker, allowing Geely
not only to upgrade its own transmissions but also to supply them to
other automakers. For the more developed markets, Li zeroed in on
Volvo, an upscale automaker he had been eying since 2002.

Volvo had originated in Sweden, where road conditions favored cars
with high body integrity. The company had built a brand around safety,
with three-point seat belts, rear-facing baby seats, and side airbags. It ap-
pealed to young urban professionals in the United States, and its models
became a favorite of families with children. But Volvo remained a niche
player, strong on driving safety but weak on fresh models, and it was slow
to introduce new lines such as an SUV. Ford Motor Company acquired
Volvo in 1999 for $6.45 billion, but the US financial crisis in 2008–2009
depressed its sales, and it lost $2.6 billion in the two years between 2008
and 2010.

When Ford CEO Alan Mulally began to refocus on Ford's traditional
brands, Li was ready to pounce, though not without trepidation. "It was
like a poor country boy chasing a famous international actress," Li admit-
ted. He anticipated that the distressed actress might now be available for
as little as $2.5 billion, and in the end he paid just $1.5 billion, with $1.1
billion coming from two local municipalities and even a $200 million loan
from Ford itself. Volvo would operate separately but become part of the
Geely family. "This is a historic day for Geely, which is extremely proud to
have acquired Volvo Cars," said Li. "This famous Swedish premium brand
will remain true to its core values of safety, quality, environmental care,
and modern Scandinavian design as it strengthens the existing European
and North American markets and expands its presence in China and
other emerging markets." Geely's evolving growth strategy, which currently includes expansion abroad, is summarized in Table 7.1.[12]

Some observers warned of a strategic misfit, given that Geely worked
the lower end of the auto market and Volvo the higher end, and others
doubted whether Volvo's workers would prove ready for Chinese bosses.
The disparities between the two automakers are summarized in Table 7.2,

TABLE 7.1 Geely's Evolving Growth Strategy

	1998–2003	2003–2007	2007–2016
Goal	Enter domestic auto market	Grow domestically; develop exports for emerging markets	Expand technological knowledge and assets; grow globally
Strategy	Charge low price; offer low-cost, limited features	Upgrade domestic technologies; export low-priced autos	Acquire in developed markets; upgrade technology
Outcome	Ninth-largest automaker in China	Export to 36 countries	Become a major maker in China and abroad

TABLE 7.2 Volvo Versus Geely in 2010

	Years Since Founding	Operational Philosophy	Branding
Geely	13 years	Utilitarian products, cost-based competition	Less differentiation, value for money
Volvo	83 years	Quality design, safety, and innovation	Distinctive, unique styling and safety features

and Li opted to sustain them separately. "Geely is Geely and Volvo is Volvo," he declared.

A "sea-turtle" who had worked overseas and then returned to China, Shen Freeman led the acquisition for Geely. He had been educated in engineering at South China University of Technology and at UCLA, and in business management at the University of Minnesota's Carlson School. He also brought experience in overseeing large-scale assets, most recently as the chief executive of Fiat Powertrain China and the president of Borg Warner in China. From that experience, he could appreciate the challenges ahead: "Geely is not a state-owned company," he said. "The job is not that secure compared to the stated-owned company. It is a privately owned business. You have to inspire people to work very hard day and night and weekends. The people need to be really motivated, not because they have a secure job, not because they have better pay," but because of the long-term goals of the company.

For guidance in integrating Volvo into Geely, Shen turned to a recent parallel: in 2008, India's Tata Motors had acquired Jaguar Land Rover, also from the Ford Motor Company. Here, too, a developing-country automaker acquired an established upscale Western auto producer, and in both cases the acquired enterprise came with a technology and a brand superior to those of the new owner. "I had a chance to actually learn a lot from them," said Shen. He knew well Tata Motors' chief executive, Carl-Peter Forster, and through calls and meetings, they agreed to share everything that they could learn from one another.

To facilitate the integration of Volvo into Geely, Shen set up a "Dialog and Cooperation Committee" for Geely and Volvo engineers and managers to exchange ideas and information on manufacturing methods, talent management, and product development. The committee focused on ways to combine Volvo's technological prowess with Geely's market knowledge in China as well as in developing countries. Shen dispatched a hundred Volvo engineers to a Geely research center, and he built a new Volvo plant in Chengdu. He also slated a Volvo product developed by Geely in China for export to the United States.

In all, Geely's acquisition of Volvo facilitated Geely's continuing growth domestically and then internationally. Its leadership moved people, technologies, and production ideas from one automaker to the other, new products and lower manufacturing costs resulted, and sales at home and abroad expanded. Yet, cross-border deals of this kind remain risky. International mergers and acquisitions face cultural and pricing problems, with expected failure rates of 50 percent or more.

Still, the Geely-Volvo decision has beat the odds so far, and as Chinese firms further learn how to effect international takeovers, they may serve as a template for further growth among other firms. Indeed, Shen Freeman turned the global trial into a lasting virtue. As he explained to us: "Push the company to become more global. If you only focus on the domestic market in China, you will not be successful. You need to go global. In most of the places in the global market, competition will be even stronger." And when "the competitors are stronger than those in Chinese markets," he added, "it will make Chinese competitors that much stronger if they are able to prosper abroad."

As Chinese companies acquire more firms internationally, much the same formula of learning-by-doing is likely to prevail, as was evident among the business leaders we interviewed whose firms had expanded abroad. A consumer-products maker entered the United States in the early 1970s, and after years of building, it emerged as a premier Chinese brand in the American market. Its chair described his working method for expanding abroad: "I would say that the essence of the China Way is observing the facts and working out realistic solutions. You need to adjust according to the business environment and market conditions. . . . When you enter foreign markets, you should not call it the China Way anymore. You need to know the local way. It might be the American Way when we enter the American market. As a company pursuing globalization, I think it's important to integrate into the world."

China's Slowdown in Growth—Is It So Bad?

In 2015, the increase in China's gross national product—the output of all individuals and enterprises in China—was the lowest in twenty-five years, just under 7 percent. That would be a blistering rate of increase anywhere else, but in a country accustomed to growing at almost 10 percent per year for almost the past two decades, it has been a source of concern not only for China but also for other countries for which China has become an important economic engine. Is this concern justified?

Danny Quah of the London School of Economics makes the obvious point that China is a much bigger economy now than it was even a decade ago. If the growth rate stays at 7 percent and productivity growth continues at its current level, almost 53 million new jobs would be added annually to the economy. It is hard to know with any certainty what China's real unemployment rate is, but the labor force is not growing. There is some evidence that it may have actually declined slightly, and government reports suggest that there are barely more applicants now than there are jobs—a pretty tight labor market. Certainly China's government is concerned about unemployment, but it no longer has the huge army of unemployed workers to deal with that it had a decade ago.[13]

What countries ought to care about is not the absolute size of their economy or their absolute growth but the size of their economy per citizen. In an economy growing at 5 percent where the population is increasing at 10 percent, the people are getting poorer at a rapid rate. In a country like China where the population is not growing, economic growth has translated into remarkable improvements in living standards for hundreds of millions of people. Yes, another percent increase in growth represents a huge amount of money in a big economy, but at some point, China will have to start worrying about the fact that adding an additional 8 million jobs, as each percentage point increase in GNP would do, will overheat its labor market and drive inflation up.

For the rest of the world, the growth in China's economy represents opportunities for exports. A 7 percent growth rate in a much bigger economy is far more significant than the 12 percent growth rate China experienced a decade ago—almost three times as big in absolute terms, according to Quah. Of course it would be nice for exporters if it was even bigger, but let's not be greedy.[14]

Conclusion

As leaders of private companies have mapped their way forward, they have defined the goals of their own Chinese ethic and the spirit of capitalism very differently from what we are familiar with in the West, both historically and contemporarily. Company growth rather than investor capitalism has become the driving agenda. And that growth is anchored in and rationalized by reference to providing more of a product to companies and the consumers who need it. In doing good by their customers, the company is doing well by itself.[15]

Moreover, the dogged quest for growth by private enterprises has come with little personal reliance on public connections. As a case in point, let's consider the following manufacturer. Now a diversified conglomerate with more than half a dozen business lines, ranging from steel making and auto parts to aviation services and wine making, the company was established in the late 1960s. With no more than an elementary-school education, the founder and long-term CEO learned, like so many others, by doing—though in his case he gave special credit to the upward tutoring of those he hired. "I treat my employees as my teacher," he explained, "since they have much more education than me. [And] due to my limited education background, my leadership style is always very open and encouraging of my team, especially the young people, to take more responsibility while I support them from the back." And what he has learned from more than four decades of management experience is to move swiftly into underdeveloped markets without the cobwebs of public entanglements.

The CEO further explained: "We can make important business decisions quickly since we don't have overly complicated decision processes. This is the most important thing if you want to stand out in the fierce competition, [and for us], competition has two aspects: cost advantage or technical advantage. Because of our simple and flexible management system, our cost is lower than that of . . . state-owned companies [and] we rarely use our government relationship to win projects. Instead, we rely on our strength and our brand." Many of the CEO's lieutenants had worked with him for decades, and one corollary of focusing on growth rather than value is that their personal rewards more often took the form of control and contributions than of cash. "The people who followed me for thirty years are now at the age of fifty to sixty. I told them that I may not be able to create more wealth for them but at least I bring a happy life to them."

The ideology of growth may be transitory in China, more a product of a historic stage than an enduring mindset. In the mid-twentieth century in the United States, for instance, informed observers of large corporations such as General Electric and General Motors saw their great scale and autonomous corporate power as a distinctive driving force, as well captured by Edward Mason's *The Corporation in Modern Society* in 1959 and later updated by Carl Kaysen's *The American Corporation Today* in 1996. But in decades to come, other observes concluded that the animating force in the United States had moved from large companies to large investors, the latter insisting that building ownership value must take precedence over building enterprise scale. And as the shares of large Chinese companies are increasingly held by professional investors worldwide in later years, the managerial ideology of corporate growth may also give way to shareholder return.[16]

In the meantime, company expansion prevails. And with that singular pursuit, the traditional Chinese norm of networking for its own sake is giving way to a more instrumental view of guanxi, especially with respect to public officials. Executive ties with civil servants are being redefined from personal to purposeful—ties that are built and nourished when they serve the company's agenda of growth but are otherwise no longer essential and, at times, even to be avoided.

In their arm's-length positioning, private Chinese companies are similar to Western enterprises that have long avoided substantial dependence on the state. Yet in their robust pursuit of expansion, they are different from Western firms, especially in the United States, that have long transcended expansion in the pursuit of shareholder value.

Growth as Gospel in the Words of the Fortune Makers

I hope [my enterprise] . . . become[s] a profitable company with continuously expanding new businesses which have close relationships with our fundamental business and market. The new businesses shall grow on top of our current business like the branch of a banyan tree, instead of like a wild flower far from the tree. And the company can last longer and be a place for all employees to apply their skills and talents to realize their dreams and personal values. Our vision is to become a "Green company for one hundred years."

—Chair, real-estate and financial-services company

In plain words, we cannot be too close to the government and also not too far. If you are too far, then the government cannot find you and may think you are not interested in their projects. In fact, you have to think . . . how to position your company with the city [and] once you have established a kind of partnership, most cities and their departments will welcome you—though some may not.

—Chair, real-estate developer

From a static perspective, we will continue to grow our business. But from a dynamic perspective, more and more young talents will replace the older executives and start to take charge of the business, especially those related to the new economy and mobile Internet. Ten years ago, anyone could look down on Jack Ma and Alibaba. But now Jack Ma is the wealthiest person in China and Alibaba has become the biggest e-commerce company. Compared to our own past, I am sure our company will become better and move forward in the ranking, but who knows what may happen with the younger-generation entrepreneurs. It's possible that we may be beaten by disruptive new technologies and business models.

I really think we can have a better future. Those international giant companies and big players have survived hundreds of years' competition and they must have their own strength. Therefore, we must always keep a humble and learning attitude no matter how strong our momentum is, how energetic our passion is, and how big our goal is.

—Chair, electrical equipment and power transmission company

CHAPTER 8

Governance as Partnership

> I disagree with maximizing shareholder value. . . . The most
> important stakeholder is our customers.

Corporate governance in China has undergone significant change during
the past three decades as the Chinese economy has liberalized and developed. Prior to the historic reforms initiated in 1978, the economy had
been state-owned and centrally planned; practically all enterprises were
government- or commune-controlled. With so many companies now privately owned, we have witnessed a sea change in Chinese corporate ownership and thus governance.[1]

The first significant changes in company ownership came in the 1980s
as small state-owned enterprises and collectively owned enterprises in rural areas began issuing shares to the public. As the reforms spread to larger
enterprises, the rapid increase in company-issued securities led the national government to create a capital market, and in 1990 it authorized the
cities of Shanghai and Shenzhen to establish national stock exchanges.

The exchanges were tiny at the start: just fourteen companies listed
themselves at the outset, and companies kept, on average, some two-
thirds of their shares off the market. Trading soared with the country's
rapid growth, however, and the government created the China Securities
Regulatory Commission (CSRC) in 1993 to impose regulatory oversight
on the burgeoning listings and the fast-growing capital market.

China instituted its first "Company Law" in 1994 to prohibit self-
dealing by executives and directors, and to require shareholder approval
of mergers. It added its "Securities Law" in 1998 to strengthen the CSRC's

oversight of the equity market and its powers to penalize improper behavior. China opened its equity market to foreign institutional investors in 2003, and in 2005 it initiated a program to convert yet-untraded shares into tradable securities.

With China's market reforms and accelerating growth, its national exchanges came into their own over the past decade. The Shenzhen Stock Exchange by the end of 2015 listed 1,743 companies with a total market value of ¥22 trillion; the Shanghai exchange hosted 1,076 companies with a collective value of ¥28 trillion. The combined exchanges with a total value of ¥50 trillion for its listed companies—$7.7 trillion—remained modest, however, by comparison with the New York Stock Exchange's $21 trillion capitalization.

Still, trading on the Chinese exchanges has become substantial by any benchmark, and in just three decades China had created a capital market from scratch that measured up reasonably well by Western standards. The World Bank and the International Monetary Fund gave high marks to China's many reforms. Still, much remained to be done, with company compliance and public enforcement of the reforms far from complete. A 2014 study by the Asia Corporate Governance Association rated China's actual governance practices ninth out of ten Asian countries. Among the negatives: relatively lax corporate governance rules, regulations, and enforcement, and less developed acceptance of corporate governance principles.[2]

A telling sign of the lingering underdevelopment of the Chinese equity market came with the precipitous decline in the stock market in 2015–2016. China's most important stock-market barometer, the SSE Composite Index, based on the Shanghai Stock Exchange listing, had more than doubled in the prior year—from 2,052 on June 12, 2014, to 5,166 on June 12, 2015. That was its highest value since an earlier cresting a year before the financial crisis of 2008, when the index touched 5,954 on October 1, 2007.

But just seven months after its mid-2015 peak, the SSE index lost nearly half its value, declining to 2,746 on February 15, 2016. Observers blamed macro factors for the precipitous drop, including underperforming bank loans, declining domestic demand, bloated real estate, and the speculative bubble itself. But the Chinese government also pointed to inadequate management of the equity market by the China Securities Regulatory Commission and its chairman, Xiao Gang.[3]

Xiao had blamed inexperienced investors for the 2015 bubble and its 2016 collapse, and that may well have contributed to both the run-up and the run-down. But on his own part, he had not reigned in stock purchases with borrowed funds during the run-up, and he had instituted faulty controls when the run-down commenced. The CSRC imposed circuit breakers on the exchange at the start of 2016, a trigger that would temporarily suspend all trading for fifteen minutes if share prices fell 5 percent—and for the entire day if they dropped 7 percent. It applied the circuit breakers twice during the first week of the new year, but instead of cooling the market, that stirred the opposite as investors rushed for the doors out of fear that the CSRC might shut down the market yet again. Finally appreciating the adverse impact, the CSRC abandoned the circuit breakers just four days later. And though its chairman was a member of the Communist Party and came with a gold-plated banking résumé—he had served as chairman of the Bank of China—the government forced him out on February 19, 2016.[4]

A Brief History of Corporate Governance in China

Private enterprise in China did not simply explode on the scene. It started with toe-in-the-water approaches, initially through state-owned enterprises. In the United States, where corporations began, modern corporate governance evolved over time, mainly through trial and error as companies experimented with different models and dealt with pushback from investors and the government as well. Typically, that happened in times of excess.

China pursued the opposite approach, a top-down model designed to steer corporate behavior even before there were many corporations. An important factor in these efforts was a focus on the public interest—some might say the government's interest—as a preeminent goal of governance. This took place through the use of state-owned enterprises as the pilots, operations that began completely under the control of the government, as opposed to the Western approach of letting models emerge and then correcting nascent problems.

In 1979, China's State Council drafted new controls to give the managers of state-owned enterprises more control over their operations and to get them to respond more to economic incentives. A series of pilot studies were undertaken, and the results were put together in a 1981 statement of goals as to how SOEs could be run more effectively—termed the SOE Management Responsibility System. The idea here was certainly not to expand capitalism but instead to borrow tools prominent in capitalism to improve SOE efficiency, a long-standing goal of the Communist Party.

In 1986, the Central Committee issued statements that helped define the head of each SOE as an independent business leader, not unlike a Western CEO. The idea was to give top executives operational autonomy over most aspects of their enterprise. Attempts to manage these new leadership roles with a series of short-term contracts basically failed, as they generated perverse incentives to hit targets at the expense of enterprise health.

A major development occurred in 1993 with the creation of the "Company Law," which began to move state-owned enterprises toward separate legal entities with ownership that included investors other than the government. As a practical matter, the SOEs were now elevated in status to being on a par with public-sector institutions, not explicitly subordinate to them. The development of a capital market with stock exchanges and listed companies followed soon after.

After joining the World Trade Organization in 2001, China issued its Code of Corporate Governance of Listed Companies in 2002. That code borrowed explicitly from Western documents and outlined the institutions of modern corporations, including boards of directors, their role, and their ethical obligations. In 2004, the State Council tightened up rules concerning the operation of China's capital markets. Company Law and Securities Law regulations issued in 2006 introduced detailed practices to be followed by listed companies in order to protect not only their shareholders but also the public.[5]

Distinctive Features of Chinese Corporate Governance

Corporate governance practices in many countries have displayed modest convergence toward Western standards in recent years. Some countries have emulated Britain's 1992 Cadbury Code or America's 2003 Sarbanes-Oxley Act and 2010 Dodd-Frank Wall Street Reform Act, but most still follow a distinct set of practices. In building its own system, China has been no exception. Three features of Chinese capitalism have affected its emergent private corporate governance, making for a notable contrast with practices

TABLE 8.1 Ownership Concentration of China's
Largest Listed Companies, 2007–2015

Year	Percentage Held by Largest Shareholder	Percentage Held by Five Largest Shareholders
2007	36.0	52.0
2008	36.3	51.8
2009	36.6	52.2
2010	36.5	53.6
2011	36.3	54.4
2012	36.9	56.0
2015	35.2	52.6

Source: China Center for Economic Research, 2015; database updated by the authors.
Note: Excludes financial companies and those with insufficient data.

in the United States: (1) highly concentrated ownership, (2) complex owner-ship structures, and (3) weak markets for corporate control.[6]

Highly Concentrated Ownership. Company ownership is widely diffused in the United States, with relatively few shareholders controlling more than several percent of the shares of any given firm. By contrast, ownership in China's listed firms remains highly concentrated. On March 31, 2015, of the 2,689 companies listed on the Shanghai and Shenzhen stock exchanges, the largest owner held 35.2 percent of the companies' shares on average, and the five largest controlled 52.6 percent—fractions that were virtually unchanged from the ownership percentages of 2007 (see Table 8.1). In-deed, the high concentration of ownership has remained relatively stable since the founding of the exchanges. And two-fifths of the listed compa-nies—39.7 percent as of March 2014—were fully controlled by the state it-self. As a consequence, the largest owners exert far more direct control over Chinese companies than is common among their Western counter-parts. Directors and executives of American firms have learned to exercise a degree of independence from their largest owners, applying their own professional judgments to management decisions that may differ from what their largest owners might seek if asked. Chinese directors and execu-tives exhibit less independence, since their largest owners are far (i.e., ten times) larger and thus are more often asked if not always heeded.[7]

Complex Ownership Structures. Most major American publicly traded companies are owned and operated as separate entities that work independently of one another to optimize investor returns. Many listed Chinese firms, by contrast, are owned or controlled by an unlisted parent, and many of the listed firms in turn control other listed companies. According to a study conducted by the Shanghai Stock Exchange in 2005, 91.2 percent of its non-state-owned firms employed such a pyramid structure, opening the way for the malfeasance of what is often termed "tunneling"—an arrangement in which a controlling firm extracts earnings or assets from subordinate firms whose lesser owners would disapprove if the transfer came to light. A 2006 study by the Shanghai Stock Exchange confirmed that such practices, often termed "connected transactions," had by then become widespread: of the 1,377 firms it studied, 35 percent had misappropriated funds, totaling ¥48 billion, from their parent companies. As a sign of the problem's vexing breadth, China declared pyramid misappropriations to be criminal offenses in its 2006 company code. Despite their criminalization, the prevalence of connected transactions had declined slowly. In 2001, 55.1 percent of all Chinese listed companies had such transactions, and ten years later that fraction had declined to only 48.6 percent. As shown in Figure 8.1, the number of companies with connected transactions rose in the period from 2000 to 2010. The implication is that directors of Chinese companies are less able than their American counterparts to exercise their monitoring function on behalf of all shareholders, not just on behalf of the small number of very large owners.[8]

Weak Markets for Corporate Control. Because two-thirds of a typical firm's shares before 2005 were held by the state or retained by companies themselves and were thus not traded, an American-style market for corporate control in which companies, hedge funds, and activist investors compete for sway over other publicly traded firms was virtually nonexistent. With the formal shift of yet-untraded company shares onto the open market completed by 2007, however, active contests for control became more feasible, and China became one of the world's fastest-growing markets for mergers and acquisitions, moving directors more into the limelight as the formal arbiters of whether to accept or resist an offer. In 2005, according to the Institute for Mergers, Acquisitions, and Alliances, 1,951 mergers and acquisitions totaled $71 billion in value for transactions that

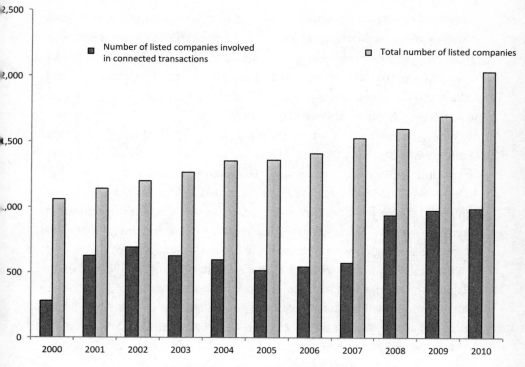

**FIGURE 8.1 Number of Chinese
Listed Companies Involved in Connected Transactions**

Source: Compiled by the authors based on information from the Shanghai Gildata Service Company.

involved at least one Chinese company, but by 2015, 5,986 transactions totaled $775 billion in value, a more than ten-fold increase in dollar amount over a decade.

Chinese Governance

As the Chinese public-equity market matured, the organization, composition, and practices of boards of some publicly listed companies in China came to acquire features similar to those of American firms. Chinese governing boards have nonetheless followed a distinctive path in the areas of (1) board structure, (2) shareholder rights, (3) disclosure and transparency, (4) corporate social responsibility, (5) and the role of directors.[9]

Board Structure. China has adopted a two-tier board structure similar to the German convention of having a supervisory board overseeing a board of directors. The Chinese supervisory board is required to have at least three members, and a third of the members must be employee representatives. In principle the supervisory board monitors the directors and management, but in practice virtually all supervisory board members are from inside the firm, and the supervisory board essentially rubber-stamps the decisions of directors and management.

The board in the American system sits at the hub of company governance, while in China the annual shareholder meeting has emerged more front and center. Chinese company law endows the shareholder meeting with powers normally reserved for the board in the United States. Still, given that those few attending the annual shareholder meeting cannot effectively exercise discretionary authority in that venue, most of the real decision-making power remains in the hands of management.

Chinese regulations require a firm to designate one individual as the "legal person representative" to act on behalf of the firm. This position is normally assumed by the chair of the board, and this rule has had the effect of investing greater power in the board chair than is common among American companies when the chair and CEO roles are separated.

Shareholder Rights. China's Company Law requires greater disclosure of information to stockholders than is common in the West. Shareholders elect directors and vote at shareholder meetings, but they also have access to company charters, shareholder lists, and meeting minutes of both the supervisory board and the board of directors.

To protect minority shareholders at companies where ownership is concentrated and pyramids prevail, companies are required to follow formal procedures for entering into related-party financial transactions. It is now mandatory, for instance, that shareholders approve a company's transactions with a controlling company, and the controlling company cannot vote their shares on such transactions. Minority shareholders have the right to introduce motions, convene, or even preside over shareholder meetings, and they can adopt a cumulative voting system for electing directors and supervisors.

Disclosure and Transparency. Compared to the disclosure requirements in most Western countries, those in China have been vague and enforcement has been weak. A 2003 study by the Shanghai Stock Exchange reported that "distortion of accounting information is quite common," and a 2007 China Securities Regulatory Commission report concluded that "there are still many cases of management entrenchment or 'insider control' in capital markets," and that "fraud, price manipulation and insider trading by securities professionals" are still evident. Reporting irregularities remain frequent as well. Among Chinese listed companies in the period from 1999 to 2007, 13.4 percent restated their financials; of those, more than a third involved restatements of key indicators and more than two-fifths adjusted their earnings as a result of accounting errors. By one appraisal, financial information disclosure at many companies remains irregular and, in some cases, whitewashed.[10]

The People's Congress strengthened the penalties for market manipulation and explicitly prohibited the widespread company practice of maintaining two sets of accounting records. The Ministry of Finance imposed a set of accounting standards that are largely in line with international reporting principles. The CSRC in 2007 imposed stricter requirements on the disclosure of company information, and the result has been improved reporting, though the pace has been modest. In a 2013 study of the amount of information disclosed by Chinese companies, an aggregate index of 62.3 in 2004 had barely budged by 2013, reaching just 63.2. This is still one more sign that non-dominant owners have substantially less than a full line of sight into their companies' management operations and financial performance, weakening their ability to monitor their investments or to insist that directors do so on their behalf.[11]

Corporate Social Responsibility. China has placed formal emphasis on corporate social responsibility, more so than is common in many Western economies. The Company Law of 2006, for instance, requires that a company "observe social norms and business ethics standards, operate honestly, accept monitoring by government and general public, and assume its social responsibility."[12]

The exchanges have gone even further. Shenzhen demands that listed companies "consider" the interests of their creditors (rather than sacrificing creditors' interests for the sake of shareholder value) and provide creditors with access to financial and operational data. Shenzhen-listed companies must also "commit themselves to social welfare services like environmental protection and community development in order to achieve social harmony."[13]

Judging from the number of company reports on listed companies' social activities, the precept of corporate responsibility is receiving greater attention. In 1999, only a single publicly listed company issued a report on its social programs. A decade later, 533 publicly traded firms did so, and by 2012, 626 companies were reporting on their social responsibility activities.[14]

Vanke's separate report on its social responsibility in 2014 is indicative of how Chinese companies have scaled up their public reporting. Founded more than three decades ago, Vanke began to publish a separate accounting in 2007. Now, its seventy-page report catalogs a host of social engagements, ranging from the 150,000 "runners" who joined organized races for personal health to housing for the elderly, support for community festivals, child care, green technologies, air purification, renewable energy, disaster relief, sustainable development (e.g., no flooring products from endangered wood species), and even protection of snow leopards and their mountain habitats in Tibet's Mount Everest region.[15]

The Role of Directors. Prior to 2001, no law or regulation required that any directors be independent of management. But the China Securities Regulatory Commission now requires that a third of the seats on a publicly listed company board be held by independent directors, and many companies have reached that threshold. A 2004 study by the Shenzhen Stock Exchange found that independent directors constituted nearly a third of the board members, and on occasion they have exercised an independent role. In one widely publicized incident, for example, an independent director challenged related-party transaction by the board chair of a prominent food maker, and upon CSRC investigation, the company ousted its chair.[16]

The 2006 Company Law strengthened the obligations of directors to be disciplined by both "duty of loyalty" and "duty of care," though it defined neither. It did state that the loyalty obligations included no use of company funds for personal use, no loans to others without authorization, and no disclosure of proprietary information, self-dealing, or bribes. It also held directors personally liable if director decisions violated state regulations or company charters.[17]

The monitoring quality of corporate governance has steadily, if slowly, improved over the past decade. Drawing on the extent to which directors are independent, appropriately paid, and empowered to act, a comprehensive governance index rose steadily, if modestly, from 52.6 in 2004 to 61.7 a

TABLE 8.2 Governance Index for China's Listed Companies, 2004–2013

Year	Index
2004	52.6
2005	53.2
2006	55.4
2007	55.7
2008	57.4
2009	57.9
2010	60.3
2011	60.8
2012	61.2
2013	61.7

Source: Nankai University, 2015.

decade later, as shown in Table 8.2. Chinese company boards are, as a result, passably more able to monitor management. The strengthened index indicates that directors are better able to speak out in the boardroom, are better compensated if the company performs well, and have greater discretion to decide independently of management without retribution.

The Boardroom as Watchdog

For more than a century, American companies have been creating and managing boards of directors—a noble concept. Boards of directors are required by state laws and regulated by US rules to ensure that the controllers are controlled. Everybody needs a watchdog, if for no other reason than to be accountable to someone.[18]

Lenovo's Governance: Building a Partnership for Globalization

While China's private-company boards have in recent years modestly strengthened the capacity of directors to oversee executive decisions and performance on behalf of company owners—the official monitoring function for the board—some companies have more fully redesigned their boards to help lead the company in partnership with the executives. Lenovo offers a case in point. Though director monitoring of management on behalf of shareholders is weaker in China than in the United States, Chinese directors have stepped forward at some companies to lead in partnership with management. And that change has been driven by company executives who have sought informed and committed inside counsel on tangible business challenges.

Before Lenovo's acquisition of the IBM Personal Computer Division in 2005, non-independent directors outnumbered independent directors by four to three. Lenovo's post-acquisition board, by contrast, was divided among five executive and non-independent directors, three private-equity directors, and three independent directors. By 2016, six of its nine directors were independent, and five of those were from outside China.[19]

Before the IBM-PC acquisition, board meetings had always been conducted in Chinese; after the acquisition, because all but one director spoke English and several spoke no Chinese, English became the medium of expression. Going into the acquisition, the executive chairman and chief executive were both Chinese; coming out of the acquisition, the executive chairman was Chinese and the CEO American. Of the top management team in 2004, all were Chinese; of the eighteen members of the top management team in 2007, six were from greater China, one from Europe, and eleven from the United States. Ma Xuezheng, the company's CFO at the acquisition moment, declared at the time: "This is going to be very much an international company operated in an international fashion."[20]

A large part of the Lenovo board's transformation entailed building an active strategy- and leadership-focused partnership between the directors and executives. "The IBM-PC acquisition is a watershed," observed Lenovo founder Liu Chuanzhi. "Before that point," he said, "the board of directors did not play much role." The board had mainly been concerned, he reported, with company audits and executive pay. Independent non-executive directors prior to the IBM acquisition were viewed by Lenovo as present largely to protect minority stockholders—in this case, investors other than the Chinese Academy of Sciences. Liu and his colleague Yang Yuanqing reconstituted the board to go well beyond that limited focus, adding international directors, improving board capacity to render guidance to the executive team, and, more generally, creating a governing body that is more globally informed, independent, and proactive—prerequisites for leading the company.

The decision to add international directors was largely driven by the reported need for the board to bring more global "vision" into the boardroom. "Now," said Yang, "internationalization is our key consideration as we are taking on international business." This required directors who would bring fresh insight into how Lenovo could make inroads into the worldwide market share of its larger rivals—Dell Computer at 18 percent and Hewlett-Packard at 16 percent in 2005—and at the same time hold on to the home market share against its smaller rivals, including Acer at 5 percent and Fujitsu at 4 percent in 2005.[21]

The restructuring of the Lenovo board following the IBM purchase also brought the directors into guiding the integration of two distinct operating styles. IBM had built up strong, enduring relations with its select corporate customers; Lenovo, by contrast, had created a largely "transactional" exchange with its many retail customers. Although large-enterprise relations had been the staple of IBM's PC sales, management anticipated greater growth among small consumers. But identifying the optimal areas for growth outside of China and specifying effective ways of reaching them were uncertain and risky judgment calls, encouraging management to seek director guidance.

Lenovo's board also became directly engaged in decisions on executive succession, an arena that had not previously been its prerogative. At the time of the purchase, the IBM executive responsible for the PC division, Stephen M. Ward, Jr., had been the logical candidate for the role of chief executive, with Yang to serve as executive chairman. Their dual appointment was largely an executive decision, but within months it became evident to the board's strategy committee—consisting of executives Liu Chuanzhi and Yang Yuanqing and directors James Coulter and William Grabe—that the former IBM executive was not the right person to lead the combined enterprise, given the specific challenges it faced, starting with the need for greater supply-chain efficiencies.

Yang and Liu worried, however, that the unexpected exit of the top American executive so soon after the acquisition could cast a shadow over their effort to internationalize the firm. Neither knew the international computer industry well enough to identify a strong replacement. Thus, it fell to American non-executive directors Coulter and Grabe to identify several candidates for succession, including William Amelio, then head of Dell Computer's Asian operations. Nor were Yang and Liu familiar with the process of replacing an American chief executive, but the private-equity directors had often done so. Coulter and Grabe and a third non-executive director, Shan Weijian of private equity (PE) firm Newbridge

Capital, worked with Liu and Yang to replace Ward with Amelio. "It would have been much more difficult to replace Stephen Ward," Liu reported, "had it not been for the help of the three PE reps."[22]

Soon, a host of other major issues was laid before the directors for vetting and decision making—among them, how long to retain the IBM logo; what acquisitions to make; which adjacencies, such as servers, to consider; and whether to build devices that bridge laptops and telephones. Lenovo subsequently considered acquiring personal-computer maker Packard Bell, for instance, and the directors took an active role in deciding on whether to proceed and what to pay. "Everybody was involved," reported non-executive director Shan Weijian, "because this is a large issue for the entire company." Lenovo decided to back off—another PC maker, Gateway, was later acquired by Taiwan's Acer—and the board's deliberations proved critical in reaching that decision.

None of this happened of its own accord. For instance, the directors and executives adopted a rule that all directors must attend all board meetings, which they rotated around the world, or send a predesignated alternate. Thus, in the wake of the IBM acquisition, directors came to play a company leadership role by quickly replacing the chief executive, deciding against an acquisition, and facilitating cross-cultural integration of widely different entities. The restructuring of the Lenovo board to more effectively serve as a partner with management, from before the acquisition of the IBM-PC line in 2003 to after it in 2007 and then a decade later in 2016, is shown in Table 8.3.

Vanke's Governance: Dispersing Ownership for Company Autonomy

Chinese executives have had to contend with an additional governance challenge—namely, having state owners that they no longer want. The reasons are varied, but they include a belief that state owners—and their representatives on the board—are likely to press for public goals such as local employment or, conversely, for private gains through tunneling or other actions that come at the expense of minority shareholders. Whatever the sources of these distortions, company leaders have pressed for greater dispersion of ownership as a means of giving them and their directors greater autonomy to pursue their own strategies for business

TABLE 8.3 Directors of Lenovo, 2003, 2007, and 2016

Executive and Non-Independent Directors, 2003			
Liu Chuanzhi	China	Executive Chairman	Founded Legend in 1984; Chairman of Legend Holdings
Yang Yuanqing	China	Chief Executive Officer	Joined Legend in 1989; became CEO in 2001
Ma Xuezheng	China	Chief Financial Officer	Joined Legend in 1992; formerly at Chinese Academy of Sciences (CAS)
Zeng Maochao	China	Non-executive director	Former director of Institute of Computing Technology at CAS
Independent Non-Executive Directors			
Chia-Wei Woo	Hong Kong	Non-executive director	Former president of Hong Kong University of Science and Technology
Lee Sen Ting	United States	Non-executive director	Managing director of WR Hambrecht, formerly Hewlett-Packard
Wai Ming Wong	United Kingdom	Non-executive director	Chartered accountant; CEO of Roly International Holdings (Singapore)

Executive and Non-Independent Directors, 2007			
William Amelio	United States	Chief Executive Officer	Formerly VP-Asia for Dell, NCR, Honeywell, and IBM
Ma Xuezheng	China	Chief Financial Officer	Joined Legend in 1992; formerly at Chinese Academy of Sciences (CAS)
Liu Chuanzhi	China	Non-executive director	Legend founder; chairman of Legend Holdings; formerly at CAS
Zhu Linan	China	Non-executive director	Joined Legend in 1989; managing director of Legend Capital
Private-Equity Directors			
James Coulter	United States	Non-executive director	Founding partner, Texas Pacific Group (TPG)
William Grabe	United States	Non-executive director	Managing director and private-equity investor at General Atlantic (GA)
Shan Weijian	China	Non-executive director	Managing director and private-equity investor at Newbridge Capital
Independent Non-Executive Directors			
John W. Barter	United States	Non-executive director	Director of BMC Software; formerly CFO at Allied Signal
Chia-Wei Woo	Hong Kong	Non-executive director	Former president of Hong Kong University of Science and Technology
Lee Sen Ting	United States	Non-executive director	Managing director of WR Hambrecht, formerly Hewlett-Packard
Wai Ming Wong	United Kingdom	Non-executive director	Chartered accountant; CEO of Roly International Holdings (Singapore)

(continues on following page)

TABLE 8.3 Directors of Lenovo, 2003, 2007, and 2016 (*continued*)

Executive Director and Non-Independent Directors, 2016			
Yang Yuanqing	China	Executive Chairman	Joined Legend in 1989, became CEO in 2001
Zhu Linan	China	Non-executive director	Joined Legend in 1989; president of Legend Capital
Gordon D. H. Orr	United Kingdom	Non-executive director	Former managing partner, McKinsey Asia
Independent Non-Executive Directors			
Nicolas Allen	United Kingdom/ Hong Kong	Non-executive director	Former partner, PricewaterhouseCoopers
William Tudor Brown	United Kingdom	Non-executive director	Founder of ARM Holdings
William O. Grabe	United States	Lead director	Advisory director and private-equity investor at General Atlantic (GA)
Ma Xuezheng	China	Former CFO	Joined Legend in 1992; formerly at Chinese Academy of Sciences (CAS)
Tian Suning	China	Non-executive director	Founder and chairman of China Broadband Capital Partners
Jerry Chih-Yuan Yang	United States	Non-executive director	Co-founder and former CEO of Yahoo; former director of Cisco Systems and Alibaba

Source: Lenovo annual reports.

growth without public distractions. We see this in Wang Shi's building of his board at Vanke, and in the primacy of company expansion over shareholder value as business leaders build the China Way.

Wang Shi founded Vanke in 1984 as a spin-off from state-owned Shenzhen Regional Development Company. And while appreciating his parentage, Wang believed that his way forward would require a governing board that was beholden to no single stakeholder. Otherwise his business decisions would be subjected to second-guessing or even overruling by directors with governing agendas different from his own for fast growth.

When the Shenzhen government started privatization of its state-owned-enterprises in 1988, four years after Vanke's founding, Wang was the first to embrace the plan, though not without strong resistance from both inside and out. Many employees feared their loss of state protection, which at the time included lifetime-job guarantees, the Iron Rice Bowl, comprehensive health care, and assured retirement benefits. If workers became just "hired hands," they faced unemployment and even destitution if the company later faltered. The regional development company, the parent, feared losing a cash cow, and Vanke was already showing strong results. But following extensive negotiations with employees and authorities, Wang's plan to privatize was accepted.

Going private, however, brought its own unexpected challenges. China had not yet established its stock exchanges, forcing Wang Shi to personally recruit investors since an initial public offering was yet undefined. With professional guidance from a Hong Kong securities firm, Wang secured buyers for all 28 million shares by his deadline, including many private investors such as Huawei founder Ren Zhengfei, who purchased some 200,000 shares. The primary buyer, however, was the Shenzhen Regional Development Company itself, acquiring a 60 percent stake in its progeny, later reduced to 30 percent.

Though now the largest single owner with a stake sufficient to exercise de facto control, the SRDC had no expertise in the real-estate industry, nor did it have capital to invest in Vanke's ambitious expansion plans. Believing that he would be burdened by a disinterested or even divergent owner, Wang worked to disperse ownership of his company. He achieved this by listing the company's A-shares—stock that could be purchased only by Chinese nationals—on the Shenzhen Stock Exchange in 1991, and then listing Vanke's B-shares in 1993 for foreign purchase, raising ¥640 million and diluting the SRDC's ownership share. He spun off Vanke's retail business to the China Vanguard Group by bringing Vanguard into a 14 percent ownership stake in Vanke. In dispersing his company ownership, Wang worked to dilute the influence of any one investor and, in so doing, erected a governing board beholden to no single interest other than Vanke itself. By 2015, its board of ten directors, chaired by Wang Shi, comprised five company executives; two representatives of a major owner, the China Resources Group; and three independent directors.

In dispersing his ownership to reduce any single shareholder's influence on it, Wang Shi had the unintended effect of making his company more vulnerable to an unwanted takeover. As the equity market in China has become more open, and firm ownership is no longer so strongly linked to its founding parent, the market for takeovers, mergers, and acquisitions has prospered. As a result, Vanke came under an unsolicited takeover targeting in 2015 by a Shenzhen-based property and finance company, Baoneng Group, which built up a 24.3 percent stake in Vanke, making it the largest single shareholder. In classic white-knight defense, Vanke encouraged a friendly investor, Anbang Insurance Group, to acquire a 7 percent stake, and in a poison-pill defense, Vanke authorized the issuance of new shares and recruited a strategic investor.[23]

Alibaba's Governance:
Restraining Ownership for Management Control

Alibaba had enjoyed dramatic profits and growth from its cluster of online businesses. Taobao and TMall were flourishing, and Alipay had become a substantial source of growth in terms of both revenues and income. Its capital needs grew as its online platforms required continued investment, and it attracted extensive attention as a prospective candidate for a public offering. There were few precedents for a public listing on the scale anticipated for the company.

Jack Ma sought to create two classes of stock, one for public investors and one for himself and thirty of his first employees. He worried about the vagaries of the capital market, and his small set of "Alibaba partners" would bring a long-term commitment to the firm and insulate it from short-term investor pressures. Ma had first considered listing his company on the Hong Kong Stock Exchange, but it insisted on its principle of "one stock for one vote." The notion of the Alibaba partners having a more influential separate class of stock was unpalatable to Hong Kong, but the New York Stock Exchange was open to a two-class offering.

For listing abroad, however, China required the creation of an offshore holding company in which international investors would own stock as well as a wholly owned foreign entity in China that would serve as an intermediary between the holding company and the operating company. After much debate, Alibaba opted to list in New York. The public offering at $22 billion—for a company whose sales were still almost entirely within greater China—drew extensive investor and media attention, attesting to its prospective performance.[24]

But the unusual governance that came with the offering also brought its critics. One advocate of shareholder sovereignty, for instance, questioned the structure's impact on investor rights in several areas. First, investors would see only returns based on transfers from the operating company to the wholly owned foreign entity in China, and that could reduce transparency into Alibaba's actual operations. Second, Alibaba partners owned just 13 percent of the stock at the time of the offering but they retained control of key decisions including director appointments, and that could open the way for related-party transactions. And finally, international investors would be able to exercise only arm's-length influence on any change in control.[25]

Jack Ma responded that investors would nonetheless benefit over the longer term because he and his partners were committed to just that. In the short run, however, the value of Alibaba's stock languished in the months after the issue. The value of its shares had dropped by 19.1 percent from the initial public offering on September 19, 2014, to May 2, 2016—a period in which the S&P 500 Index gained 2.6 percent. A potential contributing factor: China's State Administration for Industry and Commerce had reported a significant presence of counterfeit goods on the company's website, Taobao. Upon protest from Alibaba, the agency withdrew its report, but concerns about its listing of counterfeit goods evidently worried investors. Kering, a French luxury-goods dealer, alleged that Alibaba was not doing enough to identify and limit counterfeit branded products.[26]

The stock exchange and equity investors had to accept an unusual ownership model, with Alibaba's founding partners retaining control over major governance decisions including appointment of its directors—and with reduced transparency for investors, given the separation of the operating and holding companies. But Jack Ma and his partners had opted to accept the short-term market doubts as a price for their governing assurance of long-term growth.

Corporate Governance for Company Leadership

Governing boards of some non-stated-owned Chinese companies remain in the Stone Age, given to neither monitoring of nor partnering with management. This is much akin to the role that many American directors played at the height of the "managerial revolution" after the mid-twentieth-century split between owners and managers left management firmly in the driver's seat. Non-executive directors are in the room but are little engaged in the Chinese company's affairs, whatever their prescribed function. By regulatory requirement, they must review and approve financial statements, review expansionary steps, and perform their fiduciary duties in the compensation and audit committee meetings. But for partnering with management to set strategy or even direct the company, they are still missing in action.[27]

Consider governance at one of China's largest makers of electrical equipment for industry. The chief executive had founded the firm in the early 1990s and by the latter part of the decade had begun inviting non-executive directors onto its board. Though some brought prior company experience, their limited personal stakes in the company resulted in limited attention. The non-executive directors, the CEO found, "don't care for the company," never challenged his decisions, and as a consequence "don't play important roles." In his blunt summary: "I am the first shareholder, and I have complete control in making decisions."

In the similar experience of the chair of an interior design and decoration company, non-executive directors have had "limited impact" when his business was growing, which was most of the time. They had never rejected a proposal from him, and they simply did "not have much to do." The chief executive of a computer and IT equipment enterprise reported from his own experience that Chinese directors were largely under the CEO's thumb, including his own—in part, because many had come as friends. In the summary of two observers based at the French business school INSEAD, corporate governance of many listed firms in China is "still weakly developed."[28]

At other companies, however, non-executive directors have come to do far more than nothing. And for that, executives have sought those who bring distinct and diverse skill sets to the boardroom, a precondition for making a difference in the boardroom. The CEO of a computer and electronic products company sought for his board those who brought "professional competency and experience" in running companies very different from his own. It might seem odd that the outsiders came with no expertise for leading a company like his own, but that was the point. "We definitely do not want . . . senior managers from private companies," said the CEO. He instead preferred senior managers from state-owned and even foreign-owned companies, since "we ourselves are already too familiar with private-company operations. By having non-executive directors with working experience in state-owned companies, we can learn how they balance the interests among shareholders, employees, and the company."

That balancing of stakeholder interests is very different from what we often hear in the West, especially the United States, where the weighting is tilted toward the owners. Increasing total shareholder return—dividends plus growth in stock value—is the key metric and the mantra for American company performance. Executive pay is strongly contingent upon its delivery, and the director mandate is to ensure it above all else. Falling short on expected growth in total shareholder return is a sure way for an executive to be shown the exit and directors to face proxy challenge.[29]

Not so among many private companies in China. The chair of a steel company put it bluntly: "I think employees are very important stakeholders," he avowed, "so we first balance the interest of employees, and then the interest of shareholders." The balancing is not zero-sum, however, as it is premised on the logic that well-performing employees are among the drivers of value. "I think the shareholders can understand it," he said, "because employees create value for the shareholders." And his shareholders, he reported, had never challenged his priorities on this. Imagine, by contrast, the adverse reaction of equity analysts and professional investors if an American executive disclosed that employee welfare came before shareholder gain—and that company directors were in agreement.

The chair of a diversified industrial company even went so far as to characterize his firm as "not a profit-oriented business"—though it had been profitable. "My management philosophy is to bring the success to our management team, employees, and business partners," he explained, and accordingly, "my first priority is whether our partners, suppliers, and distributors are happy or not. I won't do anything to make money that leaves them unhappy." Though costly to his owners in the near term, he had opted for profit sharing with employees and generous investing in R&D. "I am not sure if this is the right management philosophy," he confessed, and "the numbers on our financial reports may not be as good as at other companies," but that was not his objective anyway. With the multi-stakeholder mindset, at the end of the day, he said, "I feel happy and good about myself."

Given that balancing among stakeholders, with shareholders not deemed as first among equals, non-executive directors on engaged boards are often asked by their executives to focus on issues of general management, whether talent development or business strategy. The chair of a personal and health care company established in the early 1990s, for instance, reported that a key source of sustainable advantage for his company had been the quality of his employees. "It is the people," he declared, and for managing his human talent he had sought guidance from his directors on how to build up the ranks.

When informed by experience and diverse in background, Chinese directors are seen by their executives as aiding the pathfinding that has defined so much of their pioneering of the China Way. We had seen this at Lenovo and Vanke, and we found it among many of the other companies at which we interviewed. The chair of a diversified industrial products company, for instance, reported that his directors have exercised a hand in major verdicts on products and investments. "There is a limitation in an individual's information-processing capability," he confessed in referencing himself. "It is hard to make a decision by gut feeling when you are overwhelmed by information," and thus, he said, "I will listen to the board before making any major decisions."

In some cases, reactive guidance has morphed into director preemption. For instance, the diversified industrial products company CEO we talked to had not thought it wise to invest in water treatment for environment protection, but his directors actively pressed him to do so, arguing that the market would one day prove strong and profitable for the company. He did not concur with their judgment, but he deferred to the board on the premise that it would at least be "a good thing for the society" if not for the company itself.

While none of our chief executives referenced the value that their non-executive directors might bring to the monitoring of management, many cited their substantive guidance, and when we probed for the criteria involved in recruiting new executives to their board for that purpose, diversity in management experience proved paramount. For Shen Freeman, vice-chair of China Geely Volvo, for example, selecting non-executive directors was a matter of bringing a range of management capabilities into the boardroom—from finance and accounting to operations and marketing—that his directors had learned at other publicly listed companies.

The chair and founder of a company providing private educational services sought non-executive directors with direct operations experience in international markets. For that, he had brought onto his board the founder and CEO of a web-services company with more than 40,000 employees as well as another individual who served as the chief executive at a large Internet company. Both brought experience in the global equity market to the board table.

In selecting non-executive directors for a company in real estate, construction materials, and tourism, its chief executive wanted "to make sure that their expertise or their background brings benefits to the whole group," and for that, the main selection criterion had been their expertise. So, too, for the human resources director of a paper-products company. In picking his outside directors, knowledge of his firm's industry was uppermost, and that had proven especially valuable during five board meetings devoted to a major joint-venture decision. For the chair of a producer of automobile and industrial glass, six non-executive directors on his board of nine vetted company decisions, such as whether to acquire a production facility in southeast China from a company also controlled by the majority shareholder. They added value to the decision since they not only were experts on the management of technology but also were independent from both the majority shareholder and local government.

On the substantive engagement of non-executive directors in company leadership, considerable variation is evident, with some executives keeping their directors largely in the dark and others enlisting their expertise. Though the monitoring potential of non-executive directors is rarely referenced, their strategic guidance is frequently cited. And for that, direct experience as executives—or at least as directors of other companies—has become a prerequisite. With that expertise, non-executives can partner with company executives in the leadership of the company.

Conclusion

We have seen governance among large private Chinese companies go from zero to sixty in just a matter of decades. Prior to the liberalization of the 1980s, no firms were publicly traded and corporate governance in its Western conception was unknown. In the quarter century since the first stock listings in Shanghai and Shenzhen, private companies have constructed a governance scaffolding that shows some resemblance to the Western canon. Yet it has also taken on a distinctive hue and constitutes still another element of China's own path forward.

With the exception of a handful of family-controlled companies in the United States, such as Estée Lauder Companies, Ford Motor Company, and the New York Times, stock ownership is now widely dispersed among the large publicly traded American firms. The largest single holding among S&P 500 companies in 2015 averaged just several percentage points, compared with more than 35 percent among large Chinese companies. Given that dominance, China has taken steps to strengthen the board's autonomous defense of investor rights, including stronger disclosure rules and minority-shareholder protections, and an insistence that at least a third of its directors are independent of management. Given the continuing dominance of single shareholders in China, however, and given the prevalence of pyramid structures and a weak market for corporate control, it comes as no surprise that the monitoring function of the board in China is less developed than that in the West.

At the same time, akin to developments in the United States and elsewhere, Chinese directors have come to play an increasing role in partnering with executives to help define and lead the company's direction. We saw this at Lenovo after it acquired the IBM Personal Computer Division in 2005 and vaulted overnight into the world market. Sparked by that, company executives transformed the board's function from one of modestly monitoring management to one of aggressively advising management. And we saw another manifestation of the same development at Vanke, where the chief executive worked to reduce the dominating presence of a single large shareholder and its representation in the boardroom so that all of his non-executive directors could bring independent, non-partisan strategic guidance to the company.

The developments that we have witnessed at Lenovo and Vanke are evident at many—though not all—private companies in China. Some still draw little guidance from their directors, supporting the board as a matter of state mandate but securing little advice from it. Yet at many other firms among the seventy-two where we interviewed top executives, we found evidence that their executives, like those at Lenovo and Vanke, are actively drawing on the management expertise of their directors.

Many American companies have only come to extoll the virtues of strategically engaged directors in recent years, a development that we have documented elsewhere. That awakening had followed as an unintended byproduct of a sustained effort by institutional holders, equity analysts, state regulators, governance raters, and activist investors to make directors more capable of embracing their formally required monitoring function. Strengthening the monitoring agenda is still only a nascent agenda among private Chinese companies, but in the meantime their directors have more fully embraced the partnership function as they have been asked by their CEO to step up to help navigate the terra incognita ahead.[30]

Like telephone services in much of the developing world that are hopping over the landlines phase to embrace mobile calling, Chinese companies have skipped over the strengthening of the monitoring function to more directly embrace the leadership function. We expect that the monitoring function will eventually be shored up as pressures from international investors for international governance standards are felt in China. But in the meantime, the China Way is characterized by company boards that help build growth with management, even if their directors are still not yet fully disciplining management to optimize total shareholder return.

Governance as Partnership in the Words of the Fortune Makers

For us, the board is fully involved and has the final decision on any strategic-level topic. Also, the non-executive directors are becoming more and more active since they have a better understanding of their responsibilities. They can look at the same question from a different viewpoint and uphold principles firmly.

— Chair, consumer-products company

[The main criteria for selecting non-executive directors?] I think the most important criteria are their independence and professional background. Their diversified background in management is good for the development of our company. Taking [our] director . . . as an example, he has always been assertive and persistent since

2007. . . . After all, we are a newly listed company and there are still a lot of problems. We need [non-executive directors] to point out the improvement areas and give recommendations so that our international company can [remain] forward-looking.

—Chair, maker and seller of branded clothing

We expect the non-executive directors to provide advice or suggestions for the major decisions.

—Chair, diversified manufacturer

I disagree with maximizing shareholder value. . . . The most important stakeholder is customers because they create the real value. The second one is employees. We pay the above-average-level salary to employees. . . . We follow the mission, vision, and core values of Fotile. A virtuous circle will be created: customers are satisfied and more willing to pay when satisfied employees create the maximum values. The shareholders will get maximum benefits. The opposite will be a vicious circle.

—Mao Zhongqun, Chair, Ningbo Fotile Kitchen Ware

We take care of our employees and give the priority to improving their working environment. Making money is not our key objective. The responsibility of business and the entrepreneur is sharing the economic value with every stakeholder.

—Chair, automobile and industrial glass maker

I don't agree that we are mainly responsible to the investors and shareholders. From my perspective, the interest of our employees always comes first and our future relies on every employee in this company. Employees are willing to follow the management because we care about them. So the business will have a bright future if the employees share the vision and interest in it.

—Chair, metals manufacturer

CHAPTER 9

What's Distinctive,
What's Sustainable

It's our responsibility to shift from
"made in China" to "designed in China."

The previous chapters outline business leadership practices in China that appear to be distinctive from what we have seen in the West—perhaps even unique. We believe that they acquired their characteristic hue because so many Chinese business executives came of age at a time when private enterprise was barely tolerated or, for those a little younger, still viewed with suspicion. It would not have made their parents proud to say as youngsters that their goal was to be a capitalist when they grew up.

That epoch shaped the kind of people who pursued the first generation of entrepreneurship, the founders of the companies we discuss in this book. It was not a group that would be defined as a privileged class. These were not the children of the Communist Party or government officials. They were ambitious and impatient and often frustrated by the lack of alternatives for social progress.

Another lasting facet of their mindset, especially among those who directly experienced the Cultural Revolution, is a lingering anxiety about uncertainty. In the first years of business development, you were on top today, but you may not be tomorrow, and many of the leaders we studied had family members who experienced that reversal, or experienced it themselves. Capitalism went rather quickly from prohibited to tolerated to accepted, but could that reverse again? We claim no special insight into the psyches of the leaders we observed, but it would seem impossible for such concerns not to have crossed their minds, especially in the early days when their companies were getting started and their values were being formed.

The Importance of Learning

A defining feature of the management mindset among the companies and executives we observed is the priority on experiential learning. Most of what the executives knew came from their own trials and tribulations, though they were also eager to top off their learnings with the wisdom of others. The executives all reported seeking information about management from business books, strategy consultants, foreign companies, and executive programs.

Knowledge about other schemes is not very useful unless one is prepared to act on it, of course, and what distinguished the leaders we studied was their readiness to do so. That stemmed from the realization that foreign competitors were ahead of them and that they needed to learn more as leaders to catch up.

Chinese culture certainly played a role in supporting the importance of formal education, but the willingness of our business leaders to take on learning as a lifelong personal mission is unprecedented in our experience. These are certainly busy people, their individual commitment to learning was impressive, and they insisted on that priority among their managers and across their companies as well, pressing their firms to learn how to learn—just as they had individually done during the many years of building their companies.

However, absorbing leadership practices from other sources was not just about their exposure to details about these practices. It began with company leaders first learning from their own experiences, something that was promoted through the widespread practice of self-reflection. Many of the founders reviewed and analyzed their own experiences, learning from and then applying their emergent understandings to the often murky, complex problems involved in business management. In some organizations this self-reflection was manifested through journal reading, self-conscious reports on personal learning, and even self-criticism. It is difficult to imagine a similar program of self-deprecation functioning in

Western companies, in part because US executives are deeply concerned about impressions of their own competence—understandably so, given the tendency of company leaders to replace "weak" managers with more assured performers.

Many of the Chinese executives we interviewed also made the point that they had been fortunate beneficiaries of the new era's great market reforms, ready labor force, and vast home market. As Lenovo founder Liu Chuanzhi pointedly told us, "If it were not for Deng Xiaoping's reform and open-door policy, none of us would be able to achieve much, regardless of how capable we are."

The Curse of Knowledge

Psychologists talk about something called the curse of knowledge—a theory that tries to explain why those who know a great deal about a particular topic are occasionally outdone by those who know nothing about it. The idea is that those who have seen something over and over come to take it for granted, perhaps do not question it anymore, and cannot imagine what it was like when they did not know it. A practical manifestation of this may be the difficulty in recognizing one's own problems. We get used to seeing how things work, even if they do not work well, and can no longer picture how things could be done differently.[1]

The Chinese business leaders we studied never suffered from this curse of knowledge in their business. They started their companies when there were no models for them to copy, at least closely. Unlike entrepreneurs in the West, they did not begin their careers working in other enterprises whose lessons they could adapt, often unconsciously. Although the government may have had the idea that entrepreneurs would first learn about business from their experiences in state-owned enterprises, that rarely happened, and when it did, the experience was often a negative one, reinforcing how they did not want their companies to operate.

These Chinese entrepreneurs certainly made mistakes initially because they knew nothing about business. Recall the twists and turns that many went through as their founders searched for a viable product. But the newness also prevented them from suffering the curse of knowledge. They had no hard-and-fast template in mind as to how their businesses should operate. This context led to three lessons implicit in the practices of the companies we studied.

The first is the learning-by-doing approach, whereby business leaders take their own experiences as paramount and their companies are willing to give something a try to find out if it works. When these companies began, everything the executives did was an experiment because they had no experience and no rule book to follow. It is not that these companies were running controlled experiments in markets, as one might see in sophisticated Western companies. They were just more willing to take risks to try something new, initially because there was no other way and eventually because they were used to doing so. Risk taking became part of their business mindset. We heard echoes of this learning-by-doing mantra in our interviews with company leaders who railed against MBA managers—typically from the United States—whose business knowledge came from a rule book rather than from experience.

The second lesson these companies learned is the importance of shopping for ideas. There was no conceit of ownership in their systems and practices because, at least initially, they had no systems or practices. The business leaders we interviewed are fiercely proud of their success and that of their companies. This experience of having so much to learn so quickly seems to have prevented the "not-invented-here" avoidance that one often sees in other countries.

The third lesson is the importance of being reflective practitioners. Just as important as learning-by-doing is learning-from-doing, an aspect of Lenovo's replay-the-game—a disciplined way of repeatedly resolving business problems for which there is no personal precedent or shared wisdom. The Chinese executives we interviewed reported that they self-consciously reflected on their actions and impacts, constructing management prescriptions from their personal experience.

There has been no single, obvious model from which to draw, as former colonies have often had from their colonial masters. When China opened its doors to the international business community, everyone came there, not the opposite. Few foreign companies served as exemplars on which the executive could model their own. Some glanced at General Electric, Apple, and others, but the executives did not adopt much from any one company or from any single business tradition. More to the point, they stayed with the underlying notion that there is much to learn from anywhere it can be sourced—especially at home, but also abroad.

The executives extended their personal commitment to "mapping their own way forward" to the workplace as a whole. But one quirky aspect of learning in these companies is that the focus is much more on traditional education than we would see in American and European companies. Career development and the work-based learning associated with it are largely missing from the Chinese companies we studied. Businesses elsewhere have moved away from education—book learning and classroom-based instruction—toward learning-by-doing. What makes the Chinese approach especially unusual is that it seems to be at odds with the leaders' stated preference for knowledge obtained through experience rather than from a classroom. It is quite likely that the Chinese companies have not had the time or the inclination to make the investment in creating hands-on learning experiences, such as rotational assignments. One reason is that such programs are expensive, require more structures (e.g., organizational development divisions), and slow down businesses. Turning abruptly is also hard to do when many managers and executives are in long-term developmental assignments.

An unusual aspect of the Chinese executives' search for lessons—one that calls to mind the "curse of knowledge"—is that they seemed to parse practices independent of the whole system. For example, they picked up ideas from General Electric about financial control without adopting the rest of the GE scheme. AnnaLee Saxenian's well-known account of the differences between American computer companies in Boston, based on a traditional corporate model, and those in Silicon Valley, based on a new model, is often taken by students to suggest that the latter completely dominates the former and should be the one copied. But the Chinese companies we observed have borrowed from both. They focus on competencies generated from within traditional corporations, but they also operate with the flat charts and lean systems of the Silicon Valley model. And they appear to have replicated the strong culture and loyalty approaches of Japanese companies without the complex systems of career development and time-consuming consensus building that one sees in those companies.[2]

Most important of all, these executives learned how to operate bigger businesses while keeping the entrepreneurial orientation of their start-up years, maintaining simpler architectures and operating models. Indeed, the human resource functions in the companies we studies are, by contemporary standards, primitive. They lack sophisticated hiring practices, development programs, programs of career progression, and organization-development functions that monitor employee morale and help manage organizational transitions. In short, these companies have just enough systems in place to ensure that they can get their work done and coordinate their operations, relying on a model where the CEO or founder is still manifestly in charge of virtually everything.

Many of these companies also lack extensive planning and strategy departments—those tasks seem to reside more with the founder or the CEO. Unlike US companies, most Chinese enterprises have not created numerous separate, autonomous operating units with their own profit-and-loss responsibilities, though Haier has certainly moved in that direction. The business leaders we spoke with are also very protective of their inner circles, but they expressed little compunction about getting rid of lower-level managers who did not fit in with company values. While the idea of corporate culture that gets everyone pointed in the same direction is very important for these executives, they have no patience for the time-consuming persuasion and influence exercises that ensure compliance with company values that one sees in Japanese companies. The Chinese CEOs and founders seem to be carrying the mission forward on their own, largely through their own personal actions and communications to employees.

What do entrepreneurial businesses do well? They identify and seize opportunities quickly, and grow by building lean organizations. That is what is perhaps most distinctive about the private companies in China. The founders and builders of these companies believe that the market fairly rewards distinctive competencies, and while that may seem obvious, acting on this belief was not easy during the early years of reform when market openings were halting. They were able to do so in part because they had more control over company strategy, and in part because they were less concerned with near-term profitability. Shifting operations away from a line of business that is currently profitable to a new market that offers long-term promise, yet entails time and risk to get there, would be anathema to many investors in the West.

Government and Business

One topic that directly relates to the questions of distinctiveness and transferability is the business executive's relationship with the government and the common perception that it can make or break an enterprise. To what extent are the leadership practices witnessed here the result of China's unique system of state-sponsored capitalism, that overlay of market enterprise on a communist system and a country culture that still stresses collective over the personal?

There is no doubt that the public officials in China could have built or broken some private companies, especially in the early years when executives were struggling to map their own way forward. With little in the way of Western-style capital markets, companies turned to state agencies and even state-owned enterprises for sponsorship and financing. They of necessity came to rely on these agencies and enterprises, and it helped to know the state provider. As the chair of a medical-devices maker explained, when he started the company "almost from zero" in the 1990s, there were no private-equity or venture funds in China, so he had to raise the capital himself. It proved very difficult to get money, he recalled, in complete contrast to the present, when he found plenty of cash in the market.

Local governments were often in a hurry to develop their real estate and incubate home-grown start-ups to generate employment. In the early years, when there were no real market prices for land or ways to value opportunities that provincial and municipal governments could provide, it was possible to make a great deal of money with government help—or to get absolutely nowhere without it. Those days, however, are largely over. Today, private financing is readily available, equity markets are well established, and competition for resources is felt everywhere. National or local backing is no longer essential for starting a business, but neither is it a guarantor of success.[3]

As we learned in our interviews, the business leaders were appropriately respectful of government authority and recognized the importance of not being out of step with state interests. As a group, though, they did not see courting government as still vital for growth. Executive relationships with public officials are still more important among Chinese firms than among Western ones, but such relationships are now less definitive.

Government is more about setting the rules of the game and enforcing them than about picking winners and sponsoring them.

As noted, a closely related attribute often cited as central to Chinese business is guanxi—personal networks of relations that give an executive access and influence. Personal ties were no doubt salient in an earlier period of the economy's opening, especially when connections with public officials were vital for setting up a company. Such webs of relations are important when free markets are less well developed; trust among individuals can provide a substitute for an absence of credible information about the reliability of transactions or the enforceability of contracts. Yet we heard very little about guanxi from the leaders we studied. They did not report it as essential for leadership of their own businesses, nor did they place a premium on it. With markets in China far more developed and information far more available, individual connections now matter less than other leadership skills, but even when they do matter, the personal has become far more impersonal—a relationship driven by the office and not by the individual.

The Boss

Given how countercultural starting a business was a generation or more ago when the founders we interviewed began their businesses, it appears that many of them were serial entrepreneurs, determined to somehow succeed in business even after failing on the first several tries. As the individuals chronicled here capitalized on the exploding opportunities afforded by China's liberalization, they in turn imposed their own personal character on their enterprises. This combination of forceful founders without prior models to emulate and impressionable employees to orchestrate led to company cultures that very much reflect the values of the founders. The fact that so many of these founders are still around and, as we have seen, have maintained their organizational culture as a company priority, suggests that their distinctive styles persist, even as homogenizing forces increase, as in the case of lateral hiring of professionals from other companies.

One thing we know about start-ups in Silicon Valley is that the founders' early imprints shape their firms for years to come, especially in terms of setting the cultural tone—the norms that tell people how to behave.

Once established, that cultural tone is very difficult to alter. In the case of Silicon Valley, norms often derive from the broader professional community of hi-tech engineers and company builders who have worked in nearby start-ups before. In the case of more recently formed companies in China, they derive from the experienced engineers and professionals who comprise their cadres. For instance, Xiaomi, the mobile phone maker founded in 2010 that achieved annual handset sales of 70 million just five years later, operated in ways akin to those Silicon Valley companies in that its culture is much drawn from the norms of the professionals it rapidly recruited.[4]

Yet there were no such pre-established professional communities when most of the companies we studied started, because there were simply very few business veterans of any kind. Filaments of national culture infused their management ideology when they began, but the relatively blank professional landscape at the time gave the founders extraordinary power to put their own cultural stamp on the enterprise. They and their early lieutenants had never worked for a private enterprise before and thus had no sense of what was appropriate. What they surely did know, however, is that what they would build would be very different from what they had known, and possibly path-breaking. They were right.

A shared theme of our interviews with these seventy-two Chinese-company leaders was their emphasis on their own roles in defining not only their firm's strategy but also its culture and architecture. While their premier role in setting strategy is hardly surprising, their stress on fostering that culture and architecture is striking, especially when compared with typical executive agendas in the West, where setting strategy has become the coin of the realm. Drawing on the experience of Alibaba, we concluded that an explanation may lie in the founders' imperative of retaining an entrepreneurial mindset even as their firms became behemoths, as so many of China's start-ups have so quickly become. Also, the velocity of change in their markets may have placed a special premium on cultures and architectures that facilitate rapid redeployment of thousands of employees as new windows open.

Many of the firms we studied had less developed pathways for delegating authority and assigning responsibility to levels of management much below the CEO, encapsulated in the continuing presence of the big-boss model. Strategic responsibility and key decisions remain concentrated at the apex. This may be partly an upshot of lingering scarcity in the market for senior talent; but whatever the source, company executives have of necessity devolved much operational authority, even if they still do not share the keys for strategy.

Common among the companies we studied was a palpable sense of urgency, a premium on timely actions and rapid decisions—perhaps driven by some combination of domestic opportunities, global openings, and fear that such prospects may not last. Products designs have diffused rapidly in the domestic market, forcing firms to compete more for market share than for product differentiation. Whether the private companies have ramped up too quickly, and may later be burdened by their scale and costs as opportunities commodify, is yet to be seen; like many global companies, they may be forced to relocate production facilities to lower-cost areas in Southeast Asia.

Where did the founders of these Chinese businesses get the values and norms that formed an enduring backbone for their companies? In more recent years, it is possible that some selected these purposefully from models elsewhere, but we know that doing so is rare among founders, even in the United States. In fact, the mindset of Chinese executives comes first and foremost from their own personal values and experience, and this helps explain the variation in some practices that we observed across firms. One of the more important norms is the extent to which employees share in the ownership of the companies. In the United States, the cultural precept of distributing ownership in start-ups across employees is so strong that it would be difficult not to do so. In the Chinese context, however, there was no norm at all, so what our founders did was more a reflection of their own values—and while some shared ownership, most did not. In this context, too, we witnessed the big-boss model whereby the particular organizational form came very much from the top.

What About Shareholders?

One of the most distinctive aspects of these Chinese leaders and their companies is their apparent lack of interest in creating shareholder value as a priority. What they do deem a priority is growth—even at the expense of earnings. Indeed, one complaint made by westerners about Chinese companies is their apparent willingness to cut prices in order to grab markets, a practice that in its extreme—where prices are set below costs—would violate US antitrust regulations that prohibit predatory pricing.

Is this orientation away from shareholders' short-term interests truly distinct? And if so, is it driven by something transitory—or, conversely, more fundamental—about Chinese business? Perhaps the first point to note in explaining this seemingly unusual orientation of the Chinese companies is that it is actually not all that rare. Our study of Indian business leaders and their companies found roughly the same behavior. Among both developing and developed economies, no country's business community is as fixed on maximizing shareholder value as that of the United States. Perhaps it is more the outlier.

One reason the Chinese companies we studied have not been very concerned with maximizing shareholder value, at least in the short term, is that the founders of these companies, who are typically still the controlling shareholders, are still in charge. We sometimes hear in the United States that if business leaders acted more like major owners, they would push harder to maximize profits to shareholders. Yet many of the Chinese business leaders we studied are already large holders, billionaires many times over. It is not that they are unconcerned with being more successful but, rather, that their view of success is different from that of professional managers and investors in the West. In our interviews with these Chinese executives, they reported no drumbeat from any quarter to optimize short-term gains for shareholders.

We might have anticipated that the timelines of the older executives would be shorter as they approach retirement, but we found that their horizons remain far longer than those of most professional investors. They stay focused on future growth and market share, and since political pressure against antitrust behavior and sector dominance are essentially nonexistent in China, company leaders are relatively unrestricted in their long-term agendas.

Chinese executives express less interest in mergers and acquisitions for the same reason that business leaders in the West often resist hostile acquisition: they want no loss of control over their enterprise. They care personally about their firm, and they care about running it regardless of any windfall financial gains. That is one reason they describe their first leadership priority as maintaining the direction of the company and its strategy, something they perceive as more important than building a personal nest egg.

It also takes eager sellers to make mergers and acquisitions happen. And it takes a more developed market for corporate control to make such transactions feasible. The ability to press shareholders of a company to sell by offering them a premium is what persuades many Western company leaders to sell even if they personally would not opt to do so. Alternatively, "golden parachutes" are offered to neutralize their will to resist. Such pecuniary tactics work far less well in Chinese companies, where the leader remains the controlling party.

Still, private-business leaders in China are starting to see value in the market for corporate control, particularly to establish a global presence, build a new brand, or enter new markets at home. We have seen that at Lenovo, with its landmark purchase of the IBM Personal Computer Division in 2004. Lenovo established its international presence overnight. And a decade later, the same global agenda drove Lenovo's purchase of IBM's server business and Google's Motorola's Mobility, the latter giving Lenovo an overnight smartphone footprint in the Americas and Europe. Similarly, Ford Motor Company was not able to manage Volvo as a European and North American brand, but in acquiring Volvo from Ford, Geely succeeded in both turning the car maker around and making itself an international player.

Shareholder activism, a key driver of the market for corporate control in the West, has been rare in China so far. It thus came as no surprise that the executives we interviewed place scant emphasis on investor and media relations. Assuming that private Chinese companies further expand their presence in the international market control, however, this function of top management will likely occupy far more executive attention.

When the Founder Retires

An important lesson researchers have observed among American start-ups is that founders of companies are often replaced at some point by professional executives. When that happens, some of the more idiosyncratic practices of the companies change. Any company where the founders stick around is likely to be different from those where they are early or easily replaced. There thus may be a distinctiveness that extends well into the future among the companies we have studied here in contrast to those that started later when the Chinese business community came to build new companies more around its own professional norms. No doubt there will be new companies coming along in the future with cultures more like Xiaomi than Huawei.

A fundamental question about the future of the companies we studied concerns what happens when this first generation of founders leaves the stage. Many have already transitioned out of day-to-day company operations, but most still control their firm's key decisions. And one of the more instructive comments we heard from these leaders is that many were planning for a professional manager rather than a family member to take over the leadership of their enterprise. That of course creates a quandary since so many of them have railed against the trend toward professional managers.

However, we believe that the objections we heard regarding professional managers were largely directed against American-style decision making, especially the financial orientation that many US executives learn in business school. The idea that there is a set of optimal decisions on how companies should be run, and the notion that such decisions can be imported from the West, runs very counter to the priorities and practices of the founders.

Moreover, it is difficult to imagine Chinese directors forcing the founder out in favor of a professional manager more focused on financial objectives. When founders let go of their companies in China, they are much more likely to remain in control of the process to ensure that a successor compatible with them is picked. Many of the founders we observed had already begun a controlled transition where they could groom and then anoint their successor, leaving their personal stamp on the company by hand-picking a replacement.[5]

The evidence from Western companies suggests that their founders leave a personal imprint on companies even if they have been pushed out and professional managers come in. Whether this first generation of Chinese leaders will leave the large legacy on the world of business that their counterparts in the United States did a century ago is more open, however.

The founders of the great American corporations like Carnegie in steel and Ford in autos were inventing the modern business form. Pierre DuPont's creation of the multidivisional company and Alfred P. Sloan's planning and control systems at General Motors, for example, were first efforts to address the fundamental challenges of building enterprises on a scale never seen before. More recently, Bill Gates at Microsoft, Steve Jobs at Apple, and Mark Zuckerberg at Facebook created whole new industries. So far at least, Chinese founders and their companies have not established legacies of that magnitude, though that, too, could be coming in the years ahead.[6]

An important and distinctive aspect of the Chinese companies we studied, and one that is shared with the first generation of US corporations, is national scale. The history of American multinational companies and their success abroad begins with the fact that America was itself already a very large market at the beginning of the twentieth century. Companies like Johnson & Johnson and Procter & Gamble grew large before they ventured abroad. The result of being big enough to serve and even dominate their vast US markets meant that they had the scale economies to drive costs and prices down, first domestically and then internationally.

The domestic market in China is already immense, with a GDP in 2015 of $10.4 trillion, second only to the American GDP of $17.4 trillion—and ahead of Japan's at $4.8 trillion and Germany's at $3.6 trillion. For mass consumer products such as housewares, cellphones, and appliances, Chinese customers vastly outnumber American buyers. A company like Haier, now the world's largest appliance maker, was already one of the world's largest refrigeration companies when it first entered the US market in 2000, and its ability to compete abroad with quality products at low prices was well established by its scale at home. A similar story can be told about Chinese electronic companies like Lenovo. Since domestic competition in China is now fierce for most private companies, those that expand into the West are typically of an established scale by the time we notice them, which helps explain why many Chinese companies are proving so successful in Western markets.[7]

What Lessons from Chinese Leaders Translate?

Some of the distinctive aspects of the Chinese business experience will not readily transfer to other countries because they derive from a China-specific context. But others are likely to translate. The latter are associated with the emergent structures of companies and the ways they operate.

The first and arguably most important of these is the ability of the Chinese businesses we studied to operate with leaner control systems than do their Western counterparts, where "lean" means fewer managers and less supervision. The reason they can do so is, first, because of the belief that employees will not shirk or cheat, at least not as much as their equivalents in the West, in part because the primacy of individualism in China has not been as pronounced. As a result, the incentive to evade accountability or self-enrich is not as great. Both the need and cost to have supervisors watching and managers monitoring have been sharply reduced.

Another factor allowing for less risk of malfeasance is the widespread sense of obligation to the company and especially its leader. In the West, we might refer to this as corporate "commitment" or "charismatic" authority. Dedicated employees are more willing to look after the interests of the company, and some of that willingness may also stem from greater faith in the big boss and the belief that their leader is looking out for them and their welfare.

This sense of obligation is particularly strong in the upper ranks. Several leaders told us that the commitment of a relatively small number of operating executives to the values and norms of the company was key to their company's leadership. How did that obligation get built? With practice over time: executives who consistently perform well and repeatedly demonstrate their honesty and commitment to the company are pulled by the CEO into his or her inner circle. And once in that circle, they are protected. The chief executive forgives their mistakes, at least modest ones, and more generally cuts them slack for under-performance; in return, the executives are more solid and candid with their bosses. They are less likely to cover up their failures since these are less personally fatal.

A lean operating system facilitates another key advantage, and that is the ability to change and adapt quickly. One contributing factor is the more modest organizational overhead: it is easier to redirect a management structure with fewer layers and controls. It is also easier to alter direction when the managers are less likely to feel at personal peril. Part of the simplicity of these organizations stems from the fact that the founder is still calling so many of the shots, resulting in fewer political struggles and less passive resistance.

That agility, in turn, helps create a competitive advantage for Chinese companies in detecting new opportunities and turning to them quickly. This is unlike many Indian companies that focus on existing customers, Japanese companies that perfect established products, and even new US companies that try fresh products. The Chinese companies we observed grew through an aggressive business strategy that sought out new opportunities for existing products and then moved into those openings before their competitors could react. Company leaders—especially their founders—spent much of their time focusing on identifying new market openings, especially where competitors were weak. They then moved into those markets quickly.

Whether these lean and agile operating measures are sustainable remains to be seen. Individualism is certainly on the rise in China, and with it a growing readiness among at least some employees to optimize their self-interest. There is little doubt that a job-hopping culture now ascendant in China, especially among private companies, will erode executive notions of loyalty and duty. Whether companies will be able to counter that incipient challenge with even stronger measures of their own is an open question. Efforts to do so would explain the great emphasis we heard from many business leaders on the importance of building and maintaining their corporate cultures.

The lean and agile approach of these Chinese companies calls to mind the importance of thinking about management as a system. The idea of systems theory can be traced back to scholars like our Wharton colleague Russell Ackoff and social scientists like Talcott Parsons. In systems thinking, many factors play a role in determining an outcome, and their specific interplay matters much. In this context, the ability to operate with less administrative oversight requires a different kind of behavior relative to that of employees, which, in turn, depends on an organizational culture of reciprocity.[8]

What's Enduring

A challenge in identifying the central aspects of leadership and management in private Chinese companies is to discern what part of the behavior we observe is temporary or transitory—a response to circumstances that soon pass, because the behavior associated with those circumstances will pass as well. Whether those practices are truly exclusive to the Chinese context is an open question. Are they simply attributes of young companies whose founders still preside, regardless of country? Or are they a product of the Chinese experience—and, even if the latter, might their best features be fruitfully borrowed and adapted by companies in other countries?

The reason this question is so relevant in the Chinese context is that so much about it has changed so quickly. Indeed, it is difficult to think of any country that has experienced as profound a set of changes as has China over the past generation. Nor is it probable that the changes China has observed will swing, like a pendulum, back in the old direction. No credible observers that we know of suggest that China will return to a centrally planned, state-operated economy.

It is fashionable now to speak of capitalism in China as being state-sponsored and to say that the government is central to the way business operates. There is much truth to such statements, but will these circumstances persist? Here we can learn lessons from the experience of Japan. Until the 1970s, Japanese business had little success in export markets. Their products were seen as low-quality and inferior. Toyota tried to sell cars in the United States but had to withdraw, finding no success.

The government became deeply involved in Japanese business, especially in determining what could be imported and exported. The agency in charge was the Ministry of International Trade and Industry (MITI). It was credited with creating industrial policy for Japan, making the decisions about where the government and indeed the private sector should invest, getting other parts of the government to push companies to cooperate in an effort to advance their collective interests, and so forth. By the 1970s, the competitiveness of Japan had changed significantly. Its companies were exporting cars to the United States and stealing market share from American companies at a rapid rate. Japanese makers like Sony started to dominate consumer electronics.

It was common at the time to give MITI credit for Japan's success in its export industries. These days, no one talks about MITI's influence (it was renamed The Ministry of Economy, Trade, and Industry in 2001) or indeed about the role of the Japanese government as a driver of Japanese

business practices. Whether or not this role was crucial two generations
ago, Japanese companies have so thoroughly established themselves in the
international economy that the government is simply no longer that important. Something very similar could be said about Korea: its government
drove an export policy for the economy through the 1980s that helped
build the giant corporations like Samsung, Hyundai, and LG that are now
international successes. Now, one no longer hears the view that Korea's
government is calling the shots for these companies.[9]

The same story may well play out in China. There is no doubt that the
first generation of private companies, many of which we studied, were
heavily influenced—and, in some cases, heavily supported—by the government. Nor is it likely that they could have survived had they opposed
government interests in any open way. That period appears to be passing,
however—much as it did for Japan and Korea. Governments everywhere
are powerful players in business, and the Chinese government is undeni-
ably even more powerful in that regard than its counterparts elsewhere.
But it is possible for a private company to start a business in China now
without any more contact with the government than one would expect in
any Western country. Access to markets, to capital, and to labor has become part of civil society. The recent and continuing crackdown on corruption, aimed at informal connections between business and government
officials, may serve to make private companies even more separate from
government (or at least government officials) than before.

Given that everything about business is ultimately transient, is this especially the case for private companies in China? Will they be able to continue this model after their founders are gone? More to the point, will it be
possible to run such agile, learning-oriented, and boss-centric operations
when the companies become bigger, more international, and more
complex?

A first caveat regarding this concern is that private Chinese companies
do not have to become much more complex. Adding complexity is an active leadership choice. We have not seen in these companies the interest
in spilling into other industries that we observed in Indian companies like
the Tata Group, which now runs everything from consulting and hotels to
steel and auto making. Continuing to remain lean is much easier if the
Chinese firms do not diversify and eschew vertical integration.

It is certainly possible for private companies in China to continue to operate as they have even when their founder passes the baton to a professional manager, as most plan to do. There is always the chance that a new leader will try to change the operations for the sake of change, to put his or her own stamp on the business. After all, American companies including Disney, IBM, and Walmart survived the hand-off from the founder with their business models relatively intact.

Maybe the biggest concern for these companies is whether operating with the model they have will continue to be possible. Indeed, a significant challenge is whether the new generation of Chinese employees, who have grown up in relative affluence and with a more individualistic culture, will be willing to work in the same way as their predecessors did, subordinating their own interests in decision making to the big boss, acting in the company's interest rather than their own. If culture no longer carries the day with employees, will the companies be forced to fall back on the more complex systems of monitoring and control and human resources that their competitors in the West adopted generations ago?

The chair of a footwear maker and clothing retailer has already anticipated this challenge: "I believe my successor will not manage the company like I am doing. He must use strategy to attract people, use profit to retain people, and use affection to touch people. . . . I believe the requirements to attract people will be different in the future."

Conclusion

After a century of corporate capitalism and multinational companies in the West that have disseminated business ideas and management principles worldwide, the idea that we would find a distinctive model in China for operating businesses represents a high hurdle. This is especially so now given the global industry of management consulting and business education, which is designed to ferret out best practices and spread them rapidly around the world.

Indeed, we have discovered something like these best practices in the China Way. The distinctiveness of the companies we studied is sui generis, in a class of its own. As in most countries, national culture, history, and legal systems in China help create those distinctive practices. Some of those practices may well dissipate as companies grow, become more complex, and expand outside their neighborhood. A private company like Lenovo has become a very significant player in China, but whether it can maintain its distinctive culture and practices as it becomes a global player remains an open question, and perhaps it may even converge with IBM, its former partner, as its operations come face to face with similar market demands and investor pressures.

But some Chinese business practices may well be retained by their originators on the world stage and may even be transferable to non-Chinese firms looking to adopt emergent practices from companies regardless of their birthplace or headquarters. Whether Western companies can learn from their Chinese counterparts depends on whether their leaders can recognize that the Western ways may not have all the answers—and then on whether they can identify their own blind spots that Chinese firms have already addressed.

We thus believe it is a fruitful time for Western business leaders to look hard at the leaders of Alibaba, Geely, Haier, Huawei, Lenovo, Vanke, Xiaomi, and the hundreds of other large private companies in China that are increasingly coming to define not only their own way of doing business but also better ways of leading business worldwide.

What's Distinctive and What's Sustainable in the Words of the Fortune Makers

It's our responsibility to shift from "made in China" to "designed in China" and to create value-add for our customers. . . . We are not the copycat and have our own creativity, [and] to achieve this ambition, we need a good business environment—but more important are our enterprises: they will be the determining factor for our future competitiveness on the world business stage.
  —Chair, footwear and diversified manufacturer

By now you basically cannot find founders among the chairmen of famous foreign companies, while it is still mostly founders as chairmen in Chinese companies. So there is a big difference in the quality and capability between the chairmen of home and abroad.

[Foreign company chairmen] are not comparable to their counter-parts in China as they are not at the same level of competency. In terms of starting a new business or company, innovation, and problem-solving capability, Chinese chairmen can score 100. Those foreign companies' chairmen are definitely below 59. There is no reason to admire them as they experience many fewer problems compared to Chinese counterparts.

—Chair, computer and electronic products maker

I think I never said that all our decisions are correct. First, the over-all market environment is still immature in China, so it is relatively easy to make money. Second, I have the ability to correct the mis-takes. Now [that] the market competition is growing, there is much less room to make mistakes. We have been more cautious in the decision-making process. I don't think I have a lot of experience in making decisions that can be leveraged because sometimes I made decisions on impulse rather than [by] careful analysis. But I have the courage to admit the mistakes and correct them quickly.

—Wang Shi, Chair, China Vanke Company

In dealing with government, we have always been sincere and hon-est. In fact we do not want to spend too much time and effort in this respect. In the end, as a private company, we need to build up our own core competence and competitive advantages in the free com-petition market. Once getting too obsessed with the benefits from good government relationship, we will lose the interest and momen-tum for self-improvement. Most of all, the resources from [the] gov-ernment relationship are not reliable and sustainable in the long run.

—Chief executive, food products company

China is quite different from other countries. In China, government is very powerful. In the past thirty years, we have been dealing with lots of local senior officials. . . . Our principle has been not to get too close to officials in the personal sense. . . . We rarely deal with offi-cials in a very close manner, as our major goals are to create value for the society, pay taxes, and create employment. As long as we deliver our results and meet the expectations of government and local officials, they are also willing to support us. This is a very important point: a company could easily get itself in trouble when getting too close to government officials and the dirty deals involved.

—Chair, agri-business enterprise

When our company celebrated its thirtieth anniversary, we made a long-term plan for the next thirty years. I believe it is important to have such a kind of long-term plan defining the company's future in the next thirty years.

—Chief executive, conglomerate manufacturing and services

Personally, I disagree with the notion of maximizing the shareholders' interest as the most important mission for a company, and I don't remember [having] a lot of arguments in this respect in our company. The foremost stakeholder is our customers, as we need to create the best value for them as a company. Then followed by our employees: we must provide them at least the above-average level salary and welfare package. We will try our best to hit the average-level benefit package for employees, even at the expense of the shareholders' interest.

—Mao Zhongqun, Chair, Ningbo Fotile Kitchen Ware

You have to ensure that everyone, regardless of their position, can all receive benefits. We cannot just send out big dividends to shareholders and exclude employees from taking fair benefits in our company's business growth.

—Yang Shaopeng, Chair, SITC International Holdings

During the start-up period, if the boss does not fully commit to the business, employees would not devote themselves, either. So at the beginning stage, I gave 100 percent of myself to the business. For example, I worked seven days a week and only took two days off for the whole year.

—Chair, real-estate and financial-services company

To be a qualified leader, I need to start with leading by example. Besides career development, my charisma and appearance are also very important. I would like to win recognition from all people for what I have done. Not to behave in complete selfishness, I should at least lead by example in doing things that others could not do. The influence of a model is huge, as one person can affect a group and a large number of people.

—Chair, maker of recycling equipment

APPENDIX 1

Growth of the China Way

In this appendix we provide several figures illustrating recent trend lines on growth in Chinese imports, exports, foreign direct investment, employment in state-owned companies, industrial output and revenue of state-owned enterprises and private companies, and annual growth in GDP.

Non-state-owned enterprises and holding enterprises include collective-owned enterprises, cooperative enterprises, limited liability corporations, and private enterprises; industrial enterprises include all state-owned enterprises and non-state-owned enterprises with annual revenue from principal businesses over ¥5 million from 1998 to 2006, industrial enterprises with annual revenue from principal businesses over ¥5 million from 2007 to 2010, and industrial enterprises with annual revenue from principal businesses over ¥20 million since 2011. Due to changes in statistical categories, we use gross industrial output value for the years 1952 to 1997 and revenue from principal businesses for the years 1998 to 2013. (For this information we consulted the National Bureau of Statistics of China.)

Private foreign direct investment (FDI) by Chinese companies in the United States includes all significant non-state-owned Chinese company ownership in American-based firms, whether the firm was created, acquired, or the target of an investment. By *significant* we mean that the Chinese firms held at least 10 percent of the American-based company assets and exercised active management.

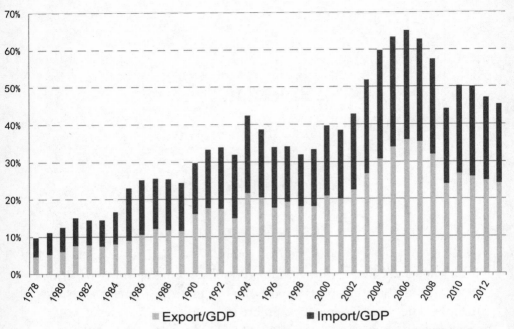

FIGURE A1.1 Chinese Import and Export Value as Percentage of GDP, 1978–2013.
Source: China Statistical Yearbook of Industry and Commerce, 2015.

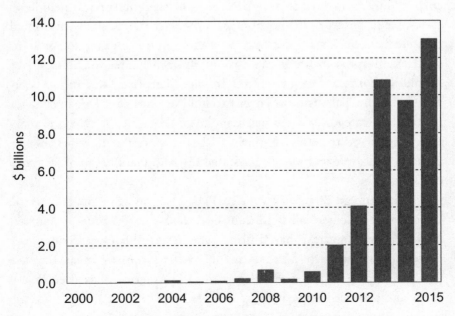

**FIGURE A1.2 Annual Foreign Direct Investment in the
United States by Private Chinese Companies, 2000–2015.**
Source: Rhodium Group, 2016.

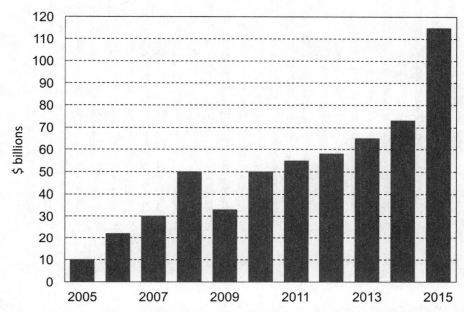

FIGURE A1.3 Value of Chinese Company Mergers and Acquisitions, 2005–2015.
Source: Dealogic, 2016.

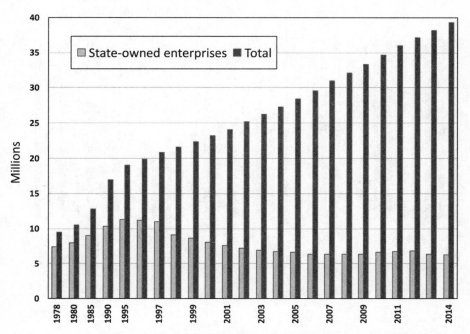

Figure A1.4 Urban Employment in State-Owned Companies,
and Total Urban Employment, in Millions, 1978–2014.
Source: China Statistical Yearbook of Industry and Commerce, 2015.

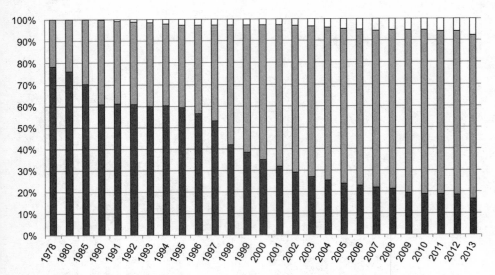

FIGURE A1.5 Fraction of Urban Enterprise Employment by Business Ownership, 1978–2013.
Source: China Statistical Yearbook of Industry and Commerce, 2015.

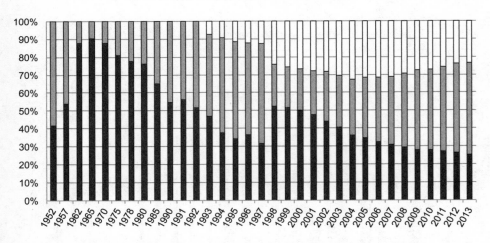

□ Enterprises funded by foreigners or by entrepreneurs from Hong Kong, Macao, and Taiwan

▨ Non-state-owned and non-state-holding industrial enterprises

■ State-owned and state-holding industrial enterprises

FIGURE A1.6 Industrial Output and Revenue by Business Ownership, 1952–2013
Source: China Statistical Yearbook of Industry and Commerce, 2015.

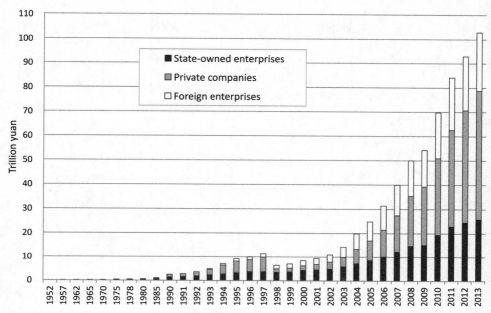

FIGURE A1.7 Chinese Company Output by Business Ownership, 1952–2013.
Source: China Statistical Yearbook of Industry and Commerce, 2015.

APPENDIX 2

Chinese Business Leaders Interviewed

Bian Pinggang, Chairman, Jiangsu Sanfangxiang Group Co., Ltd.

Cao Dewang, Chairman, Fuyao Glass Industry Group Co., Ltd.

Chai Xiangdong, General Manager, Shenzhen Neptunus Interlong Bio-Technique Co., Ltd.

Che Jianxin, Chairman and CEO, Red Star Macalline Group Corporation Ltd.

Chen Qiang, Chairman and CEO, China Huarong Energy Co., Ltd. (formerly China Rongsheng Heavy Industry)

Chen Xi, President, Sanquan Foods Co., Ltd.

Chen Zhilie, Chairman and President, EVOC Intelligent Technology Co., Ltd.

Deng Feng, Founder and Managing Director, Northern Light Venture Capital

Diao Zhizhong, Chairman, Glodon Software Co., Ltd.

Dong Caiping, Chairman and President, Zenith Steel Group Corporation Limited

Fang Hongbo, Chairman and President, Media Group Co., Ltd.

Feng Lun, Chairman, Vantone Holdings Co., Ltd.

Gao Dekang, Chairman and CEO, Bosideng International Holdings, Ltd.

Gao Tianle, Chairman, Tengen Group

Gong Yin, Vice-Chairman, Zhongli Science and Technology Group Co., Ltd.

Hai Yingjun, Chairman, Delta Group

Han, Lijun, President, Wolong Holding Group

Hu Donglong, Chairman, Walk-on Advertising Co., Ltd.

Hu Shiyong, Chairman, Jiangsu Huahong Industrial Group Co., Ltd.

Huang Nubo, Chairman, Beijing Zhongkun Investment Group Co., Ltd.

Jiang Xipei, Chairman, Far East Holdings Co., Ltd.

Jin Liangshun, Chairman, Jinggong Group Co., Ltd.

Company titles and names were current at the time of our interviews.

Kang Ming, General Manager, Sichuan Southwest Stainless Steel Co., Ltd.

Li Ming, Executive Chairman and CEO, Sino-Ocean Land Holdings Ltd.

Liang Xiaolei, Chairman, Evergreen Industries Holding Group

Liu Chuanzhi, Chairman, Legend Holding Co., Ltd.

Liu Jiren, Chairman and CEO, Neusoft Corporation

Liu Yonghao, Chairman, New Hope Group

Lou Guoqiang, President, Ningbo Jintian Copper Group Co., Ltd.

Lou Yongliang, Chairman, Zhong Tian Group

Lv Xiaoping, Vice-Chairman, Future Land Holdings Co., Ltd.

Ma Jack, Executive Chairman, Alibaba Group

Ma Weihua, Chairman, China Merchants Bank Co., Ltd.

Mao Xiangqian, CEO, ECS Technology (China), Ltd.

Mao Zhongqun, Chairman and President, Ningbo Fotile Kitchen Ware Co., Ltd.

Mei Zhefeng, Chairman, Jiangsu Jiangnan Industrial Group Co., Ltd.

Miu Hangen, Chairman and President, ShengHong Holding Group Co., Ltd.

Miu Shuangda, President, Jiangsu Shuangliang Group Co., Ltd.

Nan Cunhui, Chairman, Chint Group

Ni Lin, Chairman, Gold Mantis Construction Decoration Co., Ltd.

Qian Jinbo, Chairman, Red Dragonfly Group

Qiu Jianqiang, Vice-Chairman, Zhejiang Semir Garment Co., Ltd.

Shen Freeman, Vice-President, Zhejiang Geely Holding (Group) Co., Ltd.

Shen Guojun, Chairman, China Yintai Holdings Co., Ltd.

Sun Mingbo, Chairman, Tsingtao Brewery Co., Ltd.

Tao Qingrong, Executive Chairman and CEO, Springland International Holdings Ltd.

Tian Ming, Chairman, Landsea Group Co., Ltd.

Tseng Charles, President of Asia Pacific, Korn/Ferry International

Wang Junhao, Vice-Chairman and President, JuneYao Group

Wang Licheng, Chairman, Holley Group Co., Ltd.

Wang Shi, Chairman, China Vanke Co., Ltd.

Wang Tian, Chairman, Better Life Commercial Chain Share Co., Ltd.

Wang Wenbiao, Chairman, China Elion Resources Group

Wang Xuning, Chairman, Joyoung Co., Ltd.

Wo Pu Sum, Chairman and Founder, Central China Real Estate Ltd.

Xu Hang, Chairman and Co-CEO, Shenzhen Mindray Bio-Medical Electronics Co., Ltd.

Xu Sean, Chairman, Jiangsu Longrich Bioscience Co., Ltd.

Yang Shaopeng, Chairman and Executive Director, SITC International Holdings Co., Ltd.

Ye Meilan, Chairman and President, HuiErKang Group Co., Ltd

Yin Huaibo, President, Sichuan Jinguang Industrial Group Co., Ltd.

Yu Chunlei, Chairman, Zhejiang Jiuding Group Co., Ltd.

Yu Michael, Chairman and CEO, New Oriental Education and Technology Group

Yuan Yafei, Chairman, Sanpower Group
Zhang Hanwen, Chairman and CEO, Zhejiang Guangsha Co., Ltd.
Zhang Wuzhong, Chairman, Shandong Shiheng Special Steel Group Co., Ltd.
Zhang Zhen, Chairman, Tangshan Guofeng Iron and Steel Co., Ltd.
Zhao Tao, Chairman, Buchang Pharma
Zheng Jianjiang, Chairman, AUX Group
Zhou Jiang, CEO, Jiangsu Fasten Group Co., Ltd.
Zhou Jianping, Chairman, Heilan Group Co., Ltd.
Zhou Licheng, Chairman, New United Group Co., Ltd.
Zhou Minfeng, CEO, HuaXiang Group Co., Ltd.

We transcribed and translated all of the interviews, and have received permission from the following executives to quote or paraphrase from our interviews with them and to identify them as the source: Gong Yin, Shen Freeman, Liu Chuanzhi, Mao Zhongqun, Wang Licheng, Wang Shi, Wang Xuning, Yang Shaopeng, and Yu Michael. For quotes or paraphrases from our other interviews, we do not include the executive's name or their company's identity. We report the sources of quotes or paraphrases from public sources. For interviews with the seventy-two executives, we drew on twelve starting questions and added many follow-up questions as suggested by their responses to our starting questions:

Leadership and Strategy

1. What are the top two leadership capacities that have been most critical for the exercise of your leadership during the past five years?
2. What have been your company's most important competitive advantages? Possible follow-up questions:
    2a. How have you built up those competitive advantages?
    2b. To what extent have company-wide or corporate-group-wide resources and government relations contributed to your competitive advantages?
3. Considering your various roles as a chief executive, please identify the three that have been most important for you during the past five years.

- A guide or teacher for employees
- Chief input for business strategy
- Keeper of organizational culture
- Architect of organization structure, system, and policy
- Representative of owner and investor interests
- Representative of other stakeholders (e.g., employees and the community)
- Civil leadership within the business community
- Civic leadership outside the business community
- Diplomat (relationship builders and conflict mediators)
- Disturbance handler (managing crisis, exceptional, non-routine questions)

4. Which three tasks have been the most time-consuming during the past three years?

- Government relations, political directives, and regulatory and compliance issues
- Reporting to or managing the board
- Owner and investor relations
- Setting strategy
- Media relations
- Day-to-day management
- Employee relations, corporate culture
- Customer relations
- Building top management teams
- Securing critical resources
- Others

Governance

5. What are the two most useful practices of corporate governance at your company?
6. Who are the stakeholders that the board considers most significant? How does the board balance the interests of shareholders or investors with those of other stakeholders?
7. In your most important acquisition, divestiture, or joint venture of recent years, what roles did the board, non-executive directors, largest owner, and minority owners play?
8. What are the two most important criteria your company has used in selecting non-executive directors?

Human Resources

9. What are the top two priorities for human resources management in the company?
10. What are the two most important pieces of advice you will give your successor?
11. Projecting your company five years into the future, what will you want it to look like?

Conclusion

12. Is there any other aspect of your leadership, strategy, governance, or human resources that we should have asked you about?

ACKNOWLEDGMENTS

Luis Ballesteros, doctoral student, Wharton School, University of Pennsylvania

Jeffrey Bernstein, Managing Director, Penn Wharton China Center, Beijing, China

Ruby Chen, Deputy Director, Executive Education, and Director of Company-Specific Programs, China Europe International Business School

Maggie Cheng, General Manager and Secretary-General, China Entrepreneur Club

Charles Chow, Senior Consultant, Deloitte Consulting

Tony Fang, Associate Professor of Human Resources Management and Employment Relations, Monash University

Renata Flores, Researcher, Program Evaluation, Philadelphia and Mexico City

Gordon Gao, Deputy Director, Executive Education, and Director of Open Enrollment Programs, China Europe International Business School

Mark Hanna, Independent Researcher

David Huang, Senior Manager, Executive MBA Program, China Europe International Business School

Jianwu Jiang, School of Management, Shenzhen University

Jeffrey Klein, Executive Director, McNulty Leadership Program, Wharton School, University of Pennsylvania

Samuel Li, Director, Translation Department, China Europe International Business School

Larry Liu, Research Assistant, University of Pennsylvania

John Mahaney, Contributing Editor, PublicAffairs Books

Marshall Meyer, Professor of Management, Wharton School, University of Pennsylvania

Mukul Pandya, Executive Director/Editor-in-Chief, Knowledge@Wharton Network, Wharton School, University of Pennsylvania

Raphael Sagalyn, ICM/Sagalyn Literary Agency

Danyang Wang, Research Assistant, University of Pennsylvania

Lei Wang, Account Director, Executive Education, China Europe International
    Business School
Qinjiang Wang, Director, Alumni Relations Office, China Europe International
    Business School
John W. Wright, John W. Wright Literary Agency
Kevin Zhang, Researcher, China Entrepreneur Club
Z. John Zhang, Professor of Marketing, Wharton School, and Executive Faculty
    Director, Penn Wharton China Center
Lilian Zhang, Senior Research Assistant, China Europe International Business
    School
Weijiong Zhang, Vice President and Co-Dean, Professor of Strategy, China Europe
    International Business School
All China Federation of Industry and Commerce
China Entrepreneur Club
China Europe International Business School
        Alumni Office
        Beijing Office
        Case Center
        Executive Education Program Office
        Executive MBA Program Office
        Research Committee
        Translation Department
Knowledge@Wharton
National School of Development, Peking
Penn Wharton China Center
Wharton School, University of Pennsylvania

NOTES

1. Introduction: Not the American Way

1. Among the accounts of Zhang's life and career is Shang, 2003. The Haier Group is strictly speaking an employee-owned cooperative, although it gives every appearance of being run just as a private business. Unlike most of the leaders we interviewed, Zhang has no personal wealth associated with the company. He receives only a modest salary.

2. See http://www.chinadaily.com.cn/bizchina/2006-03/14/content_535847.htm.

3. Gutmann and Thompson, 2012; Fligstein and Zhang, 2010.

4. Chan, 2011; Zacks, 2015; Stewart et al., 2014; World Steel Association, 2015.

5. Vlasic, 2015.

6. Wong, 2015.

7. Brown and Fung, 2015.

8. Burkitt, Lublin, and Mattioli, 2015; Tsang, 2015.

9. Organisation for Economic Co-operation and Development, 2016; Wilkes, 2016.

10. Forsythe and Ansfield, 2015; Holz, 2008; Bureau of Economic Analysis, 2015.

11. Womack, Jones, and Roos, 1990.

12. Waldman et al., 2001.

13. Bray and Tsang, 2016; Revill and Spegele, 2016.

14. Yao, 2016; National Bureau of Statistics of China, 2015.

15. Due to statistical categorization changes, we use gross industrial output value for the years 1980 to 1997 and revenue from principal business for the years 1998 to 2013; ¥ = US$0.155 as of September 16, 2016.

16. Brown and Fung, 2015.

17. Economist Intelligence Unit, 2015.

18. Friedman, 2005.

19. Weber, 1958; Lenski, 1961.

20. Bendix, 2001.

21. Wiener, 2004.

22. Guillen, 1994.

23. House et al., 2004; Javidan et al., 2006; see also Martin et al., 2013, and Zhang et al., 2012.

24. Birkinshaw, 2012.

25. Hsieh, 2013; Mackey and Sisodia, 2014.

26. We have also been informed by many studies of Chinese companies, their executives, and their employment markets, including Barkema et al., 2015; Chen, 2003; Cooke, 2013; Cooke and Budhwar 2015; Fu, 2015; Haley, Haley, and Tan, 2004; Lardy, 2014; Li, Tsui, and Weldon, 2003; Sheldon, Sun, and Sanders, 2014; Tse, 2015; Tsui, Bian, and Cheng, 2014; Tsui and Lau, 2002; Varma and Budhwar, 2014; and Warner, 2009.

2. Their Own Way Forward

1. Ouchi, 1981.

2. Peters and Waterman, 1982.

3. Nee and Opper, 2012.

4. See He and Yang, 2015, for the Chinese data and Hathaway and Litan, 2014, and Li and Guisinger, 1991, for the US data.

5. Khanna and Palepu, 1997.

6. *People's Justice*, 1982.

7. Heilmann, 2008.

8. Tan and Litschert, 1994.

9. Lau, Qian, and Roland, 2000; Roland, 2002.

10. Wu and Huang, 2008.

11. He, 2000.

12. Chandler, 1962.

13. Chakravarthy and Yau, 2015; Weber, 1958; Ling, 2006; Useem and Liang, 2009.

14. Ibid.

15. Ibid.

16. Ibid.

17. Yahoo Finance, 2016.

18. Charan, Carey, and Useem, 2014.

19. Vogel, 2011, p. 447.

20. Ibid., p. 467.

21. Vogel, 2011; Kissinger, 2011; Ren, 2015.

22. Smith, 2000.

23. Kilachand, 2012; Kroll and Dolan, 2015.

24. Mitchell, 2016.

25. Mitchell, 2016; Bloomberg, 2016.

26. *Forbes,* 2016.

27. Ma, 2015; Gan, 2015.

28. Hanergy, 2016; MBA Lib, 2016; Sina Finance, 2015; Wong and Ma, 2015.

29. De Cremer and Tao, 2015; Shih, 2015.

30. Zhang et al., 2008.

31. Schein, 2010.

32. *Financial Times,* 2016; see also Wildau, 2015.

3. The Learning Company

1. Conger, 2004; Doh, 2003; Guglielmino and Guglielmino, 1994; Hiemstra, 1994; Long and Morris, 1995; McCall, 2004.

2. Edwards, 2015.

3. By 2014, however, the Chinese government was pushing foreign multinationals hard on patent protections and products that dominated local markets in order to open up more opportunities for Chinese business (Cendrowski, 2014).

4. Wei, n.d.

5. Ibid.

6. Zuo, 2015.

7. Hagerty, 2016.

4. Strategic Agility for the Long Game

1. Carew, 2016; Dou and Chu, 2016; Mozur and Isaac, 2016.

2. Fligstein, 1990.

3. Erisman, 2015; Clark, 2016.

4. Erisman, 2015, p. 10.

5. Ibid., p. 12.

6. Ibid., p. 20.

7. Fannin, 2014.

8. Erisman, 2015, p. 164; Wang, 2010.

9. This section is based on public sources.

10. Wei, n.d.; the concept of a central idea is drawn from Charan, Carey, and Useem, 2014.

11. He and Yang, 2015; Hathaway and Litan, 2014.

12. Bouchikhi and Kimberly, 2007.

5. Talent Management

1. This description is based on McGregor, 2010.

2. Warner, 1996, 2009.

3. Lansbury and McKern, 1984.

4. For a discussion of these practices, see Brugger, 1976.

5. Child and Warner, 2003.

6. Warner, 1996.

7. Mitchell, 2014.

8. Warner, 1999.

9. Kuruvilla, Lee, and Gallagher, 2011.

10. Liu, 2015; Cappelli and Keller, 2013.

11. Akhtar, 2008.

12. Zhang, 2008.

13. Zhao, Zhang, and Poon, 2012.

14. Li and Sheldon, 2010.

15. Ibid.

16. Yen, 2013.

17. Cappelli, 2014.

18. Boston Consulting Group, 2014.

19. For an example and a summary of the literature in this area, see Alves, Manz, and Butterfield, 2005.

20. See Pye, 1990.

21. Cooper, Wehrly, and Bao, 1997.

22. Ralston et al., 1999.

23. Li and Yeh, 2007; Ma and Tsui, 2015; McDonald, 2011; Redding, 1995; Tsui et al. 2004.

24. Osnos, 2014.

25. An example is the popularity of Yu Dan's *Confucius from the Heart: Ancient Wisdom for Today's World* (Yu, 2013), which adapts aspects of Confucian thought for the purpose of improving individual happiness—a distinctly non-Confucian value. A discussion of this popularity is found in Melvin, 2007.

26. See, for example, Flannery, 2012; Flannery found that the virtuous thoughts attributed to Li Ka-shing by his foundation were in fact made up.

27. Bell, 2008; Hawes, 2008; Yao, S., 2013; Pye, 1990; Rarick, 2007.

28. See, for example, Xuecon, 2015.

29. From a private interview; as neither CEO nor chair of the company, this human resources director is not included among our seventy-two leadership interviews listed at the back of the book.

30. Good background information about Alibaba's history and practices can be found in Shiying and Avery, 2009, as well as in Porter Erisman's 2012 documentary film, *Crocodile in the Yangtze* (Erisman, 2012).

31. *China Daily/Asia News Network,* 2014. One version of this account has Jack Ma explaining the company name the night the company was founded; see Barboza, 2014. The text of Alibaba and the Forty Thieves can be found at http://www.pitt.edu/~dash/alibaba.html.

32. Erisman, 2012.

33. D'Onfro, 2014.

34. Ibid.

35. Francolla, 2014.

36. Background information for this account was provided by Wharton MBA students Ronald AngSiy, Mira Batchbarova, Kunal Dag, Aman Jain, Kyul Ko, and Kelly Xu as part of their coursework for Management 612, Fall 2015; they included an interview with Xiaomi co-founder Liu De.

37. BBC News, 2014.

38. For a description of the intense devotion of the Xiaomi user base, see Mozur and Wang, 2014.

39. Cnet, 2014.

40. Mu, 2014.

41. China Europe International Business School, 2011.

42. Frear, Cao, and Zhao, 2012.

6. The Big Boss

1. McChrystal et al., 2015.

2. Knowledge@Wharton, 2009; Haier Group, 2016; Zhang, 2014; Useem, 2014.

3. Frear, Cao, and Zhao, 2012.

4. Witt and Redding, 2014.

5. Fu and Yukl, 2000; Wang, Tsui, and Xin, 2011.

6. House et al., 2004; Javidan et al., 2006; see also Martin et al., 2013, and Zhang et al., 2012.

7. Data provided by Aon Hewitt.

8. The material in this section and all the quotations are drawn from Wang and Zhang, 2011.

9. Epstein, 2011.

10. Khurana, 2004; Lublin, Zimmerman, and Terhune, 2007; Stewart, 2006.

11. Chen and Farh, 2010; Farh and Cheng, 2000.

7. Growth as Gospel

1. Wachtell et al., 2015; Pfizer, 2016; Bray, 2016.

2. Fligstein and Zhang, 2011.

3. Fan et al., 2014; Xu, 2011.

4. Zeng and Williamson, 2003.

5. Kotler and Lee, 2004; Marquis and Qian, 2014.

6. Murray and Fu, 2016; Gu, Hung, and Tse, 2008.

7. From an interview with Xu Peng, vice-CEO of Shanghai Yidian Holding Group Co. (As neither CEO nor board chair of the company, he is not included among our seventy-two leadership interviews listed at the back of the book.)

8. Private interview with bank president.

9. Kale, Singh, and Raman, 2009.

10. Thomson One Banker, 2016; Inkpen and Moffett, 2013.

11. Balcet, Wang, and Richet, 2012.

12. Young, 2010.

13. Quah, 2015.

14. See Quah, 2015, and Feng, Hu, and Moffitt, 2015.

15. Karmin, Mattioli, and Carew, 2016.

16. Mason, 1959; Kaysen, 1996.

8. Governance as Partnership

1. This section draws from Liang and Useem, 2009.

2. Allen, 2014.

3. Gough, 2016.

4. Bradsher, 2016; Wei, 2016; Forsythe, Bradsher, and Buckley, 2016.

5. Organisation for Economic Co-operation and Development, 2011.

6. Ding, Zhang, and Zhang, 2007; Fan, Wong, and Zhang, 2007; Fan, Wong, and Zhang, 2005; Gul, Kim, and Qiu, 2010; Liu, 2006.

7. China Association for Public Companies, 2014.

8. Research Center of Shanghai Stock Exchange, 2012.

9. This section draws from Liang and Useem, 2009.

10. Research on the Quality of China's Listed Companies' Information Disclosure, 2008.

11. Corporate Governance Database of Nankai University, China Corporate Governance and Development Report, 2013.

12. Standing Committee of the Tenth National People's Congress of the People's Republic of China, 2011.

13. Shenzhen Stock Exchange, 2006.

14. Comprehensive Research Institute of Shenzhen Stock Exchange, 2011.

15. Vanke, 2014.

16. Shenzhen Stock Exchange, 2006.

17. Ibid.

18. This section draws from Charan, Carey, and Useem, 2014.

19. Much of what follows is drawn from Useem and Liang, 2009, and Charan, Carey, and Useem, 2014.

20. Ibid.

21. Ibid.

22. Liang, Useem, and Zhao, 2014.

23. Yu, 2015; *South China Morning Post*, 2016.

24. US Securities and Exchange Commission, 2014; Palepu et al., 2015.

25. Bebchuk, 2014.

26. Demos, 2015; Liang, 2015; Sugawara, 2015; Tang, 2015; Yahoo Finance, 2016.

27. Berle and Means, 1991; Charan, Carey, and Useem, 2014.

28. Witt and Redding, 2014.
29. Davis, 2011; Mayer, 2013; Useem, 1996, 1998.
30. Charan, Carey, and Useem, 2014.

9. What's Distinctive, What's Sustainable

1. Camerer, Loewenstein, and Weber, 1989.

2. One of the biggest differences was that the Boston companies were disproportionately in the hardware business, which faded, while the Silicon Valley companies were disproportionately in the software business. See Saxenian, 1996.

3. For a more recent example of the declining relevance of political connections, see Zhao and Lu, 2016.

4. Baron and Hannan, 2002.

5. For ideas about factors that drive founders out of their companies in the West, see Wasserman, 2003.

6. See Nelson, 2003.

7. Haier is partly government owned and certainly heavily influenced by the government, but its subsidiaries are listed on stock exchanges in Shanghai and Hong Kong.

8. See, for example, Parsons, 2005, and Ackoff, 1974.

9. See Johnson, 1982, and Henderson, 1983, for the opposing view.

REFERENCES

Ackoff, Russell, *Redesigning the Future: A Systems Approach to Societal Problems,* Wiley, 1974.

Akhtar, Syed, Daniel Z. Ding, and Gloria L. Ge, "Strategic HRM Practices and Their Impact on Company Performance in Chinese Enterprises," *Human Resource Management,* 47, 2008, 15–32.

All China Federation of Industry and Commerce, various years, http://www.china chamber.org.cn/web/c_00000002.

Allen, Jamie, "CG Watch 2014—Market Rankings," Asian Corporate Governance Association, 2014, http://www.acga-asia.org/public/files/CG_Watch_2014_ Key_Charts_Extract.pdf.

Alves, Jose C., Charles C. Manz, and D. Anthony Butterfield, "Developing Leadership Theory in Asia: The Role of Chinese Philosophy," *International Journal of Leadership Studies,* 1, 2005.

Aon Hewitt, *Top Companies for Leaders,* 2015, http://www.aon.com/human-capital -consulting/thought-leadership/talent/aon-hewitt-top-companies-for-leaders -highlights-report.jsp.

Balcet, Giovanni, Hua Wang, and Xavier Richet, "Geely: A Trajectory of Catching Up and Asset-Seeking Multinational Growth," *International Journal of Automotive Technology and Management,* 12, 2012, 360–375.

Barboza, David, "The Jack Ma Way: At Alibaba, the Founder Is Squarely in Charge," *New York Times,* September 6, 2014.

Barkema, Harry G., Xiao-Ping Chen, Gerard George, Yadong Luo, and Anne S. Tsui, "West Meets East: New Concepts and Theories," *Academy of Management Journal,* 58, 2015, 460–479.

Baron, James N., and Michael T. Hannan, "Organizational Blueprints for Success in High-Tech Start-Ups," *California Management Review,* 44, 2002, 8–36.

BBC News, "China's Xiaomi Becomes Most Valuable Tech Start-Up," December 30, 2014, http://www.bbc.com/news/business-30629883.

Bebchuk, Lucian, "Alibaba's Governance Leaves Investors at a Disadvantage," *New York Times,* September 16, 2014.

Bell, Daniel A., *China's New Confucianism: Politics and Everyday life in a Changing Society,* Princeton University Press, 2008.

Bendix, Reinhard, *Work and Authority in Industry: Managerial Ideologies in the Course of Industrialization,* Transaction Publishers, 2001 (originally published in 1956).

Berle, Adolf Augustus, and Gardiner C. Means, *The Modern Corporation and Private Property,* Transaction Publishers, 1991 (originally published in 1932).

Birkinshaw, Julian, "Management Ideology: The Last Bastion of American Hegemony," *Business Strategy Review* (London Business School), June 2012, http://bsr.london.edu/blog/post-54/index.html.

Bloomberg, "Yong Hui Li, Chairman/CEO, AutoChina International Ltd.," 2016, http://www.bloomberg.com/profiles/people/16666818-hui-li-yong.

Boston Consulting Group, The BCG Global Manufacturing Cost-Competitiveness Index, BCG Perspectives, 2014, https://www.bcgperspectives.com/content/biinteractive/lean_manufacturing_globalization_bcg_global_manufacturing_cost_competitiveness_index.

Bouchikhi, Hamid, and John R. Kimberly, *The Soul of the Corporation: How to Manage the Identity of Your Company,* Pearson Prentice Hall, 2007.

Bradsher, Keith, "Xiao Gang, China's Top Securities Regulator, Ousted over Market Turmoil," *New York Times,* February 19, 2016.

Bray, Chad, "Pfizer and Allergan Call Off Merger," *New York Times,* April 6, 2016.

Bray, Chad, and Amie Tsang, "ChemChina Makes $43 Billion Offer for Syngenta," *New York Times,* February 3, 2016.

Brown, Eliot, and Esther Fung, "Building Homes in the U.S., Selling in China," *Wall Street Journal,* December 30, 2015.

Brugger, Walter, *Democracy and Organization in the Chinese Industrial Enterprise, 1948–1953,* Cambridge University Press, 1976.

Bureau of Economic Analysis, US Department of Commerce, National Economic Accounts, 2015, http://www.bea.gov/national/index.htm#gdp.

Burkitt, Laurie, Joann S. Lublin, and Dana Mattioli, "China's Haier to Buy GE Appliance Business for $5.4 Billion," *Wall Street Journal,* January 15, 2015.

Camerer, Colin, George Loewenstein, and Martin Weber, "The Curse of Knowledge in Economic Settings: An Experimental Analysis," *Journal of Political Economy,* 97, 1989, 1232–1254.

Cappelli, Peter, private conversations with students at Chinese universities, 2014.

Cappelli, Peter, and Laura Huang, "Are Entrepreneurs Different Than the Rest of Us?" *Wall Street Journal,* November 3, 2014.

Cappelli, Peter H., and J. R. Keller, "A Study of the Extent and Potential Causes of Alternative Employment Arrangements," *Industrial and Labor Relations Review,* 66, 2013, 874–901.

Cappelli, Peter, Harbir Singh, Jitendra Singh, and Michael Useem, *The India Way: How India's Top Business Leaders Are Revolutionizing Management,* Harvard Business Press, 2010.

———, "The India Way: Lessons for the U.S.," *Academy of Management Perspectives,* 24, 2010, 6–24.

———, "Leadership Lessons from India: How the Best Indian Companies Drive Performance by Investing in People," *Harvard Business Review,* March 2010, 90–97.

———, "Indian Business Leadership: Broad Mission and Creative Value," *Leadership Quarterly,* 26, 2015, 7–12.

Carew, Rick, "The Road to the Uber-Didi Deal," *Wall Street Journal,* August 2, 2016.

Cendrowski, Scott, "Cold War on Business: Beijing Pulls Back the Welcome Mat," *Financial Times,* October 8, 2014.

Chakravarthy, Bala, and David Yau, "Leading Chinese Companies on to the International Stage," *Perspectives for Managers,* 2015.

Chan, Anita, ed., *Walmart in China,* Cornell University Press, 2011.

Chandler, Alfred D., Jr., *Strategy and Structure: Chapters in the History of American Enterprise,* Beard Books, 1962.

Charan, Ram, Dennis Carey, and Michael Useem, *Boards That Lead,* Harvard Business School Press, 2014.

Chen, C. C., and J. L., Farh, "Developments in Understanding Chinese Leadership: Paternalism and Its Elaborations, Moderations, and Alternatives," in Michael Harris Bond, ed., *Handbook of Chinese Psychology,* Oxford University Press, 2010.

Chen, Ming-Jer, *Inside Chinese Business: A Guide for Managers Worldwide,* Harvard Business Review Press, 2003.

Child, John, and Malcolm Warner, "Culture and Management in China," in Malcolm Warner, ed., *Culture and Management in Asia,* Routledge, 2003.

China Association for Public Companies, Report on Corporate Governance for Listed Companies in China, Economic and Management Publication House, Beijing, 2014.

China Center for Economic Research, Peking University, database, 2015, http:// ccer.pku.edu.cn.

China Corporate Governance, *Related Party Transactions and Horizontal Competition,* 2001.

China Daily/Asia News Network, "Inside Alibaba's 'Kung Fu' Culture," October 10, 2014.

China Entrepreneur, "Liu Chuanzhi's Catchword 'Replay the Game': Lenovo's Critical Methodology," June 2013.

———, "Secret of Lenovo Management: The 4-Steps Replay-the-Game Methodology," July 2013.

China Europe International Business School, Chinese Executive Survey, Shanghai, 2011.

China Statistical Yearbook of Industry and Commerce, 2015, http://www.stats.gov.cn/tjsj/ndsj/2015/indexeh.htm.

Clark, Duncan, *Alibaba: The House That Jack Ma Built*, Ecco, 2016.

Cnet, "Xiaomi's Hugo Barra: True World Phones in 2 Years, Android All the Way," March 24, 2014, http://www.cnet.com/news/xiaomi-world-phone-in-2-years-android-all-the-way-says-hugo-barra.

Comprehensive Research Institute of Shenzhen Stock Exchange, Research Report on Corporate Governance: Status Quo, Key Areas and the Role of the Stock Exchange, 2011, https://www.szse.cn/main/files/2011/05/12/8455129 32999.pdf.

Conger, Jay A, "Developing Leadership Capability: What's Inside the Black Box?" *Academy of Management Executive*, 18, 2004, 136–139.

Cooke, Frank Lee, *Human Resource Management in China: New Trends and Practices*, Routledge, 2013.

Cooke, Frank Lee, and Pawan Budhwar, "Human Resource Management in China and India," *Handbook of Human Resource Management in Emerging Markets*, Elgar, 2015.

Cooper, Terry L., Mark Wehrly, and Yongjian Bao, "Organization Loyalty and Personal Ethics: The Moral Properties of Chinese Cadres," *International Journal of Public Administration*, 20, 1997, 1791–1820.

Corporate Governance Database of Nankai University, China Corporate Governance and Development Report, 2013, http://www.chinacsrmap.org/Org_Show_EN.asp?ID=1030.

Davis, Gerald F., *Managed by the Markets: How Finance Re-Shaped America*, Oxford University Press, 2011.

Dealogic, Annual China Outbound M&A Volume, 2016, http://www.dealogic.com/media/market-insights/ma-statshot.

De Cremer, David, and Tian Tao, "Leading Huawei: Seven Leadership Lessons of Ren Zhengfei," *European Business Review*, September 17, 2015.

Demos, Telis, "Alibaba's Dealings with Chinese Regulator Draws SEC Interest," *Wall Street Journal*, February 14, 2015.

Ding, Yuan, Hua Zhang, and Junxi Zhang, "Private vs State Ownership and Earnings Management: Evidence from Chinese Listed Companies," *Corporate Governance: An International Review*, 15, 2007, 223–238.

Doh, Jonathan P., "Can Leadership Be Taught? Perspectives from Management Educators," *Academy of Management Learning and Education*, 2, 2003, 54–67.

D'Onfro, Jillian, "We Talked to the Man Who Knows More About Alibaba's Beginning Than Any Other American," *Business Insider*, 2014, http://www.business insider.com/porter-erisman-crocodile-in-the-yangtze-2014-5.

Dou, Eva, and Kathy Chu, "Uber's Efforts to Build Chinese Business Ultimately Fail Against Homegrown Rival Didi," *Wall Street Journal*, August 1, 2016.

Dullforce, Anne-Britt, *Financial Times*, "FT 500 2015 Introduction and Methodology," June 19, 2015, http://www.ft.com/intl/cms/s/2/1fda5794--169f-11e5-b07f -00144feabdc0.html.

Economist Intelligence Unit, Long-Term Macroeconomic Forecasts: Key Trends to 2050, 2015, http://pages.eiu.com/rs/783-XMC-194/images/EIU_Long-term Forecasts_KeyTrends2050_FINAL2.pdf?mkt_tok=3RkMMJWWfF9ws RouvqnAZKXonjHpfsX56usoUaC2lMI%2F0ER3fOvrPUfGjI4GT8ZlI%2B SLDwEYGJlv6SgFTbjGMbht2bgMUhU%3D.

Edwards, Suzanne, "The Dawn of Chinese Consultancy Companies?" *China Business Review*, March 10, 2015.

Epstein, Gady, "Alibaba.com CEO, COO Resign; Read Jack Ma's Letter to Staff," *Forbes*, February 21, 2011.

Erisman, Porter, *Alibaba's World*, Macmillan, 2015.

———, *Crocodile in the Yangtze* (documentary film), 2012, http://www.crocodile intheyangtze.com/production.html.

Fan, Joseph P. H., T. J. Wong, and Tianyu Zhang, "The Emergence of Corporate Pyramids in China," Chinese University of Hong Kong, 2005, http://www .rieti.go.jp/users/peng-xu/project/asia/pdf/fan_wong_zhang.pdf.

Fan, Joseph P. H., Tak Jun Wong, and Tianyu Zhang, "Organizational Structure as a Decentralization Device: Evidence from Corporate Pyramids," 2007, SSRN 963430.

Fan, Shenggen, Ravi Kanbur, Shang-Jin Wei, and Xiaobo Zhang, *The Oxford Companion to the Economics of China*, Oxford University Press, 2014.

Fannin, Rebecca, "A Look at What Makes Alibaba's Jack Ma Tick, and How He Did It," *Forbes*, September 21, 2014.

Farh, Jiing-Lih, and Bor-Shiuan Cheng, "A Cultural Analysis of Paternalistic Leadership in Chinese Organizations," in Anne S. Tsui and J. T. Li, eds., *Management and Organizations in Context*, Macmillan, 2000.

Feng, Shuaizhang, Yingyao Hu, and Robert Moffitt, "Long-Run Trends in Unemployment and Labor Force Participation in China," NBER Working Paper, 2015.

Financial Times, "Global MBA Ranking 2016," 2016, http://rankings.ft.com/ businessschoolrankings/global-mba-ranking-2016.

Flannery, Russell, "8 (Genuine!) Tips for Success from Asia's Richest Man Li Kashing," *Forbes.com*, March 7, 2012.

Fligstein, Neil, *The Transformation of Corporate Capital*, Harvard University Press, 1990.

Fligstein, Neil, and Jianjun Zhang, "A New Agenda for Research on the Trajectory of Chinese Capitalism," *Management and Organization Review*, 7, 2010, 39–62.

Forbes, "Li Hejun," 2016, http://www.forbes.com/profile/li-hejun.

Forsythe, Michael, and Jonathan Ansfield, "Fading Economy and Graft Crackdown Rattle China's Leaders," *New York Times,* August 22, 2015.

Forsythe, Michael, Keith Bradsher, and Chris Buckley, "Chinese Securities Regulator Is Out, But Little May Change," *New York Times,* February 20, 2016.

Francolla, Gina, "Alibaba: Bigger Than 494 of the S&P 500 Companies," CNBC, November 10, 2014, http://www.cnbc.com/2014/11/10/alibaba-bigger-than-494-of-the-sp-500-companies.html.

Frear, Katherine A., Yang Cao, and Wei Zhao, "CEO Background and the Adoption of Western-Style Human Resource Practices in China," *International Journal of Human Resource Management,* 2012, 23, 4009–4024.

Friedman, Thomas L., *The World Is Flat: A Brief History of the Twenty-First Century,* Farrar, Straus and Giroux, 2005.

Fu, Ping Ping, and Gary Yukl, "Perceived Effectiveness of Influence Tactics in the United States and China," *Leadership Quarterly,* 11, 2000, 251–266.

Fu, Xiaolan, *China's Path to Innovation,* Cambridge University Press, 2015.

Gan, Jie, "How Hanergy Has Exposed Weaknesses in Hong Kong's Stock Market, *Forbes,* April 1, 2015.

Gough, Neil, "China G.D.P. Growth at Slowest Pace Since 2009, Data Shows," *New York Times,* January 18, 2016.

Gu, F. F., K. Hung, and D. K. Tse, "When Does Guanxi Matter? Issues of Capitalization and Its Dark Sides, *Journal of Marketing,* 72, 2008, 12–28.

Guglielmino, Lucy M., and Paul J. Guglielmino, "Practical Experience with Self-Directed Learning in Business and Industry Human Resource Development," *New Directions for Adult and Continuing Education,* 1994, 39–46.

Guillen, Mauro F., *Models of Management: Work, Authority, and Organization in a Comparative Perspective,* University of Chicago Press, 1994.

——, *The Limits of Convergence: Globalization and Organizational Change in Argentina, South Korea, and Spain,* Princeton University Press, 2010.

Gul, Ferdinand A., Jeong-Bon Kim, and Annie A. Qiu, "Ownership Concentration, Foreign Shareholding, Audit Quality, and Stock Price Synchronicity: Evidence from China," *Journal of Financial Economics,* 95, 2010, 425–442.

Gutmann, Amy, and Dennis Thompson, *The Spirit of Compromise: Why Governing Demands It and Campaigning Undermines It,* Princeton University Press, 2012.

Hagerty, James R., "A Class of Cultures at Alabama Factory," *Wall Street Journal,* February 28, 2016.

Haier Group, website, May 7, 2016, http://www.haier.net/en/about_haier.

Haley, George T., Usha C. V. Haley, and Chin Tiong Tan, *The Chinese Tao of Business: The Logic of Successful Business Strategy,* Wiley, 2004.

Hanergy, News, 2016, http://www.hanergy.com/en/news/news_hn.html.

Hathaway, Ian, and Rober E. Litan, "Declining Business Dynamism in the United States: A Look at States and Metros," *Economic Studies at Brookings,* May 2014, 1–7.

Hawes, C., "Representing Corporate Culture in China: Official and Academic Perspectives," *The China Journal,* 59, 2008, 31–62.

He, Canfei, and Rudai Yang, "Determinants of Firm Failure: Empirical Evidence from China," *Growth and Change,* 47, 2015, 72–92.

He, Zengke. "Corruption and Anti-Corruption in Reform China," *Communist and Post-Communist Studies,* 33, 2000, 243–270.

Heilmann, Sebastian, "From Local Experiments to National Policy: The Origins of China's Distinctive Policy Process, *The China Journal,* 59, 2008, 1–30.

Henderson, David R., "The Myth of MITI," *Fortune,* August 8, 1983, 113–116.

Hiemstra, Roger, "Self-Directed Learning," *The Sourcebook for Self-Directed Learning,* 1994.

Holz, Carsten A., "China's Economic Growth 1978–2025: What We Know Today about China's Economic Growth Tomorrow," *World Development,* 36, 2008, 1665–1691.

House, Robert J., Paul J. Hanges, Mansour Javidan, Peter Dorfman, and Vipin Gupta, *Culture, Leadership, and Organizations: The Globe Study of 62 Societies,* Sage Publications, 2004.

Hsieh, Tony, *Delivering Happiness: A Path to Profits, Passion, and Purpose,* Grand Central Publishing, 2013.

Inkpen, Andrew, and Michael Moffett, "Volvo and Geely," Thunderbird School of Global Management, 2013, http://caseseries.thunderbird.edu/case/volvo-and-geely.

Institute for Mergers, Acquisitions, and Alliances, M&A Statistics, China, 2016, https://imaa-institute.org/statistics-mergers-acquisitions/#Mergers-Acquisitions-China.

International Monetary Fund, World Economic Outlook, October 2015, http://knoema.com/IMFWEO2015Oct/imf-world-economic-outlook-weo-october-2015.

International Monetary Fund, World Economic Outlook, October 2016, http://www.imf.org/external/pubs/ft/weo/2016/01/weodata/index.aspx.

Javidan, Mansour, Peter W. Dorfman, Mary Sully du Luque, and Robert J. House, "In the Eye of the Beholder: Cross Cultural Lessons in Leadership from Project GLOBE," *Academy of Management Perspectives,* 20, 2006, 67–90.

Johnson, Chalmers A., *MITI and the Japanese Miracle: The Growth of Industrial Policy, 1925–1975,* Stanford University Press, 1982.

Kale, Prashant, Harbir Singh, and Anand Raman, "Don't Integrate Your Acquisitions, Partner with Them," *Harvard Business Review,* December 2009.

Karmin, Craig, Dana Mattioli, and Rick Carew, "Anbang's Curious Starwood Courtship," *Wall Street Journal,* April 4, 2016.

Kaysen, Carl, ed., *The American Corporation Today,* Oxford University Press, 1996.

Khanna, Tarun, and Krishna G. Palepu, "Why Focused Strategy May Be Wrong for Emerging Markets," *Harvard Business Review,* 75, 1997, 41–51.

Khurana, Rakesh, *Searching for a Corporate Savior: The Irrational Quest for Charismatic CEOs,* Princeton University Press, 2004.

Kilachand, Sean, "Forbes History: The Original 1987 List of International Billionaires," *Forbes,* March 21, 2012.

Kissinger, Henry, *On China,* Penguin, 2011.

Knowledge@Wharton, "Haier Group's Zhang Ruimin: Standing at the 21st Century's 'Global Crossroads,'" June 24, 2009, http://knowledge.wharton.upenn.edu/article/haier-groups-zhang-ruimin-standing-at-the-21st-centurys-global-crossroads.

Kotler, Philip, and Nancy Lee, *Corporate Social Responsibility,* Wiley, 2004.

Kroll, Luisa, and Kerry A. Dolan, "The World's Billionaires," *Forbes,* 2015.

Kuruvilla, Sarosh, Ching Kwan Lee, and Mary E. Gallagher, *From Iron Rice Bowl to Informalization: Markets, Workers, and the State in a Changing China,* Cornell University Press, 2011.

Lam, W. Raphael, Xiaoguang Liu, and Alfred Schipke, "China's Labor Market in the 'New Normal,'" International Monetary Fund Working Paper, 2015.

Lansbury, Russell D., and Bruce D. McKern, "Management at the Enterprise Level in China," *Industrial Relations Journal,* 15, 1984, 56–63.

Lardy, Nicholas R., *Markets over Mao: The Rise of Private Business in China,* Peterson Institute for International Economics, 2014.

Lau, Lawrence J., Yingyi Qian, and Gerard Roland, "Reform Without Losers: An Interpretation of China's Dual-Track Approach to Transition," *Journal of Political Economy,* 108, 2000, 120–143.

Lenski, Gerhard, *The Religious Factor,* Doubleday, 1961.

Li, Jiatao, and Stephen Guisinger, "Comparative Business Failures of Foreign-Controlled Firms in the United States," *Journal of International Business Studies,* 22, 1991, 209–224.

Li, J. T., Anne S. Tsui, and Elizabeth Weldon, eds., *Management and Organization in the Chinese Context,* Palgrave, 2003.

Li, Shaomin, and Kuang S. Yeh, "Mao's Pervasive Influence on Chinese CEOs," *Harvard Business Review,* 85, 2007, 16–17.

Li, Yiqiong, and Peter Sheldon, "HRM Lives Inside and Outside the Firm: Employers, Skill Shortages and the Local Labour Market in China, *International Journal of Human Resource Management,* 21, 2010, 2173–2193.

Liang, Jonathan R. "Alibaba: Why It Could Fall 50% Further," *Barron's,* September 12, 2015.

Liang, Neng, and Michael Useem, "China," *The Handbook of International Corporate Governance,* Institute of Directors, 2009.

———, "Corporate Governance in China," *Nankai Business Review,* 2009.

Liang, Neng, Michael Useem, and Ziqian Zhao, "Lenovo 2009: The Role of Board Chairman in a Turnaround," China Europe International Business School, 2014.

Ling, Zhijun, *The Lenovo Affair,* Wiley, 2006.

Liu, Qiao, "Corporate Governance in China: Current Practices, Economic Effects and Institutional Determinants," *CESifo Economic Studies,* 52, 2006, 415–453.

Liu, Xiangmin, "How Institutional and Organizational Characteristics Explain the Growth of Contingent Work in China," *Industrial and Labor Relations Review,* 68, 2015, 372–397.

Long, Huey B., and S. Morris, "Self-Directed Learning in Business and Industry: A Review of the Literature, 1983–1993," in Huey B. Long, ed., *New Dimensions in Self-Directed Learning,* Oklahoma Research Center for Continuing Professional and Higher Education, 1995.

Lublin, Joanne S., Ann Zimmerman, and Chad Terhune, "Behind Nardelli's Abrupt Exit," *Wall Street Journal,* January 4, 2007.

Ma, Hao, Shu Lin, and Neng Liang, *Corporate Political Strategies of Private Chinese Firms,* Routledge, 2012.

Ma, Li, and Anne S. Tsui, "Traditional Chinese Philosophies and Contemporary Leadership," *Leadership Quarterly,* 26, 2015, 13–24.

Ma, Wayne, "Hanergy Thin Film to Cut Workforce by More Than a Third in Restructuring," *Wall Street Journal,* August 30, 2015.

Mackey, John, and Rajendra Sisodia, *Conscious Capitalism,* Harvard Business Review Press, 2014.

Marquis, Christopher, and Cuili Qian, "Corporate Social Responsibility Reporting in China: Symbol or Substance?" *Organizational Science,* 25, 2014, 127–148.

Martin, Gillian S., Mary A. Keating, Christian J. Resick, Erna Szabo, Ho Kwong Kwan, and Chunyan Peng, "The Meaning of Leader Integrity: A Comparative Study Across Anglo, Asian, and Germanic Cultures," *Leadership Quarterly,* 24, 2013, 445–461.

Maslow, Abraham H., "Theory Z," *Journal of Transpersonal Psychology,* 1, 1969, 31–47.

Mason, Edward S., ed., *The Corporation in Modern Society,* Harvard University Press, 1959.

Mayer, Colin, *Firm Commitment: Why the Corporation Is Failing Us and How to Restore Trust in It,* Oxford University Press, 2013.

MBA Lib, "Jun Li River Profile," 2016, http://wiki.mbalib.com/wiki/%E6%9D%8E%E6%B2%B3%E5%90%9B.

McCall, Morgan W., "Leadership Development Through Experience," *Academy of Management Executive,* 18, 2004, 127–130.

McChrystal, Stanley, with Tantum Collins, David Silverman, and Chris Fussell, *Team of Teams: New Rules of Engagement for a Complex World,* Portfolio, 2015.

McDonald, Paul, "Maoism Versus Confucianism: Ideological Influences on Chinese Business Leaders," *Journal of Management Development*, 30, 2011, 632–646.

McGregor, Richard, *The Party: The Secret World of China's Communist Rulers*, Harper, 2010.

Melvin, Sheil, "Yu Dan and China's Return to Confucius," *New York Times*, August 29, 2007.

Mitchell, Tom, "Walmart Wins China Labour Dispute," *Financial Times*, June 26, 2014.

———, "Li Yonghui, Chinese SelfMade 'Everyman,'" *Financial Times*, January 3, 2016.

Mozur, Paul, and Mike Isaac, "Uber to Sell to Rival Didi Chuxing and Create New Business in China," *New York Times*, August 1, 2016.

Mozur, Paul, and Shanshan Wang, "The Rise of a New Smartphone: China's Xiaomi," *New York Times*, December 14, 2014.

Mu, Eric, "Xiaomi Employee's Snobbery Backfires," *Forbes Asia*, August 5, 2014, http://www.forbes.com/sites/ericxlmu/2014/08/05/xiaomi-employees-snobbery-backfired/#72d597fa38c9.

Murray, Janet Y., and Frank Q. Fu, "Strategic Guanxi Orientation: How to Manage Distribution Channels in China," *Journal of International Management*, 22, 2016, 1–16.

Nankai University, Tianjin, 2015, privately provided data.

National Bureau of Statistics of China, *China Statistical Yearbook*, 2015, China Statistics Press.

Nee, Victor, and Sonja Opper, *Capitalism from Below: Markets and Institutional Change in China*, Harvard University Press, 2012.

———, "Markets and Institutional Change in China," Center for the Study of Economy and Society, Cornell University, 2013.

Nelson, Teresa, "The Persistence of Founder Influence: Management, Ownership, and Performance Effects at Initial Public Offerings," *Strategic Management Journal*, 24, 2003, 707–724.

Organisation for Economic Co-operation and Development, *Corporate Governance of Listed Companies in China: Self-Assessment by the China Securities Regulatory Commission*, OECD, 2011.

———, *Latin American Economic Outlook 2016: Toward A New Partnership with China*, OECD, 2016.

Osnos, Evan, "Confucius Comes Home," *The New Yorker*, January 13, 2014.

Ouchi, William, *Theory Z: How American Management Can Meet the Japanese Challenge*, Addison, 1981.

Palepu, Krishna, Suraj Srinivasan, Charles C. Y. Wang, and David Lane, "Alibaba Goes Public," Harvard Business School, November 2015.

Parsons, Talcott, *The Social System*, 2nd ed., Routledge, 2005.

People's Justice, "The Case of Ma Hanwen," September 1982.

Peters, Thomas J., and Robert H. Waterman, Jr., *In Search of Excellence: Lessons from America's Best-Run Companies,* Harper & Row, 1982.

Pfizer Inc., "Pfizer Announces Termination of Proposed Combination with Allergan," April 6, 2016, http://www.pfizer.com/news/press-release/press-release-detail/pfizer_announces_termination_of_proposed_combination_with_allergan.

Pye, Lucian W., "China: Erratic State, Frustrated Society," *Foreign Affairs,* Fall, 1990.

Quah, Danny, "The Simple Arithmetic of China's Growth Slowdown," in (blog) *Future Development: Economics to End Poverty,* Brookings, 2015.

Ralston, David A., Carolyn P. Egri, Sally Stewart, Robert H. Terpstra, and Yu Kaicheng, "Doing Business in the 21st Century with the New Generation of Chinese Managers: A Study of Generational Shifts in Work Values in China," *Journal of International Business Studies,* 30, 1999, 415–427.

Rarick, Charles A., "Confucius on Management: Understanding Chinese Cultural Values and Managerial Practices," *Journal of International Management Studies,* 2, 2007.

Redding, Gordon, *The Spirit of Chinese Capitalism,* Walter de Gruyter, 1995.

Ren, Daniel, "Beijing to End Price Controls for Most Products, *South China Morning Post,* May 8, 2015.

Research Center of Shanghai Stock Exchange, China Corporate Governance Report 2011: Related Party Transaction and Horizontal Competition, Shanghai People's Publication, Shanghai, 2012.

Research on the Quality of China's Listed Companies' Information Disclosure, 2008.

Revill, John, and Brian Spegele, "Syngenta Agrees to $43 Billion ChemChina Takeover," *Wall Street Journal,* February 3, 2016.

Rhodium Group, "Chinese FDI in the US: 2015 Recap," 2016, http://rhg.com/notes/chinese-fdi-in-the-us-2015-recap.

Roland, Gerard, "The Political Economy of Transition," *Journal of Economic Perspectives,* 16, 2002, 29–50.

Saxenian, AnnaLee, *Regional Advantage: Culture and Competition in Silicon Valley and Route 128,* Harvard University Press, 1996.

Schaffmeister, Niklas, *Brand Building and Marketing in Key Emerging Markets,* Springer, 2015.

Schein, Edgar H., *Organizational Culture and Leadership,* Jossey-Bass, 2010.

Senge, Peter, *The Fifth Discipline: The Art and Practice of the Learning Organization,* Doubleday, 2006 (originally published in 1990).

Shang, Jeannie Jin, *The Haier Way,* Homa & Sekey Books, 2003.

Shanghai Gildata Service Co., Ltd., TK, Shanghai, 2015, www.gildata.com.

Sheldon, Peter, Jian-Min James Sun, and Karin Sanders, "Special Issue on HRM in China: Differences Within the Country," *International Journal of Human Resource Management*, 25, 2014, 2213–2217.

Shenzhen Stock Exchange, "Shenzhen Stock Exchange," 2006, http://www.szse.cn/main/en/RulesandRegulations/SZSERules/GeneralRules/10636.shtml.

Shih, Gerry, "China's Huawei Leads International Patent Filings: WIPO," Reuters, March 19, 2015.

Shiying, Liu, and Martha Avery, *Alibaba : The Inside Story Behind Jack Ma and the Creation of the World's Biggest Online Marketplace,* Collins Business, 2009.

Sina Finance, "Li Hejun's Certainties and Uncertainties," 2015, http://finance.sina.com.cn/zl/energy/20150212/113721538161.shtml.

Smith, Craig S., "China's High-Flying Capitalist Crashes to Earth," *New York Times,* May 31, 2000.

Soros, George, "The Capitalist Threat," *Atlantic Monthly,* February, 1997.

South China Morning Post, "China Vanke Seeks Ally in Shenzhen Metro After Baoneng's Hostile Takeover Bid," March 13, 2016.

Srinivas, Nidhi, "Epistemic and Performative Quests for Authentic Management in India," *Organization,* 19, 2012, 145–158.

Standing Committee of the Tenth National People's Congress of the People's Republic of China, "Companies Law of the People's Republic of China," 2011, http://www.china.org.cn/china/LegislationsForm2001-2010/2011-02/11/content_21898292.htm.

Stewart, John, *Disney War,* Simon & Schuster, 2006.

Stewart, Terence P., Elizabeth J. Drake, Jessica Wang, Stephanie M. Bell, and Robert E. Scott, "Surging Steel Imports Put Up to Half a Million U.S. Jobs at Risk," Economic Policy Institute, 2014, http://www.epi.org/publication/surging-steel-imports.

Sugawara, Toru, "Slowing Growth, Clashes with Regulators Cloud Alibaba's Future, *Nikkei Asian Review,* February 5, 2015, http://asia.nikkei.com/magazine/20150205-Changes-in-the-air/Business/Slowing-growth-clashes-with-regulators-cloud-Alibaba-s-future.

Sun, Zhongjuan, W. Xie, K. Tian, and Y. Wang, "Capability Accumulation and the Growth Path of Lenovo," Technology and Management for Development Centre Working Paper, Oxford University, 2013.

Tan, J., and R. J. Litschert, "Environment-Strategy Relationship and Its Performance Implications: An Empirical Study of Chinese Electronics Industry," *Strategy Management Journal,* 15, 1994, 1–20.

Tang, Stephy, "Kering v Alibaba Sounds the Alarm on China's Online Counterfeits," *Managing Intellectual Property,* June 29, 2015.

Thomson One Banker, Mergers and Acquisitions database, 2016.

Trading Economics, China Wages, 2016, http://www.tradingeconomics.com/china/wages.

Tsang, Amie, "G.E. to Sell Appliance Division to Haier for $5.4 Billion," *New York Times,* January 15, 2015.

Tse, Edward, *China's Disruptors: How Alibaba, Xiaomi, Tencent, and Other Companies Are Changing the Rules of Business,* 2015, Portfolio.

Tsui, Anne S., Yanjie Bian, and Leonard Cheng, eds., *China's Domestic Private Firms: Multidisciplinary Perspectives on Management and Performance: Multidisciplinary Perspectives on Management and Performance,* Routledge, 2014.

Tsui, Anne S., and Chung Ming Lau, eds., *The Management of Enterprises in the People's Republic of China,* Springer, 2002.

Tsui, Anne S., Hui Wang, Katherine Xin, and Lihua Zhang, "Let a Thousand Flowers Bloom: Variation of Leadership Styles Among Chinese CEOs," *Organizational Dynamics,* 33, 2004, 5–20.

Useem, Michael, *Investor Capitalism: How Money Managers Are Changing the Face of Corporate America,* HarperCollins/Basic Books, 1996.

———, "Corporate Leadership in a Globalizing Equity Market," *Academy of Management Executive,* 12, 1998, 43–59.

———, interview with Peng Jiajun, Director, Management Research Institute, Haier Group, Beijing, June 13, 2014.

———, "From Classwide Coherence to Company-Focused Management and Director Ascendance," in Paul Hirsch, Glenn Morgan, and Sigrid Quack, eds., *Elites on Trial,* in the series titled *Research in the Sociology of Organizations,* edited by Michael Lounsbury, Emerald Group Publishing, 43, 2015, 399–421.

Useem, Michael, and Neng Liang, "Globalizing the Company Board: Lessons from China's Lenovo," in Jay Conger, ed., *Leading Corporate Boardrooms: The New Realities, the New Rules,* Jossey-Bass, 2009.

US Securities and Exchange Commission, Alibaba Group Holding Limited, F-1 Registration Statement, May 6, 2014, https://www.sec.gov/Archives/edgar/data/1577552/000119312514184994/d709111df1.htm.

Vanke, Corporate Social Responsibility Report, 2014, http://www.vanke.com/en/upload/file/2016-05-09/367797f6-cc69-42af-9c25-c987a91a6dae.pdf.

Varma, Arup, and Pawan S. Budhwar, eds., *Managing Human Resources in Asia-Pacific,* Routledge, 2014.

Vlasic, Bill, "G.M. Will Import Buicks Made in China to the U.S.," *New York Times,* December 4, 2015.

Vogel, Ezra F., *Deng Xiaoping and the Transformation of China,* Harvard University Press, 2011.

Wachtell, Lipton, Rosen & Katz, "Hedge Fund Activism and Long-Term Firm Value," 2015, http://www.wlrk.com/webdocs/wlrknew/WLRKMemos/WLRK/WLRK.24990.15.pdf.

Waldman, D. A., G. G. Ramirez, R. J. House, and P. Puranan, "Does Leadership Matter? CEO Leadership Attributes and Profitability Under Conditions of

Perceived Environmental Uncertainty," *Academy of Management Journal*, 44, 2001, 134–143.

Wang, Changsheng, and Gang Zhang, "The Story Behind the Dismissal of Alibaba CEO David Wei by Jack Ma," *China Entrepreneur*, March 28, 2011.

Wang, Helen H., *The Chinese Dream: The Rise of the World's Largest Middle Class and What It Means to You*, CreateSpace Independent Publishing Platform, 2010.

Wang, Hui, Anne S. Tsui, and Katherine R. Xin, "CEO Leadership Behaviors, Organizational Performance, and Employees' Attitude," *The Leadership Quarterly*, 22, 2011, 92–105.

Warner, Malcolm, "Chinese Enterprise Reform, Human Resources and the 1994 Labour Law," *International Journal of Human Resource Management*, 7, 1996.

———, "Human Resources and Management in China's 'Hi-Tech' Revolution: A Study of Selected Computer Hardware, Software and Related Firms in the PRC," *International Journal of Human Resource Management*, 10, 1999, 1–20.

———, "Making Sense of HRM in China: Setting the Scene," *International Journal of Human Resource Management*, 20, 2009, 2169–2193.

Wasserman, Noam, "Founder-CEO Succession and the Paradox of Entrepreneurial Success," *Organizational Science*, 14, 2003, 149–172.

Weber, Max, *The Protestant Ethic and the Spirit of Capitalism*, Talcott Parsons, trans., Scribner's, 1958 (originally published in German in 1905).

Wei, Lingling, "China's Top Securities Regulator Replaced," *Wall Street Journal*, February 19, 2016.

Wei, Zhe, "From a Professional Manager to a Business Partner—My 'Grown-Up Night,'" in Fei Zeng, ed., *The Ali Smell: Reflections*, Alibaba Group, n.d.

Wiener, Martin J., *English Culture and the Decline of the Industrial Spirit, 1850–1980*, Cambridge University Press, 2004.

Wildau, Gabriel, "Wang Chunqui, China's First MBA Graduates," *Financial Times*, January 25, 2015.

Wilkes, William, "China's Deal Makers Have German Tech Firms in Their Sights," *Wall Street Journal*, June 9, 2016.

Witt, Michael A., and Gordon Redding, "China: Authoritarian Capitalism," in Michael A. Witt and Gordon Redding, eds., *The Oxford Handbook of Asian Business Systems*, Oxford University Press, 2014.

Womack, James P., Daniel T. Jones, and Daniel Roos, *The Machine That Changed the World: The Story of Lean Production*, Free Press, 1990.

Wong, Chun Han, "China Rolls Out First Large Passenger Jet," *Wall Street Journal*, November 2, 2015.

Wong, Jacky, and Wayne Ma, "Hanergy Plunge: The Man Who Lost $14 Billion in One Day," *Wall Street Journal*, May 21, 2015.

World Bank, Foreign Direct Investment, 2015, http://data.worldbank.org/indica-tor/BX.KLT.DINV.CD.WD.

World Steel Association, *World Steel in Figures 2015*, 2015, https://www.world steel.org/dms/internetDocumentList/bookshop/2015/World-Steel-in -Figures-2015/document/World%20Steel%20in%20Figures%202015.pdf.

Wu, Jinglian, and Shaoqing Huang, "Innovation or Rent-Seeking: The Entrepreneurial Behavior During China's Economic Transformation," *China and World Economy*, 16, 2008, 64–81.

Wulf, Julie M., "Alibaba Group," Harvard Business School Case 710-436, Harvard Business School, 2010.

Xie, Wei, and Steven White, "Sequential Learning in a Chinese Spin-off: The Case of Lenovo Group Limited," *R&D Management*, 34, 2004, 407–422.

Xu, Chenggang, "The Fundamental Institutions of China's Reforms and Development," *Journal of Economic Literature*, 49, 2011, 1076–1151.

Xuecon, Muron, "China's Tradition of Public Shaming Thrives," *New York Times*, March 20, 2015.

Yahoo Finance, 2016, http://finance.yahoo.com/echarts?s=LNVGY+Interactive#.

Yao, Souchou, *Confucian Capitalism: Discourse, Practice and the Myth of Chinese Enterprise*, Routledge, 2013.

Yao, Yang, "The Chinese Growth Miracle," in Philippe Aghion and Steven N. Durlauf, eds., *Handbook of Economic Growth*, Elsevier, 2016.

YCharts, Alibaba data, 2016, https://ycharts.com.

Young, Doug, "Geely's Folksy Li Known as China's Henry Ford," Reuters, July 22, 2010, http://www.reuters.com/article/us-geely-volvo-newsmaker-idUSTRE 66L2ER20100722.

Yu, Dan, *Confucius from the Heart: Ancient Wisdom for Today's World*, Atria Books, 2013.

Yu, Rose, "Builder China Vanke Acts to Block Takeover," *Wall Street Journal*, December 30, 2015.

Yuen, Lotus, "Why Chinese College Graduates Aren't Getting Jobs," *The Atlantic*, 2013.

Zacks, "U.S. Steel Imports Up in July on China Glut: More Pain Ahead?" 2015, http://www.zacks.com/stock/news/188236/us-steel-imports-up-in-july-on -china-glut-more-pain-ahead.

Zeng, Ming, and Peter J. Williamson, "The Hidden Dragons," *Harvard Business Review*, 81, 2003, 92–103.

Zhang, Lu, "Lean Production and Labor Controls in the Chinese Automobile Industry in an Age of Globalization," *International Labor and Working-Class History*, 73, 2008, 24–44.

Zhang, Ruimin, "Management Model Innovations of the Internet Era," Wharton Global Alumni Forum, Beijing, June 14, 2014.

Zhang, Xiaojun, Pingping Fu, Youmin Xi, Lei Li, Liguo Xu, Chunhui Cao, Gui-quan Li, Li Ma, and Jing Ge, "Understanding Indigenous Leadership Research: Explication and Chinese Examples," *The Leadership Quarterly,* 23, 2012, 1063–1079.

Zhang, Zhi-Xue, Chao-Chuan Chen, Leigh Anne Liu, and Xue-Feng Liu, "Chinese Traditions and Western Theories: Influences on Business Leaders in China," in Chao-Chuan Chen and Yueh-Ting Lee, eds., *Leadership and Management in China: Philosophies, Theories, and Practices,* Cambridge University Press, 2008.

Zhao, Hongzin, and Juangyong Lu, "Contingent Value of Political Capital in Bank Loan Acquisition: Evidence from Founder-Controlled Private Enterprises in China," *Journal of Business Venturing,* 31, 2016, 153–174.

Zhao, S., J. Zhang, W. Zhao, and T. S. C. Poon, "Changing Employment Relations in China: A Comparative Study of the Auto and Banking Industries," *International Journal of Human Resource Management,* 23, 2012, 2051–2064.

Zuo, Many, "The Secret Behind How Chinese Entrepreneur Che Juianxin Outdid His Foreign Rivals," *South China Morning Post,* July 16, 2015.

INDEX

Michael Useem is a professor of management and the director of the Center for Leadership and Change Management at the Wharton School of the University of Pennsylvania. His university teaching includes courses on management and leadership, and he offers programs on leadership and governance for managers in the United States, Asia, Europe, and Latin America. He is the author of *The Leader's Checklist, The Leadership Moment, Executive Defense, Investor Capitalism, Leading Up,* and *The Go Point;* the co-author and co-editor of *Learning from Catastrophes;* and the co-author of *The India Way, Boards That Lead, Leadership Dispatches,* and the forthcoming *Catastrophic Risk: How Corporate America Copes with Disruption* (Oxford University Press). He is also the co-anchor for a weekly program, *Leadership in Action,* on SiriusXM Radio Channel 111, Business Radio Powered by Wharton, and he can be reached at useem@wharton.upenn.edu.

Photograph by Tommy Leonardi

Harbir Singh is a professor of management and the co-director of the Mack Center for Technological Innovation at the Wharton School. He has been chair of the Business Policy and Strategy Division of the Academy of Management and Wharton's vice-dean for Global Initiatives. He holds a bachelor's degree in technology from the Indian Institute of Technology, an MBA from the Indian Institute of Management–Ahmedabad, and a PhD from the University of Michigan. He is widely published in the areas of strategy, governance, acquisitions, joint ventures, and restructuring, and is the co-editor of *Innovations in International and Cross-Cultural Management.* He can be reached at singhh@wharton.upenn.edu.

Photograph by The Wharton School

Neng Liang is a professor of management, the director of the Case Development Center at China Europe International Business School, and the president of the International Association of Chinese Management Research (IACMR). Before returning to China, he was a tenured professor of international business at Loyola University of Maryland. His university teaching includes MBA and executive-MBA courses on international business and strategy as well as succession planning, and he offers programs on corporate governance for boards of directors in China. He also serves as a consultant to multinational firms and as independent director for several listed and unlisted firms. He is the author of *On the Globalization Process* and *International Business,* the co-author of *Corporate Political Strategies of Private Chinese Firms* and "Corporate Governance in China" in the *International Handbook of Corporate Governance,* and the editor of *Corporate Governance: Chinese Practice and American Experiences.* He can be reached at liangneng@ceibs.edu.

Photograph by China Europe International Business School

Peter Cappelli is a professor of management and the director of the Center for Human Resources at the Wharton School of the University of Pennsylvania. He is a research associate at the National Bureau of Economic Research, served as senior adviser to the Kingdom of Bahrain for Employment Policy from 2003 to 2005, and since 2007 has served as Distinguished Scholar of the Ministry of Manpower for Singapore. He is the author of *The New Deal at Work: Managing the Market-Driven Workforce, Talent Management: Managing Talent in an Age of Uncertainty, Why Good People Can't Get Jobs,* and *Will College Pay Off?* and the co-author of *The India Way* and *Managing the Older Worker.* He is also the co-anchor of a weekly radio program, *In the Workplace,* on SiriusXM Radio Channel 111, Business Radio Powered by Wharton, and he can be reached at cappelli@wharton.upenn.edu.

Photograph by The Wharton School

PublicAffairs is a publishing house founded in 1997. It is a tribute to the standards, values, and flair of three persons who have served as mentors to countless reporters, writers, editors, and book people of all kinds, including me.

I. F. STONE, proprietor of *I. F. Stone's Weekly*, combined a commitment to the First Amendment with entrepreneurial zeal and reporting skill and became one of the great independent journalists in American history. At the age of eighty, Izzy published *The Trial of Socrates*, which was a national bestseller. He wrote the book after he taught himself ancient Greek.

BENJAMIN C. BRADLEE was for nearly thirty years the charismatic editorial leader of *The Washington Post*. It was Ben who gave the *Post* the range and courage to pursue such historic issues as Watergate. He supported his reporters with a tenacity that made them fearless and it is no accident that so many became authors of influential, best-selling books.

ROBERT L. BERNSTEIN, the chief executive of Random House for more than a quarter century, guided one of the nation's premier publishing houses. Bob was personally responsible for many books of political dissent and argument that challenged tyranny around the globe. He is also the founder and longtime chair of Human Rights Watch, one of the most respected human rights organizations in the world.

· · ·

For fifty years, the banner of Public Affairs Press was carried by its owner Morris B. Schnapper, who published Gandhi, Nasser, Toynbee, Truman, and about 1,500 other authors. In 1983, Schnapper was described by *The Washington Post* as "a redoubtable gadfly." His legacy will endure in the books to come.

Peter Osnos, *Founder and Editor-at-Large*